INTERRUPTING CLASS INEQUALITY IN HIGHER EDUCATION

Interrupting Class Inequality in Higher Education explores why socioeconomic inequality persists in higher education despite widespread knowledge of the problem. Through a critical analysis of the current leadership practices and policy narratives that perpetuate socioeconomic inequality, this book outlines the trends that negatively impact low- and middle-income students and offers effective tools for creating a more equitable future for higher education. By taking a solution-focused approach, this book will help higher education students, leaders, and policy makers move from despair and inertia to hope and action.

Laura M. Harrison is Associate Professor of Counseling and Higher Education at Ohio University, USA.

Monica Hatfield Price is an Adjunct Professor of Communication Studies at Ohio University-Chillicothe, USA, and has more than a decade of corporate training and consulting experience.

INTERRUPTING CLASS INEQUALITY IN HIGHER EDUCATION

Leadership for an Equitable Future

*Laura M. Harrison and
Monica Hatfield Price*

NEW YORK AND LONDON

First published 2017
by Routledge

711 Third Avenue, New York, NY 10017
and by Routledge
2 Park Square, Milton Park, Abingdon, Oxon, OX14 4RN

Routledge is an imprint of the Taylor & Francis Group, an informa business

© 2017 Taylor & Francis

The right of Laura M. Harrison and Monica Hatfield Price to be identified as the authors of this work has been asserted by them in accordance with sections 77 and 78 of the Copyright, Designs and Patents Act 1988.

All rights reserved. No part of this book may be reprinted or reproduced or utilised in any form or by any electronic, mechanical, or other means, now known or hereafter invented, including photocopying and recording, or in any information storage or retrieval system, without permission in writing from the publishers.

Trademark notice: Product or corporate names may be trademarks or registered trademarks, and are used only for identification and explanation without intent to infringe.

Library of Congress Cataloging in Publication Data
Names: Harrison, Laura M., author. | Price, Monica Hatfield, author.
Title: Interrupting class inequality in higher education : leadership for an equitable future / by Laura M. Harrison and Monica Hatfield Price.
Description: New York : Routledge, 2017.
Identifiers: LCCN 2016046471 | ISBN 9781138669000 (hardback) | ISBN 9781138669017 (paperback) | ISBN 9781315618340 (master) | ISBN 9781317210672 (web PDF) | ISBN 9781317210665 (ePub) | ISBN 9781317210658 (mobipocket)
Subjects: LCSH: Educational equalization—United States. | Education, Higher—Social aspects—United States. | Educational leadership. | Classism—United States.
Classification: LCC LC213.2 .H39 2017 | DDC 379.2/6—dc23
LC record available at https://lccn.loc.gov/2016046471

ISBN: 978-1-138-66900-0 (hbk)
ISBN: 978-1-138-66901-7 (pbk)
ISBN: 978-1-315-61834-0 (ebk)

Typeset in Bembo
by Swales & Willis Ltd, Exeter, Devon, UK

Laura:
To my wife, Christy Zempter, and my dad, Dan Harrison, both of whom exemplify lives built on treating all people as ends, not means.

Monica:
To my sons, Hayden, Hunter, and Cooper, who inspire me to consider my actions through the lens of generations that follow.

CONTENTS

Preface	*viii*
Acknowledgments	*xv*

PART I
Understanding the Problems — 1

1	The Perpetuation of Class Inequity through Policy	3
2	The Consequences of Unexamined Practices on Class Inequality	23
3	The Role of Diminished Public Funding in Class Inequality	40
4	Class Inequality as a Higher Education Leadership Problem	57

PART II
Forging the Solutions — 77

5	Leading Collaboratively	79
6	Telling a Better Story	98
7	Gaining the Public Trust	120
8	Charting a More Equitable Course	142

Index — *162*

PREFACE

Introduction

The image of a rising tide that lifts all boats captures the promise of American higher education. Understood as a goal to which young people should aspire, college means opportunity, growth, and discovery. The unwritten, but widely known deal has been that college empowers students to turn a corner in their lives. Adolescents may have attended underresourced schools, grown up in tough neighborhoods, and overcome myriad other hurdles but if they could make it to college, their future would be brighter than their past.

This story drove higher education for over 70 years. From the passage of the Servicemen's Readjustment Act (GI Bill) in 1944 to the greater inclusion of students with disabilities in the 2008 Higher Education Act Reauthorization, the explicit goal has been to expand access to college. Society generally and higher education leaders specifically often fell short of this goal as racism, sexism, able-ism, and other forms of discrimination impeded this vision of inclusivity. Nonetheless, we argue there was at least some agreement that equal opportunity to higher education was the goal to which we ought to aspire.

While university leaders still generally espouse values of parity, policies and practices within higher education have exacerbated economic class polarization in recent years. The shift from need to merit-based financial aid, aggressive recruitment of full pay, out of state students, and astronomical salary increases for the executive class are just some of the trends reflecting a diminished commitment to equity in higher education.

These practices reflect a broader social phenomenon of unbridled privilege for the few and progressively smaller pieces of the proverbial pie for the many. In her provocatively titled book *White Trash: The 400-Year Old Untold History of Class in*

America, Nancy Isenberg (2016) exposes the historical acceptance of the notion of disposable humans. She details the ways in which those in power created classes of people to perform society's hardest and most dangerous work in the earliest days of what would become the United States:

> Whatever else their lies entailed, vagrants, children of beggars, and ex-soldiers who might be transported to the New World and transplanted onto its soil were thought to be fertilizing wasteland with their labor. Their value was calculated not in humane (or even human) terms, but as a disembodied commercial force. If that proposition seems cold and calculating, it was. In death, they were, to use the operative modern phrase, collateral damage. They had more value to the realm as dead colonists than as idle waste in England.
>
> *(Isenberg, 2016, p. 24)*

It would be politically untenable to make a case for disposable human beings in our own times. We proclaim allegiance to the notion of equal opportunity, but it would be difficult to argue there is not some tacit acceptance of the idea of throwaway people operating in our society. Evidence abounds—from the tolerance of grossly unequally funded schools to a minimum wage people generally agree does not provide enough income on which to live. We may feel genuine sympathy for the less fortunate and may even choose to do something like donate to charities or volunteer in soup kitchens. We do not minimize these acts; they provide vital help to the most economically vulnerable people in our society. Yet philanthropy is optional. Those of us in the middle and upper classes can choose to contribute when our heart strings are pulled and go on with our lives the rest of the time.

The tacit acceptance of waste people allows us to donate our kids' old clothes to a clothing drive while making sure our kids and their kids never live in the same neighborhood or attend the same school. Sometimes this process is conscious, but more often it's the result of largely coded discussions about finding a home in a nice neighborhood with good schools. Benign as the words "nice" and "good" seem, they suggest the existence of "bad" neighborhoods and schools. We understand the desire to avoid bad neighborhoods and schools, but why do we accept the idea that any child has to be there, even if it's not our own?

We accept untenable living and schooling conditions for other peoples' kids because we accept the idea that some people are disposable. We don't like to think about this truth, which is precisely the reason we feel the need to raise it as starkly as possible. This ugly truth is extremely palpable in higher education, where parents scramble relentlessly to obtain the very best for their own child. The very idea of "the best" is predicated on "the worst." Hurst (2010) articulated this problem eloquently, writing, "Meritocracies depend upon losers as well as producing winners. The 'brightest' will only shine against a contrasting background of dull lights and undifferentiated dullness" (pp. 73–74). Until we grapple with this conundrum honestly and directly, we will keep taking half measures that fail to adequately address the root of the problem.

Higher education can no longer afford to be an elitist enterprise in either reality or perception. The education divide reflected in the 2016 presidential election demonstrates clearly what can happen when we deprive significant portions of the country access to the tools for critical thinking. We argue neither that everyone who voted for Trump did so out of ignorance, nor that there is any excuse for hateful rhetoric. We do believe the results of this election indicate a stark need for higher education to recommit to its role in inculcating informed citizenship.

Hopefully, the moral implications of accepting the idea of waste people are obvious. We argue the notion of disposable people fails to work on any level, even the practical. The challenges we face as a world require the ability of all people to realize their potential. We need more peoples' minds working on issues ranging from climate change to infectious diseases to political instability. To accomplish this goal, we must protect colleges and universities from becoming places only the wealthy can afford to access.

Purpose

We argue that higher education has reached a crossroads where a re-commitment to the basic principle of equity is necessary to maintaining a laudable track record as a force for good. One would be hard pressed to find an individual working in our field who is unaware that participation in higher education is largely effected by family wealth. Mythical beliefs that students have equal opportunities to prepare for and participate in college have been handily rebuked (see, for example, McNamee & Miller, 2014). Illusions that socioeconomic status is not heavily considered in college admissions have been stripped away (see, for example, Soares, 2007). And decades of enrollment and student performance data demonstrate the strong relationship between high socioeconomic status and college success (see, for example, NCES, 2015). Therefore, this book is not intended to cover that same proving-ground. Instead, we intend to launch a new conversation into why, if we know socioeconomic inequalities exist in higher education, have conditions not changed?

In this book we challenge the assumption that leaders and professionals in higher education are not aware of the socioeconomic injustice that has long been occurring. We assert leaders know that differences exist for the wealthy and the poor students, but that higher education is not premised on an equitable design. Therefore, this book is intended to launch a different conversation. We will explore why the discrepancies between college for the wealthy and poor continue, and what could be done to finally make higher education the rising tide that lifts all boats.

A central argument we posit is that higher education's continued commitment to a corporate model is (re)producing inequality. We identify what causes us not to hold the corporate model accountable while we accept other forms of criticism (like vilification of teachers, for example). We suggest that 30 years of running higher education under a business model has yielded ample evidence to conclude a poor fit. Now, we encourage a critical analysis of the corporate model, the leadership approaches, and the policy narratives that are perpetuating socioeconomic inequality in higher education.

Our purpose in writing this book is two-fold. First, we debunk the notion of class stratification as inevitable. By revealing the precise policies and practices that contribute to higher education's role in classism, we will demonstrate their optional nature. Too often, we accept business as usual because we fail to recognize that different paths exist. We succumb to hierarchical decision making, for example, because we misunderstand it as some sort of natural order rather than an artificial construction for which we could create an alternative if we had the vision to do so. Hence we aim to help readers interrupt the self-replicating patterns that have produced class inequality and develop the more creative practices necessary to expand higher education's reach for all students.

Our second goal is to expose specific policies and practices that result in higher education's complicity in classism. Our experience working in universities leads us to believe the consequences are largely unintended; people generally do not seek to promote class stratification in higher education. Yet uncritical acceptance of some contemporary policy trends creates unintended consequences that negatively impact low- and middle-income students. We identify these trends specifically in the chapter descriptions.

Audience

We strove to write a book that is useful to higher education students, leaders, and/or policy makers working within and outside university settings. We assume a spirit of goodwill among our audience, even among our potential detractors. We do not imagine those who disagree with us as necessarily against the principle of equal opportunity in higher education. We approach our audience with a sense of humility, understanding the problems we identify in this work are complex and the potential solutions are neither clear nor uncontested. Hence the spirit of this book is more invitation than critique; we offer an analysis based on our understanding of both the scholarship as well as our lived experience in higher education. We conceptualize our readers as scholars who bring their own research and experience to the conversation, hopefully using our book as an additional tool in their own work toward interrupting the cycle of inequality in higher education.

We wrote the majority of this book at the height of what has turned out to be one of the most polarizing and negative political seasons of our lifetimes. In contrast to much of the rhetoric swirling around us, we do not buy into the notion that those who see things differently from us do so out of a desire to promote inequality. We assume anyone who picks up our book is probably interested in learning more about what drives inequality in higher education and how we might change course. Through the themes and examples presented in the book, we seek to illuminate these drivers and potential interventions.

Organization

Too many scholarly works are skewed heavily toward discussing problems, with a short recommendation section at the end of the text. In contrast, we take a solution-focused approach that helps readers move from despair and inertia to hope and action. Hence our book is divided into two equal parts. The first half of the book will address the historical and contemporary contributors to the problem of classism in American higher education. In the second half of the book, we will provide readers with frameworks and tools for creating a more equitable future for colleges and universities.

In the opening chapter, we introduce the issue of class inequality in higher education and discuss how policies can perpetuate the problem. We discuss the policy and practice implications resulting from the decrease in public funding for higher education. Using the frameworks of policy theorists, such as the Social Construction of Target Population Framework (Schneider & Ingram, 1993; Schneider, Ingram, & deLeon, 2014), we illuminate the underexplored aspects of higher education policy and their implications for class inequity.

In Chapter 2, we draw attention to the often unexamined operational practices that influence the way students of lower socioeconomic status experience college. We identify practices that have not kept pace with the changing needs of the economically diversified student body. Regardless of whether institutions provide greater access to higher education for lower-income students, until the experience of college is made more equitable for all classes the cycle of inequity will continue.

Chapter 3 recovers a not so distant time when public financing of higher education was fairly uncontroversial. The citizenry looked to university presidents as intellectual leaders and viewed higher education institutions as beneficial to the public through their research, teaching, and service functions. However, contemporary higher education is experiencing decreased public support which contributes to funding practices that are disproportionately consequential for low socioeconomic status students.

In Chapter 4, we frame the issue of class inequality in higher education as a leadership problem. We will use Heifetz, Grashow, and Linsky's (2009) concepts of technical versus adaptive leadership systems theory to reveal the vicious circle created first by public divestment in higher education, followed by misguided institutional reactions that fail to address the root of the problem.

In Chapter 5, we transition from problems to potential interventions, considering alternative paradigms and best practices for addressing inequality. Drawing on the emerging field of Critical Management Studies, this chapter offers new frameworks for creating more equitable leadership norms in higher education.

Chapter 6 focuses on the role of story and changing the narrative as an effective strategy for combatting inequality. Narratives that are consciously created to improve the framing of socioeconomically diverse students can bring about much needed policy changes at the federal, state, and institutional levels. This chapter provides examples and analysis of policy narratives that frame class inequality in higher education in a more empowering way.

Chapter 7 provides strategy for regaining the vital public support needed to chart a more equitable future path for higher education. Scholars routinely dismiss the lack of public support as a *fait accompli*, preemptively dismissing it in favor of short-term solutions that exacerbate class inequality. Yet higher education has not always been viewed as a private commodity unworthy of state and federal support. In this chapter, we examine the past and future trends that might help us understand our present challenges as real today, but not inevitable.

In Chapter 8, we discuss promising new practices emerging as institutions recommit to their public-serving missions. We consider leadership, policy, and practice strategies that are showing potential to interrupt the cycle of class inequality in higher education. One specific strategy we offer is addressing the intersections of inequality. As President Lyndon Johnson famously stated, "If you can convince the lowest white man he's better than the best colored man, he won't notice you're picking his pocket. Hell, give him somebody to look down on, and he'll empty his pockets for you" (as cited in Moyers, 1988). Any real solution cannot pit one group against another in an endless and circular battle for scarce resources. We must interrupt that paradigm by interrogating and confronting the source of the resource scarcity in the first place.

References

Heifetz, R., Grashow, A., & Linsky, M. (2009). *The practice of adaptive leadership: Tools and tactics for changing your organization and the world*. Boston, MA: Harvard Business Press.

Hurst, A. L. (2010). *The burden of academic success: Loyalists, renegades, and double agents*. Lanham, MD: Lexington Books.

Isenberg, N. (2016). *White trash: The 400-year old untold history of class in America*. New York, NY: Viking.

McNamee, S., & Miller Jr., R. (2014). *The meritocracy myth* (3rd ed.). Lanham, MD: Rowman & Littlefield Publishers.

Moyers, B. (1988, November 13). What a real president was like. *Washington Post*. Retrieved from www.washingtonpost.com/archive/opinions/1988/11/13/what-a-real-president-was-like/d483c1be-d0da-43b7-bde6-04e10106ff6c/.

NCES [National Center for Education Statistics]. (2015). *Postsecondary attainment: Differences by socioeconomic status*. US Department of Education: Institute of Education Sciences. Retrieved from http://nces.ed.gov/programs/coe/indicator_tva.asp.

Schneider, A., & Ingram, H. (1993). Social construction of target populations: Implications for politics and policy. *American Political Science Review, 87*(2), 334–347.

Schneider, A., Ingram, H., & deLeon, P. (2014). Democratic policy design: Social construction of target populations. In P. A. Sabatier & C. M. Weible (Eds), *Theories of the policy process* (3rd ed., pp. 105–149). Boulder, CO: Westview Press.

Soares, J. (2007). *The power of privilege: Yale and America's elite colleges*. Stanford, CA: Stanford University Press.

ACKNOWLEDGMENTS

Special thanks to our editor, Heather Jarrow, for her wise counsel throughout the long process of imagining, pitching, writing, creating, releasing, and promoting this book. We express our gratitude for everyone at Routledge/Taylor & Francis Group who brought our book into being. Writing this book made us think more intentionally about the limits of individualism, amplifying the appreciation we feel for the community that makes work like this possible.

Laura: I wish to thank the following individuals for the knowledge they contributed to this work: Carissa Anderson, Joe Carver, Tamara Leech, Mike Mather, Pete Mather, Jacob Okumu, Katharine Sprecher, Amanda Sohl, and Christy Zempter. I also wish to thank Shelley McClain and Lillie Roberts for both the administrative support and comic relief they provided as I was working on this book. Finally, I thank my co-author, Monica Hatfield Price, whose quick mind and limitless energy made writing this book both fulfilling and fun.

As a professor, I feel inclined to thank my students, but I hope they read this and know this isn't some sort of perfunctory acknowledgement. The relationship I have with my students is uniquely and deeply satisfying in ways that are difficult to describe. First, they motivate me beyond my wildest dreams. They are such good people that I want to do and be my best for them. Second, they are inspiringly smart and creative. Nearly every good idea, thought, and source that made it into this book came from them in some way, either directly or indirectly. Sometimes it was a class discussion; other times it was something they wrote in a paper. Finally, I don't know that there is a bond stronger than the one you share with people who love the same thing you do. My students love fairness and opportunity and learning in ways that resonate with who I am and how I want to spend my time on this earth. Heartfelt thanks to you all for making my life so rich.

Monica: I wish to thank a community of scholars that have inspired deeper thinking: Ohio University Cohort XII, David Horton, Scott Titsworth, Michael Williford, and Pamela Wilson. I am thankful for the conversations and ideas shared from such extraordinarily thoughtful minds. Special thanks go to my co-author, Laura Harrison. She embodies the best of what it means to be an inquisitive scholar and compassionate educator.

PART I
Understanding the Problems

1
THE PERPETUATION OF CLASS INEQUITY THROUGH POLICY

Calls to address the educational disparities between lower and higher socioeconomic status (SES) students have been made for decades. As far back as 1947, the Truman Commission declared, "It is the responsibility of the community, at the local, State, and National levels, to guarantee that financial barriers do not prevent any able and otherwise qualified young person from receiving the opportunity for higher education" (PCHE, 1947, p. 23). However, the gap between the educational attainment of low SES students and high SES students is growing (Pell Institute, 2015). The time has come for the higher education community to reverse the trends and close the education attainment gap between low and high SES students. This chapter suggests that a better understanding of the higher education policy arena may ensure that the policy system changes to incorporate the values and needs of stakeholders concerned about the education of economically diverse students.

Higher Education Policy Primer

Policies are rules to direct behavior and resources. As such, policies are a mechanism for (in)equity. Public policy, as the name implies, pertains to matters that have been deemed to affect the public good. There are numerous public policy topic areas. Public policy is designed for fields such as natural resources, health care, social welfare, and education. Therefore, higher education policy is situated within the larger context of public policy.

Some higher education policies are made and enforced at the federal level while others function at the state, local, or institutional level. However, there is no mention of education in the US Constitution. Technically, the responsibility for educating citizens falls to the states (US Department of Education, n.d.).

In reality, the federal government's role in higher education is increasingly bureaucratic and the states' financial responsibilities are increasingly unmet. Some states are better than others at considering the socioeconomic levels of their citizens and providing support for those who need it. Similarly, particular institutions within a state are better than others at considering the SES of their students and providing aid. However, overall recent trends demonstrate that higher education policies are not adequately supporting low SES students.

Ensuring that the higher education system improves rather than exacerbates the socioeconomic divide in the US will take collective effort. Small, isolated campus programs are certainly wonderful for the students they help. However, to address this inequality problem, large-scale thinking is also appropriate. As think tanks and advocacy groups have long understood, a key to large-scale change is policy makers. Federal, state, and institutional policy makers are influencing the upward mobility of students in myriad ways. Understanding how the issue of higher education is framed for policy makers may shed light on why the system continues to reinforce the class divide.

A Goal of Equity

Stone (2012) contends that there are five primary goals for policies: equity, efficiency, welfare, liberty, and security. The focus of this book is equity, yet, we acknowledge additional arguments could be made that the perpetuation of socioeconomic inequality are matters of efficiency, welfare, liberty, and security as well. For example, in a global economy, we gain more US economic security when the country invests in increased numbers of college graduates rather than economically relying on the shrinking number of families that can currently afford higher education for their student.

A challenge with equity, as with all the policy goals, is that disagreement exists about what is equitable. Even in higher education policy scholarship, equity is not clearly defined (Dar, 2014). Equity concerns fairness. However, fairness in distributing something may not always involve equality. Equal is not always equitable. For example, in education, some students are advanced and some are behind. If everyone is given the same support (equality), then some students will not have enough support to succeed. Equity, on the other hand, means providing differentiated support to help everyone succeed.

When questions of equity arise, Stone (2012) advocates the consideration of three dimensions: recipients, items, and process. A starting point for understanding equity in a policy issue entails clarifying the recipients. This means identifying who is intended to receive the benefits from the policy and how the recipients will prove eligibility. Understanding equity also entails clarifying the items that are intended to be distributed. What precisely is the benefit that is meant to be distributed? Finally, consideration of the distribution process builds understanding of equity in a policy issue. This means identifying what process will be used to distribute the intended benefits to the intended recipients. Exploring the dimensions of recipients, distribution items, and process can illuminate (in)equity in policy.

To demonstrate that it is helpful to scrutinize recipients, items, and process to illuminate (in)equity, consider the trends in policy to provide free community college. While the free community college policy trend is growing across the country (Harnisch & Lebioda, 2016), there are differences in how the states address equity. In some states, the free community college programs are designed to contribute the "last dollar." After a student has used all existing federal and state financial aid they qualified for, the last dollar programs cover any tuition expenses that remain. Although the process dimension is the same across all students, the dimensions of recipients and items vary.

The last dollar programs have made higher-income students the benefit recipients under their free community college policy design. Existing federal and state financial aid programs already cover the community college tuition of low-income students. However, compared to low-income students, higher-income students qualify for less federal and state aid. Therefore, the largest student group with tuition not covered by existing federal and state financial aid is comprised of higher-income students. Higher-income students are not the student group that policy makers heralded as the recipients benefiting from the free community college policy.

Then, consider the item actually intended for distribution in the free community college policy issue. Free community college policy for the states with a last dollar design is about tuition. However, for other states, the item intended for distribution is a broader interpretation of financial aid. States interpreting financial aid more broadly acknowledge that for the poorest students, the non-tuition expenses associated with college attendance are as prohibitive as tuition. The last dollar programs have a narrow definition of the item for distribution. To them, the item is simply tuition. As a result of last dollar free community college programs, as Harnisch and Lebioda (2016) argue, "state resources will be re-directed from the poorest students at community colleges needing help with non-tuition expenses, as well as those needy students choosing to attend public four-year universities" (para. 27). This example of last dollar free community college policies illustrates how recipients and items distributed are identified differently across the states, and how questions of equity can arise from the different policy approaches.

Addressing issues of equity and improving the education of economically diverse students is paramount for the US because now the majority of public school students are from low-income families (Southern Education Foundation, 2015). State data collected by the National Center for Educational Statistics (NCES) reveal that 51 percent of public school students are eligible for free or reduced-price lunches. For higher education professionals who may not be familiar with these indicators, free lunches are available to families whose income is less than 135 percent of the poverty income threshold, and reduced price lunches are available to families whose income is less than 185 percent of the poverty income threshold.

For decades the number of low-income students being served by the country's public education system has grown, but now it has reached a majority level. In 1989, less than 32 percent of the students were low income. By 2000, the number had climbed to over 38 percent. Six years after that the rate was 42 percent. But after the Great Recession, in 2011, 48 percent of public school students were low income. Then, in 2013, low-income students became the new majority in America's public schools (Southern Education Foundation, 2015). As the Association of American Colleges and Universities (AAC&U) (Witham, Malcom-Piqueux, Dowd, & Bensimon, 2015) summarizes, "the population of young people on whom the nation's future depends will increasingly be comprised of children from groups who have been historically excluded from, tracked out of, and served most poorly by existing higher education structures" (p. 7). These figures help demonstrate the imperative of providing higher education to low SES students.

Higher education policies that are increasingly unrepresentative of the students the US needs to educate raise the issue of equity. Because education is cumulative and the higher education pipeline is filled from the nation's K-12 system, the growing number of low-income K-12 students requires policy makers to revisit the accessibility of higher education for economically diverse students. Again, referring to the Truman Commission's suggestions almost 70 years ago, the Commission asserts:

> There must be developed in this country the widespread realization that money expended for education is the wisest and soundest of investments in the national interest. The democratic community cannot tolerate a society based upon education for the well-to-do alone. If college opportunities are restricted to those in the higher income brackets, the way is open to the creation and perpetuation of a class society which has no place in the American way of life.
>
> *(PCHE, 1947, p. 23)*

The Commission's statement makes a strong argument for equity in US higher education, yet the systemic differences between education for the well-to-do and the poor continue today.

The purpose of reflecting on the sentiments expressed years ago by the Truman Commission is not to suggest that prior eras appropriately addressed issues of equity. Reflecting on these earlier sentiments demonstrates how deeply engrained the issue of (in)equity is for higher education. It is worth remembering that once upon a time, college was exclusively reserved for the education of wealthy men who were being groomed as civic leaders and clergymen (Brubacher & Rudy, 2008). Higher education in our country did not begin as an equitable venture. At the time they were provided, the Commission's recommendations to improve access by eliminating financial, race, sex, and religious barriers were seen "as an absolutely terrible idea by many leaders in higher education" (Gilbert & Heller, 2013, p. 428). Exclusion has a long history in US higher education.

That former leaders felt eliminating financial, race, sex, and religious barriers to higher education was an "absolutely terrible idea" reminds us that policy is an entirely human construct. Policy makers are just people. Some policy makers are highly educated, and some are not. Some policy makers are conservative and some are liberal in their outlook. Some policy makers are very experienced and some are brand new. The point is, policy makers are simply people crafting rules. Just like the rest of us, their beliefs and their decisions are a reflection of what motivates them and what makes sense to them. Therefore, it is helpful to consider the socially constructed nature of policy.

Social Construction in the Policy Process

Schneider and Ingram (1993) introduced the Social Construction Framework to help explain how the policy process works. Within the framework, a target population is the intended recipient of benefits or burdens of a policy. Schneider and Ingram posit that policy makers socially construct target populations in either positive or negative terms and then allocate benefits and burdens that reflect and perpetuate these constructs (Ingram, Schneider, & deLeon, 2007). Ingram, Schneider, and deLeon contend that the framework is helpful in explaining "why public policy, which can have such a positive effect on society, sometimes—and often deliberately—fails in its nominal purposes, fails to solve important public problems, perpetuates injustice, fails to support democratic institutions, and produces an unequal citizenship" (2007, p. 93). Thus, the framework can be helpful in exploring why higher education policy continues to perpetuate socioeconomic inequality.

The Social Construction Framework provides five propositions that are helpful in considering how higher education policy perpetuates economic inequality. The propositions concern allocation, feedback, origins, changing social constructions, and policy change (Schneider, Ingram, & deLeon, 2014). The last two propositions, changing social constructions and policy change, will be discussed in Chapter 6. In the present chapter, we use the first three propositions to explore the socially constructed nature of higher education policy. Understanding the socially constructed nature of policy reveals how changeable policy is.

Allocation

The first proposition of the Social Construction Framework concerns allocation. The framework posits that "The allocation of benefits and burdens to target groups by public policy depends on the extent of their political power as well as their positive or negative social construction" (Schneider, Ingram, & deLeon, 2014, p. 109). This means that the framework considers two dimensions of the

8 Understanding the Problems

target population construction: the political power of the group and the positive or negative social construction of the group.

As Figure 1.1 depicts, target groups who have high political power and positive social construction are known as "advantaged" (Schneider, Ingram, & deLeon, 2014, p. 110). The proposition suggests that the advantaged group will receive more policy benefits and less policy burdens than the other three groups. In higher education, an example target population that is advantaged is merit scholars. O'Shaughnessy (2011) reports that merit scholarships are often awarded based on grade point averages (GPAs), standardized test scores, and the strength of the student's high school curriculum. High standardized test scores are positively correlated to SES (Bowen, Chingos, & McPherson, 2011). And the strength of a student's high school curriculum is linked to the SES of the community the high school serves (Bowen, Chingos, & McPherson, 2011). Therefore, merit scholars tend to come from higher socioeconomic groups, and higher socioeconomic groups have more power in the policy arena than lower socioeconomic groups.

Next, from Figure 1.1, consider the target group with low political power and positive social construction referred to as "dependents" (Schneider, Ingram, &

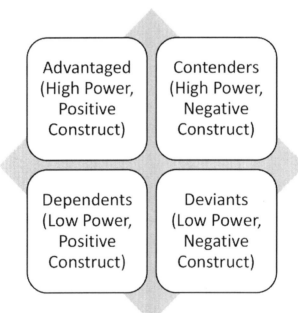

FIGURE 1.1 Power and construct matrix of Social Construction of Target Population Framework

Source: Adapted from "Democratic policy design: Social construction of target populations," by A. Schneider, H. Ingram, & P. deLeon, 2014, p. 111.

deLeon, 2014, p. 112). The Social Construction of Target Populations Framework suggests that the dependent group will receive fewer benefits and more burdens than the two groups (advantaged and contenders) who have more political power. However, due to the positive social construction of the group, this target population tends to receive policy benefits that are rhetorical but not substantive. For example, financially needy students tend to be in the dependent target population. With fewer financial resources and a lack of formal organization, these need-based students and their families have lower political power in the policy arena. However, it would be a public relations mistake for a policy maker to openly disparage need-based students. Therefore, many political speeches include pledges to address the financial needs of low-income students, but enacting policy that distributes more privileges to the low power target population tends to be a low priority.

If, as the Social Construction Framework suggests, the allocation of benefits and burdens is based on the political power and the social construction of the target population, then we can see why higher education policy perpetuates socioeconomic inequality. Low SES students and their families do not have the financial or organizational resources to drive policy change. However, the group does have a positive social construction, unlike the "deviant" and "contender" (Schneider, Ingram, & deLeon, 2014, pp. 111, 112) groups who have negative social construction.

Commandeering the dependent group's positive social construction can become a policy ploy for some in the contender group. Contenders have political power; however, the group is generally seen as selfish, immoral, and untrustworthy. Included in the contenders are groups like Wall Street brokers, firearms industries, wealthy political donors, and groups receiving congressional earmarks (Schneider, Ingram, & deLeon, 2014). As a result of their high political power, the contenders group does receive more policy benefits and fewer burdens. Schneider, Ingram, and deLeon state that the contenders receive benefits that are "buried in the details of legislation and difficult to identify. Benefits to contenders are hidden because no legislators want to openly do good things for shady people or be accused of manipulating the rules to favor a few through special allocations" (2014, pp. 111–112). So, if a contender group can convince the public that a policy issue is about the dependent group, when it is actually about benefits for the contender group, the dependent group does not receive the benefits and continues to face inequities.

Education technology (edtech) groups provide an example of commandeering the positive social construct of the dependent group. Picciano and Spring (2013) provide a compelling argument in their book, *The Great American Education-Industrial Complex*, that the hidden connections and power of private education technology companies are impacting education policy. Edtech groups have been successful in altering policy to ensure that their products are a requirement for education institutions.

Edtech groups have been influential in the movement toward online education under the assertion that it will make education more accessible to low-income students. However, when the research organization Public Agenda (2013) surveyed students, they found 41 percent wanted to take fewer courses online. Additionally, Jaggars (2012) examined the outcomes for tens of thousands of students and found that, compared to face-to-face courses, students enrolled in online courses had lower completion rates, earned lower grades, and were less likely to successfully graduate community college or transfer to a four-year school. In deeper analysis, Xu and Jaggars's (2013) findings suggest that male, Black, and lower-levels of academically prepared students experience the highest negative grade and persistence associations with online courses. The discrepancy between the students' desires and outcomes, and the edtech groups' successful policy influence, raises questions of democracy and educational equity (Jaggars, 2014).

The first proposition of the Social Construction Framework highlights the importance of power and positive construction in the policy arena. But the most influential of the two is power. Despite having a positive social construction, financially needy students and their families lack the power to drive substantial change in the policy arena. The individuals and groups who are advantaged in the policy arena do have the opportunity to drive policy change. Mindful higher education policy makers and leaders can use their advantaged position to drive changes in policy that reflect concern for equity.

Feedback

The second proposition of the Social Construction Framework concerns feedback. The framework posits that "Policy designs have both material and symbolic (reputational or interpretive) effects on target populations that impact their attitudes and political participation. These effects occur through structuring of opportunities that shape life experiences and subtle messages about how government works and how they are likely to be treated" (Schneider, Ingram, & deLeon, 2014, p. 116). Thus, the proposition suggests that policies themselves can be a starting point for impacting attitudes and political participation.

Several higher education policies allow consideration of how policy can affect attitudes and participation. The first example is provided by policies that are changing the makeup of state flagship universities. By original design, state flagship universities were intended to provide democratized access to higher education for the state's residents. The states collected taxes from their residents and then used the tax revenue to support the public higher education institutions within its borders. By directing income collected from their residents into public higher education, the states were intended to provide accessible higher education opportunities for their residents. However, as the states' expenditures on higher education have declined (Desrochers & Hurlburt, 2016), the public higher education institutions have begun to make up for state funding reductions in ways that negatively impact the accessibility and affordability for in-state residents. Now, as the *New York Times* reported, "Many of the most elite public universities are steadily restricting the number of students who are allowed to pay in-state tuition in the first place" (Carey, 2015, para. 4). By restricting the number of in-state tuition paying students, the public state institutions have increased the competition for fewer in-state tuition paying slots, and reduced the options for students to attend research institutions at the lower, in-state tuition rate. These changes perpetuate the challenges for lower-income students in higher education.

Restricting the number of in-state tuition paying students at flagship institutions affects participation in unconsidered ways. Elite public universities are research intensive, doctorate awarding institutions. Reduced access to institutions that award advanced graduate degrees changes who will have the education to get the most secure employment. Reduced access also changes who will have the education to secure faculty positions in higher education institutions, which then changes the diversity of the socioeconomic backgrounds of future faculty. Thus, restricted access to flagship institutions has multigenerational impact.

Restricting access to public flagships also affects the political power loop. Because public flagships provide residential college experiences, they tend to expose students to numerous civic and political engagement opportunities. Public flagship students can learn how to navigate the political arena and make political contacts. Evidence suggests that adults who have bachelor's degrees engage in more community-based and political engagement activities than adults with high school diplomas or associate's degrees (Newell, 2011). As higher-degree awarding institutions, public flagships contribute to the pool of degree-holding citizens who are knowledgeable of and influential in the political arena. Limiting access to these institutions then affects the future makeup of the state's political leadership.

Restricting access to public flagship universities can have material effects on the students. The state's excluded students may experience reduced future earnings potential, less powerful social networks, and fewer opportunities to learn civic engagement. But there can also be symbolic effects on the students. Exclusion from public institutions can promote feelings of unworthiness in those who are outside the inclusion parameters. In this way, the exclusion serves as a message to keep the excluded groups demoralized by their exclusion. The agency to speak out is lessened through the fostering of beliefs that the system/exclusion was fair. As Freire (1970) details in *Pedagogy of the Oppressed*, repeated messages of unworthiness contribute to the student's lowering of self-worth. The exclusion sends a symbolic message about one's place and power which discourages political participation. After all, who would students complain to when they are excluded from their state's public higher education system?

A second higher education example illustrates how policy design can affect the target populations' attitudes and participation. The Free Application for Federal Student Aid, known as "FAFSA," is the form students and their families must fill out to access all forms of federal student aid. The form is intended to establish the extent of the student's eligibility for federal student aid. However, research reveals that filling out the FAFSA form is a deterrent for low-income students (Bettinger, Long, Oreopoulos, & Sanbonmatsu, 2009). The FAFSA form is viewed as complicated and requires document verification that can be difficult for low-income students to obtain. Therefore, a substantial number of students who would qualify for aid do not complete the form.

Not filling out the FAFSA form prohibits low-income students from accessing aid they would otherwise qualify for. But a lack of timeliness in filling out the FAFSA also prohibits students from accessing aid. Feeney and Heroff (2013) identified that low-income students were less likely to complete the FAFSA in time to qualify for need-based aid. Their research also showed that increases in Expected Family Contribution (money the family is able to contribute based on their financial condition) significantly increased the likelihood that the student would complete the FAFSA in time to qualify for aid. Additionally, having at least one parent who attended college significantly increased the likelihood that the student would fill out the FAFSA in time to qualify for aid.

The FAFSA example shows the perpetuation of privilege in higher education. Students from wealthier families, and students with at least one parent who attended college, have the cultural capital to maneuver the FAFSA form and the deadlines. For low-income students and their families who lack experience with and knowledge of the financial aid process, even the initial entry steps can be deterrents. Research suggests it need not be this way.

Bettinger, Long, Oreopoulos, and Sanbonmatsu (2012) report results from their randomized field experiment in which low-income individuals received personal assistance in completing the FAFSA. Their results showed that high school seniors whose parents had received the FAFSA assistance were 40 percent more likely to file the FAFSA. Among the high school seniors whose parents received FAFSA assistance, college enrollment increased by over 23 percent. And those enrolled students whose parents had received FAFSA assistance were more likely to persist. Three years after the FAFSA assistance, the educational attainment rates for the participant group were higher than the control group who did not get help with the FAFSA. Based on the experiment results, the researchers concluded that personalized assistance may be an effective and economical way to increase participation in programs that require forms for eligibility.

The second proposition in the Social Construction Framework draws attention to the importance of policy design. The policy design itself can negatively affect the participation levels and attitudes of target populations. Then, the cycle of exclusion continues because the target population becomes alienated from the policy process. The advantaged group continues to experience the advantages and the dependent group continues to experience the burdens. Scrutinizing the feedback component of higher education policies can help explain why higher education perpetuates socioeconomic inequality in its current design.

Origins

The third proposition of the Social Construction Framework concerns the origins of social constructions. The framework posits that "Social constructions emerge from emotional and intuitive reactions and then are justified with selective attention to evidence. Policymakers, especially elected politicians, respond to (and exploit) these emotional and intuitive judgments in their rationales and selection of policy elements" (Schneider, Ingram, & deLeon, 2014, p. 121). If, as the framework suggests, the social constructions are formed from emotion and intuition, then attempts to understand the policy arena solely through a lens of rationality will fall short.

Emotion and intuition act as heuristics, or mental shortcuts, to help people make sense of the world. Narratives can be a means to influence emotion and intuition and thus affect the social construction of a target population. Therefore, considering narratives in the policy arena can reveal the justifications policy makers rely on when higher education policies (re)produce socioeconomic inequality.

Narratives are a way for us to understand issues. They provide a scaffold of sorts that help us build our perceptions of the world around us. Narratives are not neutral; they reveal positions and world frames. Some narratives highlight a villain, while others highlight a victim or a hero. In particular, policy narratives are the stories used in policy contests. Through analysis, policy narratives can suggest power structures and imbalances (Roe, 1994). Schneider, Ingram, and deLeon (2014) assert:

> People tend to exaggerate the positive and negative traits of groups and create narratives, myths, and rationales that justify the domination of some groups over others. In time, these stories become inculcated in the culture and embodied in policies so that their authenticity is unquestioned and they are accepted as fact.
>
> *(p. 123)*

Several higher education narratives help demonstrate myths that tend to go unquestioned by policy makers and contribute to the perpetuation of socioeconomic inequality.

Myth: Higher education is a meritocracy

The narrative of higher education as a meritocracy is premised on the idea that access, opportunities, and outcomes are the result of an individual student's own merit. The AAC&U contends that "The disparities in access and success experienced by students who are socioeconomically disadvantaged are perpetuated by deeply entrenched beliefs about the primacy of merit as a logic guiding admissions and financial aid practices" (Witham, Malcom-Piqueux, Dowd, & Bensimon, 2015, p. 27). The narrative of higher education as a meritocracy reveals assumptions about what is meritorious. In higher education, the assumption is that students are evaluated equally and through direct comparison some students are deemed "better" and therefore have more merit. In the dualism created from a meritocracy narrative, a student is either meritorious or not. The student is either in or out. But who gets to tell this story? Who is the narrator? In American higher education, the group with the most economic, cultural, and social capital is dominant and defines what it means to be meritorious (Bourdieu, 1984).

For the most part, the general public agrees with the notion that higher education should operate as a meritocracy (Carnavale & Rose, 2004; McNamee & Miller, 2014). When Carnavale and Rose (2004), in partnership with Princeton Survey Research Associates, conducted a nationwide poll of more than 2,100 adults, they found "broad agreement that individual academic achievement, and the character traits of hard work and personal motivation it requires, should govern the distribution of opportunity in higher education" (p. 27). However, McNamee and Miller (2014) point out that many Americans hold simultaneously conflicting beliefs. Many Americans believe in meritocracy, the notion that individual merit should drive benefit distribution, and simultaneously believe in inheritance rights, which are individual rights to distribute one's wealth as they see fit. This means many Americans believe on one hand that if someone has accumulated wealth, that person has the right to use that wealth to help their children get ahead in life and on the other hand that each individual's merit should determine who gets ahead in life. This conflict is similar to believing everyone should start a race at the same starting line while at the same time believing some selected racers can start yards ahead of the other racers. McNamee and Miller (2014) contend that, "Simply put, to the extent that income and wealth are distributed on the basis of inheritance, they are not distributed on the basis of merit" (p. 2). This conflict between ideals is often missing from discussions on meritocracy. Several other aspects of meritocracy are also obscured from the common narrative.

The meritocracy narrative conceals that systemic issues contribute to the merit evaluation. From womb to tomb, SES matters. Beginning in the earliest years of life, family economic status empowers or constrains. Educationally, grade school and high school preparation differ based on socioeconomic levels. The K-12 education available to each student depends greatly on the local property taxes. High-value real estate neighborhoods provide greater financial and community resources to students (Lieberman, 2015). Schools servicing lower-income neighborhoods tend to be staffed with lower skilled teachers (Crotty, 2014). Such schools also provide fewer Advanced Placement (AP) course options compared to schools servicing high-income neighborhoods (Wildhagen, 2014). Therefore, the zip code in which a student's family can afford to reside is highly influential in preparing students for success in higher education, yet the meritocracy narrative suggests that it is the student's ability that differs instead of their exposure to preparation.

The meritocracy narrative also conceals that college admissions are highly influenced by SES. As was just discussed: low-income students have less access to AP classes. However, Wildhagen (2014) found that when AP classes become more available to disadvantaged students, the AP classes become less valuable to those disadvantaged students in the college admissions process. So, when few disadvantaged students had access to AP classes, the AP credential was more valuable for their college admissions folder. Yet, as AP classes become more democratized, they become less valuable in the disadvantaged student's admissions folder. Changing the value of a commodity once more people have access to it is a form of social closure. It is akin to convening a club in a secret location and when non-club members find the location and try to join, the club location is changed.

The narrative that college admissions is meritocratic also conceals that using standardized tests, such as the SAT, in admissions decisions favors higher economic status students. The narrative that the SAT is an accurate reflection of student ability does not include important caveats. SAT scores are highly correlated with the student's family wealth. Wealthy students have the resources to take SAT preparation courses and hire SAT tutors. Wealthy students also have the resources to take the SAT multiple times to increase their scores.

The connectivity of SAT scores and family wealth contributes to the perpetuation of higher education socioeconomic inequality. Higher education institutions that are attempting to secure students whose families can afford to pay full tuition can use the SAT as a budget tool. The link between SAT scores and family wealth is essentially what makes it helpful to some universities. In *The Power of Privilege: Yale and America's Elite Colleges*, Soares (2007) explores the way elite institutions have used the SAT over the years. Soares writes that Yale, as an elite institution, continued to publicize the SAT scores for the entering class annually. He contends that "It did so knowing the SAT's poor capacity to predict first-year college grades, and with an awareness of the linear relationship between SAT scores and a family's SES" (Soares, 2007, p. 136). Knowing that SAT scores were not good predictors of first-year success, which was the proposed benefit the SAT provided, the elite school continued to use SAT scores in admission decisions. Soares (2007) concludes:

> Yale, despite its vast resources and commitment to academic excellence, never bothered to research whether the SAT was more contaminated by SES bias than were other available substitutes. Perhaps the SAT was too convenient to Yale's goal of capturing approximately 60 percent of each undergraduate cohort as full-fee paying clients for the OIR [Office of Institutional Research] to raise the idea that the SAT's linear relationship to SES was anything other than an unfortunate and inescapable reality of educational standards.
>
> *(p. 136)*

While the meritocracy narrative suggests that students have the same opportunity to perform well on standardized tests like the SAT, the narrative conceals many caveats. Performance on the SAT is linked to family wealth. From the institutional perspective, if SAT scores are linked to wealth, then the financial income of the institution can be improved when higher scores are required for admission. Importantly, these types of caveats are not highlighted in the meritocracy narrative.

Myth: Community college is an equivalent entry point for students aspiring to a bachelor's degree

Over 80 percent of students entering community college intend to transfer and earn a bachelor's degree (Horn & Skomsvold, 2012). Yet, only 25 percent of community college students actually transfer to a four-year college within five years (Jenkins & Fink, 2015). Ultimately, of the over 80 percent of community college students who intended to earn a bachelor's degree, only 17 percent earn that bachelor's degree within six years of transferring (Jenkins & Fink, 2015). However, among students who start at a public four-year degree-granting institution, 58 percent earn their bachelor's degree within six years (NCES, 2015). The numbers suggest that despite aspirations of a bachelor's degree, students who start that journey at a community college achieve the goal of a bachelor's degree at less than half the rate.

Our intent is not to disparage community colleges. Our argument is that if a student aspires to earn a bachelor's degree, beginning that journey at a community college decreases the student's changes of achieving that goal. The narrative that community colleges are an educationally equalizing option for low SES students conceals many realities.

Community colleges have been lauded by policy leaders as an economical and effective route to a four-year college degree (see, for example, Fain, 2014; Obama, Office of the Press Secretary, 2015). However, the majority of students who begin higher education at a community college do not transfer to a four-year institution even though that was their original intent (Monaghan & Attewell, 2015). More research is necessary to identify *why* students who aspired to a bachelor's degree and earn approximately 60 credit hours at the community college do not transfer to four-year institutions (Monaghan & Attewell, 2015). At present, what research does suggest is that transfers from community college to four-year college happen in lower numbers than the policy makers' narratives imply.

The narrative that community college is an equivalent entry point for students aspiring to a bachelor's degree also conceals the challenges stemming from the transfer process. Many students who transfer from community college to four-year public college lose substantial credit hours in the process. Monaghan and Attewell (2015) found "only 58% of community college transfers were able to bring over 90% or more of their college credits to the 4-year institution" (p. 83).

They also found that 14 percent of students essentially have to start from scratch after transferring because the four-year institution accepts less than 10 percent of their credits. Research suggests that student uncertainty about their major and their future institution is a primary contributor to loss of credits, as well as a lack of early, personalized academic advice (Hodara, Martinez-Wenzel, Stevens, & Mazzeo, 2016). Transferring students must then take additional hours to make up for the credit hours they lost in the transfer process. The narrative that community college is an economical and effective route to a bachelor's degree conceals the challenging realities of transferring.

Myth: Inequity in higher education is simply about financial aid

Increasing financial aid for students is helpful in addressing financial barriers; however, financial aid alone will not significantly improve outcomes for low SES students. Research on graduation rates of students with Pell Grants reveals that students receiving the grant complete degrees at a 14 percent lower rate than non-Pell students (Nichols, 2015). Yet, institutional level analysis indicates that the average gap within institutions is only 5.7 percent (Nichols, 2015). This means that the largest differences between Pell Grant and non-Pell students is a result of the differences between institutions themselves. Nichols (2015) contends:

> But even if all institutional-level gaps in completion between Pell and non-Pell students were eliminated, there would still be a considerable national gap because too many Pell students attend institutions where few students of any sort graduate, and too few attend institutions where most students graduate.
>
> (p. 1)

If students receiving Pell Grants continue to attend institutions that have poor graduation rates, both taxpayers and students suffer.

Higher education institutions that do not graduate high percentages of their low-income students have strong financial incentives to maintain a narrative that steers attention toward the students' preparation-levels and financial challenges. Currently, low-performing institutions that graduate few students collect money from the students but do not experience financial penalties when they produce few graduates. A narrative that narrowly focuses on the low-income student's need for financial aid can conceal the inadequate performance of some higher education institutions.

The third proposition of the Social Construction Framework encourages scrutiny of the origins of social constructions. Unquestioned myths in policy narratives can perpetuate inequalities. The examples of policy narrative myths included in this chapter demonstrate how distorting unquestioned policy narratives can be.

Clinging to Limiting Constructs

The idea that more histograms or scatter plots depicting inequality will finally disrupt the cycle that perpetuates socioeconomic inequality in higher education seems fanciful. Policy makers, like the rest of us, tend to select evidence that supports an existing mindset. Change at the mindset or worldview level could be instrumental in making higher education more equitable. But changing mindsets means exploring some convenient constructs policy makers use to maintain the policy status quo. One construct that policy makers use to limit changes is known as the "iron triangle" (Immerwahr, Johnson, & Gasbarra, 2008, p. 4).

The iron triangle is the notion that higher education cost, quality, and access exist in a reciprocal relationship (Immerwahr, Johnson, & Gasbarra, 2008). With the three elements existing in tension with one another, when a change is made to one element, the other elements are impacted. Higher education policy leaders have described the iron triangle as a way to communicate the challenges facing higher education.

The notion that cost, quality, and access exist in a reciprocal relationship is an example of a social construct. Cost, quality, and access are concepts in their own right. Each concept has variables within it and has been studied in the context of higher education. Yet, when the three concepts are tied together in the iron triangle, they provide a defensive, nearly impenetrable shield from assertions that improvements can be made. The notion of an iron triangle is a limiting construct.

An analogy from healthcare may help demonstrate the way tying concepts together in iron triangles is limiting. Imagine a patient in a doctor's office. The doctor advises the patient about his worrisome lab results. The doctor advises the patient to stop smoking, lose some weight, and reduce his stress levels. The patient invokes an iron triangle defense. The patient argues if he stops smoking he is going to gain weight, not lose it. He continues that the only way to reduce his stress is to smoke more. And he argues that making time in his schedule to eat better would increase his stress because he already has too many time constraints. The iron triangle, therefore, limits possibilities.

We acknowledge there are relationships between policies that impact cost, quality, and access in higher education. But we challenge the idea that they must exist in tension with one another. The concepts can be addressed in conjunction with one another and not at the expense of one another. Could some policies that impact cost affect access? Yes; just like some patients who stop smoking gain weight. But that need not be the case. There are higher education institutions that strive to address all three issues of cost, quality, and access. If policy makers and institutional leaders reconsider the notion that the iron triangle is an appropriate construct, perhaps more solutions can be created for providing accessible, affordable, high quality college educations to low SES students.

Conclusion

As a mechanism for the (re)production of socioeconomic inequality in higher education, policy requires scrutiny. Currently, policy makers at the institution, state, and federal levels are influencing the access and experience of low SES college students. In this chapter, we have drawn attention to the socially constructed nature of policy to stress the ultimately changeable nature of rules and distributions. There have been, and will continue to be, differences in how equity is defined with regard to benefit distribution in higher education. However, using the Social Construction Framework, we discussed the idea that political power and social construct drive policy to draw attention to the disconnect between equity and those concepts. We provided examples of how policies perpetuate the socioeconomic inequality in higher education. By highlighting myths and constructs that have limiting effects on higher education policy makers, we suggest the importance of considering heuristics and mindsets that influence policy making.

In an article reflecting on their 45 years of scholarly work focused on higher education equity, the esteemed researchers Alexander and Helen Astin argue that for those who work in higher education, the greatest contribution to improving equity may be at the student level. They reflect that through the years they have seen little evidence of the structural changes that have been repeatedly recommended. Now, they suggest redirected focus to the student level. Astin and Astin (2015) write that they have

> come to the conclusion that since the structural barriers that stand in the way of achieving greater equity for students—a hierarchical system of institutions, the continuing heavy reliance on standardized test scores, diminishing state support for public institutions, to name just a few—show little sign of changing, it makes little sense to continue focusing our current energies on trying to change these structures.
>
> (p. 72)

Instead of focusing on structural changes, they argue that higher education professionals will have the greatest impact on equity by fostering a new generation who are more caring, aware, and committed to social justice than prior generations.

We understand frustrations about the unchanging structural elements of higher education that perpetuate inequality. However, in this chapter, we argued that the role social construction plays in policy making is encouraging for the prospect of change. Underlying the structural elements are human decisions based on social constructions that we contend are changeable. While Astin and Astin's (2015) contention is that inroads can be made by working with students to foster caring, awareness, and commitments to social justice, we argue that inroads can be made by similarly working with higher education policy makers. Waiting for the "next generation of leaders, public servants, and engaged citizens" (Astin & Astin, 2015, p. 73), as the Astins suggest, excuses this generation of leaders and policy makers of their responsibilities.

References

Astin, A., & Astin, H. (2015). Achieving equity in higher education: The unfinished agenda. *Journal of College and Character, 16*(2), 65–74.

Bettinger, E., Long, B., Oreopoulos, P., & Sanbonmatsu, L. (2009). *The role of simplification and information in college decisions: Results from the H&R Block FAFSA experiment.* National Bureau of Economic Research. NBER Working paper no. 15361. Retrieved from www.nber.org/papers/w15361.

Bettinger, E., Long, B., Oreopoulos, P., & Sanbonmatsu, L. (2012). The role of application assistance and information in college decisions: Results from the H&R Block FAFSA experiment. *Quarterly Journal of Economics, 127*(3). Retrieved from http://isites.harvard.edu/fs/docs/icb.topic1232998.files//Bettinger_et_al_2012_Role_of_Application_Assistance_and_Info.pdf.

Bourdieu, P. (1984). *Distinction: A social critique of the judgment of taste.* Cambridge, MA: Harvard University Press.

Bowen, W., Chingos, M., & McPherson, M. (2011). *Crossing the finish line: Completing college at America's public universities.* Princeton, NJ: Princeton University Press.

Brubacher, J., & Rudy, W. (2008). *Higher education in transition: A history of American colleges and universities* (4th ed.). New Brunswick, NJ: Transaction Publishers.

Carey, K. (2015, May 18). The in-state tuition break, slowly disappearing. *New York Times.* Retrieved from www.nytimes.com/2015/05/19/upshot/the-in-state-tuition-break-slowly-disappearing.html?_r=0.

Carnavale, A., & Rose, S. (2004). *Socioeconomic status, race/ethnicity, and selective college admissions.* New York, NY: A Century Foundation Paper. Century Foundation. Retrieved from www.eric.ed.gov/contentdelivery/servlet/ERICServlet?accno=ED482419.

Crotty, J. (2014, April 29). Students in poor and minority school districts less likely to be taught by highly effective teachers. *Forbes.* Retrieved from www.forbes.com/sites/jamesmarshallcrotty/2014/04/29/report-students-in-poor-and-minority-school-districts-less-likely-to-be-taught-by-highly-effective-teachers/#289e159a2ea8.

Dar, L. (2014). Toward a better understanding of equity in higher education finance and policy. In M. B. Paulsen (Ed.), *Higher education: Handbook of theory and research: Volume 29.* (pp. 535–571). Dordrecht, Netherlands: Springer Science+Business Media Dordrecht.

Desrochers, D., & Hurlburt, S. (2016). *Trends in college spending: 2003–2013. Where does the money come from? Where does it go? What does it buy?* Washington, DC: Delta Cost Project at American Institutes for Research.

Fain, P. (2014, August 26). Aggressive pragmatism. *Inside Higher Ed.* Retrieved from www.insidehighered.com/news/2014/08/26/bill-haslams-free-community-college-plan-and-how-tennessee-grabbing-spotlight-higher.

Feeney, M., & Heroff, J. (2013). Barriers to need-based financial aid: Predictors of timely FAFSA completion among low-income students. *Journal of Student Financial Aid, 43*(2), 65–85. Retrieved from http://publications.nasfaa.org/cgi/viewcontent.cgi?article=1204&context=jsfa.

Freire, P. (1970). *Pedagogy of the oppressed*. New York, NY: Seabury Press.
Gilbert, C., & Heller, D. (2013). Access, equity, and community colleges: The Truman Commission and federal higher education policy from 1947 to 2011. *Journal of Higher Education, 84*(3), 417–443.
Harnisch, T., & Lebioda, K. (2016). *Top 10 higher education state policy issues for 2016*. Washington, DC: American Association of State Colleges and Universities.
Hodara, M., Martinez-Wenzl, M., Stevens, D., & Mazzeo, C. (2016). *Improving credit mobility for community college transfer students: Findings and recommendations from a 10-state study*. Portland, OR: Education Northwest. Retrieved from www.luminafoundation.org/files/resources/improving-credit-mobility.pdf.
Horn, L., & Skomsvold, P. (2012). *Community college student outcomes 1994–2009 (NCES Report 2012-253)*. US Department of Education. Retrieved from http://nces.ed.gov/pubs2012/2012253.pdf.
Immerwahr, J., Johnson, J., & Gasbarra, P. (2008). *The iron triangle: College presidents talk about costs, access, and quality*. A report from the National Center for Public Policy and Higher Education and Public Agenda. Retrieved from www.highereducation.org/reports/iron_triangle/IronTriangle.pdf.
Ingram, H., Schneider, A. L., & deLeon, P. (2007). Social construction and policy design. In P. A. Sabatier (Ed.), *Theories of the policy process*. Boulder, CO: Westview Press.
Jaggars, S. (2012). Online learning in community colleges. In M. G. Moore (Ed.), *Handbook of distance education* (3rd ed., pp. 594–608). New York, NY: Routledge.
Jaggars, S. (2014). Democratization of education for whom? Online learning and educational equity. *Diversity & Democracy, 17*(1). Retrieved from www.aacu.org/diversitydemocracy/2014/winter/jaggars.
Jenkins, D., & Fink, J. (2015). *What we know about transfer*. New York, NY: Columbia University, Teachers College, Community College Research Center.
Lieberman, A. (2015, January 15). *Equitable funding: Which states are leading the way?* Washington, DC: New America EdCentral. Retrieved from www.edcentral.org/equitable-funding-states.
McNamee, S., & Miller, R., Jr., (2014). *The meritocracy myth* (3rd ed.). Lanham, MD: Rowman & Littlefield Publishers.
Monaghan, D., & Attewell, P. (2015). The community college route to the bachelor's degree. *Educational Evaluation and Policy Analysis, 37*(1), 70–91.
NCES. (2015). *The condition of education 2015 (NCES 2015-144), Institutional retention and graduation rates for undergraduate students*. US Department of Education. Retrieved from https://nces.ed.gov/fastfacts/display.asp?id=40.
Newell, M. (2011). *An exploration of civic engagement of community college students and graduates*. Dissertation. Retrieved from https://rpgroup.org/resources/exploration-civic-engagement-community-college-students.
Nichols, A. (2015, September). *The Pell partnership: Ensuring a shared responsibility for low-income student success*. The Education Trust. Retrieved from https://edtrust.org/wp-content/uploads/2014/09/ThePellPartnership_EdTrust_20152.pdf.
Obama; Office of the Press Secretary. (2015, January 9). *Fact sheet: White House unveils America's College Promise proposal: Tuition-free community college for responsible students*. Retrieved from www.whitehouse.gov/the-press-office/2015/01/09/fact-sheet-white-house-unveils-america-s-college-promise-proposal-tuitio.
O'Shaughnessy, L. (2011, August 23). How colleges determine merit scholarships. US News & World Report. Retrieved from www.usnews.com/education/blogs/the-college-solution/2011/08/23/how-colleges-determine-merit-scholarships.

PCHE [President's Commission on Higher Education]. (1947). *Higher education for American democracy: Volume II, Equalizing and expanding individual opportunity*. A report of the President's Commission on Higher Education. Washington, DC: US Government Print Office.

Pell Institute. (2015). *Indicators of higher education equity in the United States: 45 year trend report*. Retrieved from www.pellinstitute.org/downloads/publications-Indicators_of_Higher_Education_Equity_in_the_US_45_Year_Trend_Report.pdf.

Picciano, A. G., & Spring, J. (2013). *The great American education-industrial complex: Ideology, technology, and profit*. New York, NY: Routledge.

Public Agenda. (2013). *What employers and community college students think about online education*. New York, NY: Public Agenda.

Roe, E. (1994). *Narrative policy analysis: Theory and practice*. Durham, NC: Duke University Press.

Schneider, A., & Ingram, H. (1993). Social construction of target populations: Implications for politics and policy. *American Political Science Review, 87*(2), 334–347.

Schneider, A., Ingram, H., & deLeon, P. (2014). Democratic policy design: Social construction of target populations. In P. A. Sabatier & C. M. Weible (Eds), *Theories of the policy process* (3rd ed., pp. 105–149). Boulder, CO: Westview Press.

Soares, J. (2007). *The power of privilege: Yale and America's elite colleges*. Stanford, CA: Stanford University Press.

Southern Education Foundation. (2015). *A new majority: Low income students now a majority in the nation's public schools*. Retrieved from www.southerneducation.org/getattachment/4ac62e27-5260-47a5-9d02-14896ec3a531/A-New-Majority-2015-Update-Low-Income-Students-Now.aspx.

Stone, D. (2012). *Policy paradox: The art of political decision making* (3rd ed.). New York, NY: W. W. Norton & Company.

US Department of Education. (n.d.). *Laws & guidance: Overview*. Retrieved from www2.ed.gov/policy/landing.jhtml.

Wildhagen, T. (2014). Unequal returns to academic credentials as a hidden dimension of race and class inequality in American college enrollments. *Research in Social Stratification and Mobility, 38*, 18–31.

Witham, K., Malcom-Piqueux, L., Dowd, A., & Bensimon, E. (2015). *America's unmet promise: The imperative for equity in higher education*. Washington, DC: Association of American Colleges and Universities.

Xu, D., & Jaggars, S. (2013). The impact of online learning on students' course outcomes: Evidence from a large community and technical college system. *Economics of Education Review, 37*, 46–57.

2
THE CONSEQUENCES OF UNEXAMINED PRACTICES ON CLASS INEQUALITY

In addition to the policy issues raised in the previous chapter, there are practices common in higher education institutions today that contribute to the growing inequality in students' learning experiences. Even on the same college campus, research suggests that lower SES students experience higher education differently than their wealthy counterparts (Armstrong & Hamilton, 2013). Many operational practices have not kept pace with the changing needs of the economically diversified student body. Regardless of whether institutions provide greater access to higher education for lower-income students, until the experience of college is made more equitable for all classes, the cycle of inequity will continue. In this chapter, we draw attention to the often unexamined operational practices that influence the way students of lower SES experience college.

Practices Resulting from Public Divestment

University leaders face complex and competing pressures, which sometimes translate into organizational practices that result in parts of a higher education institution working at cross-purposes. For example, institutional public relations departments frequently extol the merits of equal opportunity while admissions offices are mandated to recruit students who can pay the tuition, preferably at the much higher out-of-state rate. Another example occurs in the student affairs realm where students are offered an increasingly vast array of activities many of them can no longer afford with rising tuition rates necessitating more hours spent working. The result of these (and other) contradictions is a system of practices that exacerbate rather than mitigate inequality in higher education.

In this chapter, we identify these problematic institutional practices and posit public divestment in higher education as their source. As universities have attempted to compensate for budget shortfalls, they have looked to solutions like aggressive fundraising, recruitment of high achieving and/or full pay students, and increased grant activity. While these strategies may be appropriate in some contexts, we argue their current overemphasis creates mission creep. As we will further discuss in Chapter 3, the public rightly questions why it should support institutions that are in danger of becoming bastions for the elite.

The very practices higher education institutions have engaged to compensate for the lack of state and federal funding are now undermining their credibility with the public whose support they need. If increased attention to fundraising, commercial research, grant activity, and lucrative student recruitment had paid off, it would be difficult to argue that public funding is better than these alternatives. Universities turned to these practices with the hope that they would be financially beneficial. The prevailing logic is that while some of these strategies may be unseemly, they are necessary evils as a means to a greater end. The problem is that they have not achieved this greater end and have become ends in themselves.

Fundraising

Fundraising seems like a logical way to replace funds lost due to public divestment in higher education. After all, public universities are non-profit entities with long histories of soliciting donations from their alumni. The problem with contemporary fundraising in many public institutions lies in its shift from means to end. Traditionally, institutions raised funds as a means to an end defined and driven by the college. Now, donors play a greater role in defining that end, not surprisingly in accordance with their self-interest and/or ideological leanings. Rather than private funds augmenting a public good, the public entity is re-shaped to the private donors' wishes.

This point extends far beyond buildings named after wealthy benefactors; concerns about this practice seem almost quaint given the power of today's donors. Contemporary donors can influence activities once seen as too sacred to sell on the open market, such as the curriculum. For example, Marshall University accepted a $1 million gift with the caveat that Ayn Rand's *Atlas Shrugged* be taught in the business school (Jaschik, 2008). The Koch brothers gave more than $12.7 million to 163 colleges and universities in 2012 with the goal of "reinvigorating the teaching of America's founding principles and history" (Strauss, 2014, para. 11).

University officials have claimed that such gifts come with no strings attached, but this does not appear to be entirely true. Florida State University, for instance, accepted a Koch-appointed advisory committee in exchange for a $1.5 million gift, according to a *Tampa Bay Times* report (Hundley, 2011). The committee's work included faculty hiring decisions and annual reviews, activities generally considered not for sale in public institutions.

The aforementioned examples represent the most egregious conflicts of interest that result from an overemphasis on private donors' roles in public institutions. These cases are important and worth studying as cautionary tales because they erode public confidence and undermine the case for public support. In *Beyond the University*, Michael Roth (2014) analyzes the historical connection between institutions' ability to provide a civically-minded, liberal arts education and the need for public financing: "This was why Jefferson argued that taxpayers should foot the bill, rather than count on churches or rich benefactors to see to the people's education" (p. 25).

But the subtler forms of donors' outsized influence are equally significant because they drain human and financial resources from the more substantive work of the university. Consider the enormous amount of money spent on college sports, a cost often justified for its purported contribution to school spirit and potential to boost alumni giving. While it is not possible to know what role athletics play in alumni giving, it would be hard to make the case that it's anywhere close to the $10.3 billion public universities invested in their sports programs over the past five years (Wolverton, Hallman, Shifflett, & Kambhampati, 2015). Much of this money comes from athletics fees paid by students already struggling to pay tuition, room/board, book, and other costs.

Commercial Research and Grants

The pressure to engage in sponsored research and procure grants has intensified as universities look for alternative funding sources. As in the case of fundraising, this seems like a logical solution given the attractive revenue streams potentially afforded by increased participation in commercial research and grant activity. Unfortunately, there have been several unintended consequences of universities counting too heavily on commercial research and grants.

In the biggest picture, the most significant negative outcome has been the lack of return on the investment of institutional resources spent on commercial research. The current debate about technology transfer illustrates this point. *Technology transfer* refers to the process by which technologies developed in university labs are made into commercial products. In their seminal work on academic capitalism, Slaughter and Rhoades (2004) explain how emulation of top tier universities' technology transfer activities has not paid off for the vast majority of higher education institutions:

> A relatively small number of universities are responsible for the lion's share of patenting activity and run their technology transfer efforts in the black. In the 1990s, the one hundred largest universities received more than 90 percent of all patents awarded. Incomes from patents was also concentrated in the top one hundred institutions; the most recent survey indicates

that two-thirds of the monies were generated by thirteen institutions. However, most doctoral granting institutions maintained technology transfer offices, as did a few comprehensive universities. In other words, a number of universities bore the expense of technology transfer offices but reaped relatively few rewards.

(Chapter 12, para. 23)

We raise the financial issue first because the monetary benefit is often used as a preemptive strike against the other concerns that have been raised about contemporary universities' attraction to commercial research. The logic is that commercial research may not be ideal in organizations which purportedly exist for a public good, but its economic benefits outweigh those costs. Yet as world class economic scholars Sheila Slaughter and Gary Rhoades point out, these benefits only exist for the most elite institutions. Compared to the entire breadth of higher education, large, elite institutions have disproportionate resources. The large, elite institutions have know-how, well-funded labs, publishing clout, and financial packages to attract premiere faculty. Using data collected from technology licensing offices, DiGregorio and Shane (2003) found intellectual eminence of the faculty was a key determinant in how effective an institution is at exploiting university knowledge into profitable technology licensure.

Technology transfers' costs, however, impact all colleges and universities that participate in these activities. Some of the costs include the marginalization of academic departments less favorably positioned to produce commercial products (for example, the humanities), lack of funding for research that supports public aims but may not be financially lucrative, and drain on faculty time and attention that could be spent on teaching.

These costs are equally true in higher education institutions that give grant writing an outsized role. While attractive as alternative funding sources, grants generate their own costs in terms of the increased staff needed to research, write, and manage them. Large grants tend to be labor intensive, requiring significant time in both writing and administrative compliance.

We believe there are roles for both commercial research and grant activity in the academy in contexts where public and private interests are thoughtfully weighed. Problems result when these strategies are used as a replacement for the public funding necessary for universities to fulfill their teaching and public research missions.

Lucrative Students

Recruiting lucrative students has now become a popular strategy in the effort to make up for budget shortfalls resulting from public divestment. We generally mean *lucrative* here as able to pay full tuition, ideally at the out-of-state rate. Lucrative students can also be those whose SAT scores, high school GPA, and class ranking help raise the profile of the college they attend. These students are lucrative to higher education institutions because they allow these universities to rise in the rankings, thus making them more competitive and allowing them to raise tuition, recruit star faculty, etc. Given the strong relationship between a student's family income and their SAT score, there is great overlap between these two groups, but it's not a perfect correlation so we make this distinction in our use of the term, *lucrative*.

The commodification of higher education has heightened the pressure to move up in the rankings as colleges and universities compete for student-customers. While heavy competition may benefit consumers in the private sector, it tends to create perverse incentives in higher education. Pressured to appear more selective and prestigious, universities intensively recruit high achieving students with full merit scholarships while becoming less accessible to students who may be talented, but lack the AP courses and expensive test preparation classes their wealthier counterparts can afford. Thus the rankings frenzy further exacerbates higher education's ability to address class inequality.

Unbridled competition not only favors financially advantaged students, it incentivizes practices that actively exclude struggling students. Mount St. Mary's President, Simon Newman, recently came under fire for pushing a policy to improve the college's retention rates by encouraging students to drop out of school before the institution had to report its numbers to the Department of Education. According to Jaschik's (2016) *Inside Higher Ed* story, student journalists obtained an email in which Newman responded to faculty objections by arguing "This is hard for you because you think of the students as cuddly bunnies, but you can't. You just have to drown the bunnies . . . put a Glock to their heads" (para. 4).

While Newman's rhetoric was harsher than most, the ethos behind his words has become commonplace. This is perhaps no more true than in the international student market, where Chinese students in particular are routinely referred to as "cash cows." Attractive for the new wealth that has generated the ability for many Asian (particularly Chinese and Korean) families to be able to pay the full, out-of-state rate, these students are heavily recruited by many American colleges and universities.

Aside from the obvious ethical problem of treating students as means to financial goals rather than ends in their own right, the strategy is starting to backfire as Asian students report dissatisfaction with their American higher education experience. Stuck in language programs and isolated from other students, research indicates many Asian students experience heightened stress due to lack of institutional support (Yan & Berliner, 2013). This lack of investment in truly and substantively serving these students is the economic problem with "cash cow" thinking. As a result of these poor ethical and business practices, the US is becoming a less attractive choice for Asian students considering international education (Fischer, 2014).

Classism within Institutions of Higher Education

Even when low-income students overcome the myriad obstacles to accessing higher education, their experience while in college contains significantly more challenges than those faced by their middle- and upper-class counterparts. While some of the causes are well-known, others are either unclear and/or distorted by taken-for-granted institutional attitudes and practices.

Lacking a Sense of Belonging

The most obvious form of classism within institutions of higher education comes from low-income students' self-reporting about exclusion from both the classroom and the co-curriculum. As with other aspects of diversity, the majority of those working on college campuses do not intentionally marginalize those from socioeconomic class backgrounds different from their own. Yet many universities' cultural norms stimulate feelings of isolation and confusion for low-income students because they reflect middle/upper-class experiences.

Something as simple as the co-curriculum can reproduce the privilege with which middle- and upper-class students enter college. Co-curricular activities have many benefits, particularly for low-income students whom researchers found actually derive more positive outcomes than their middle- and upper-class counterparts (Pascarella, Pierson, Wolniak, & Terenzini, 2004). Yet the co-curriculum is often inaccessible to working-class students for many reasons, including both the need to work and lack of student organization experience. Low-income students frequently receive relatively little investment in their K-12 schools, causing them to lack both the knowledge and confidence necessary to take on leadership experiences. Coupled with the pressure to save money by commuting and completing college quickly and efficiently, low-income students often find themselves paying for opportunities they have little chance of accessing.

In terms of academic cultural disconnects, talking to faculty can be an activity that comes more easily to middle- and upper-class students due to the congruence between the cultural norms of their childhood and those of most university environments. Middle- and upper-class parents tend to instill values of autonomy and independence, encouraging their children to navigate the adult world fairly early in life (Lareau, 2011). Working-class families are less likely to see authority as accessible or negotiable, placing a higher value on both respect and interdependence with one's relatives.

Lareau is careful to point out that neither cultural practice is necessarily better or worse. Middle- and upper-class children's upbringing affords some benefits like social capital, but also some costs in the form of entitlement and lack of resilience. Likewise, working-class children may benefit from being raised to be more thoughtful and generous, but suffer from the lack of experience that comes from advocating for oneself. Acknowledging the assets many working-class students bring to college would be a positive development on campuses that may unwittingly overvalue middle- and upper-class students' cultural experiences.

To return to the example of talking to faculty, then, one can see how working-class students may experience a cultural disconnect unless intentional efforts have been made to sensitive members of the campus community to recognize and appreciate students from all class backgrounds. Even without intending to discriminate, faculty often perceive middle- and upper-class students as more intelligent simply because they frequently speak the same language (Crossley, 2008). Consequently, professors sometimes express lower expectations and assumptions of intellectual deficits based on issues of cultural capital rather than academic ability (Espinoza, 2011). These situations create a vicious cycle for low-income students who internalize these experiences as confirmation that they do not in fact belong in college, a suspicion with which many of them begin their freshman year (Barratt, 2011).

Though culture change is notoriously difficult, it can be done through concerted effort and institutional commitment. As Soria and Bultmann (2014) found, simple awareness and open communication about socioeconomic class can create a more welcoming campus climate for low-income students. Unfortunately, faulty perceptions and cultural norms do not account for all of the reasons working-class students experience more formidable challenges in their experience of higher education. Low-income students' overrepresentation in underresourced K-12 schools plays a significant role that must be both acknowledged and addressed if universities are to interrupt rather than reproduce class inequality in education.

College Readiness

There has been an increase in pressure to promote college readiness, defined as one's capacity to complete academic work at the postsecondary level without remediation. There are many indicators of college readiness, though the ones most frequently referenced tend to be high school GPA and SAT/ACT scores. Attendance in secondary schools that emphasize college preparation for all students, knowledge of how to choose between higher education institutions, information about financial aid processes, and understanding of academic expectations at the postsecondary level are less measurable, but equally important to consider when examining college readiness holistically.

Not surprisingly, K-12 schools in the neighborhoods where most low-income young people live often lack both the culture of college preparation and the resources necessary to create college ready students. Holland and Farmer-Hinton (2009) define college cultures as "environments that are accessible to all students and saturated with ever-present information, resources, and ongoing formal and informal conversations that help students to understand the various facets of preparing for, enrolling in, and graduating from postsecondary academic institutions as those experiences specifically pertain to the students' current and future lives" (p. 26). These elements of culture and resource are intricately connected, forming a system of inequality that disadvantages poor and minority students from the beginning of their educational careers. Schools need reasonable student/guidance counselor ratios, experienced teachers, and time in the day to create the personalized learning community necessary to foster these qualities essential to cultures that promote college readiness.

Burdens placed on underresourced schools under the No Child Left Behind Act undermine educators' ability to foster climates that promote college readiness. The extreme amount of time and energy spent on standardized test preparation, for example, depletes resources that might be used to provide students with information about colleges, financial aid, and what they need to do to prepare themselves for the transition.

Less obvious, but equally important is the issue of stigma. When underresourced schools are labeled as failing and deficient, a host of problems that impact their ability to promote a culture of college readiness occur. Hamstrung by the negative labels, teachers and students alike become demoralized about college as a possibility in marginalized communities. Teacher turnover in poor schools exacerbates the issue, making it difficult for students to trust the very adults they need to mentor them through the often daunting process of gaining information about higher education. K-12 schools are even more important sources of college knowledge for low-income students, who are less likely to have parents or siblings familiar with what they need to know to navigate college choice, financial aid, etc.

Higher education faculty and administrators need to understand these issues of college readiness in order to attempt to level the playing field once students from all K-12 schools enter their campuses. If higher education leaders are not sensitive to the grossly unequal K-12 schools their students experienced, it becomes easy to blame the victim by pathologizing either low-income students or their underresourced schools. Yet the blame should land squarely at the feet of the politicians who allow these gross inequities to occur. In our home state of Ohio, for example, the inequality in school funding was declared unconstitutional over 15 years ago. Not only has there been no follow up to fix the problem, legislators recently introduced a bill to amend Ohio's constitution rather than actually address the problem substantively (Kasler, 2014).

University leaders need to be better advocates for their K-12 counterparts in situations like the Ohio school funding issue. Not only would closer ties create better goodwill and mutual support, but both K-12 and postsecondary institutions benefit when all students have a greater opportunity to be college ready. In the smaller picture, there are proactive measures higher education institutions can take to acknowledge and mitigate college readiness issues low-income students may face. Mentoring and summer bridge programs, for example, have yielded positive results in boosting recruitment and retention rates for low-income students. Institutions must make a commitment to all students rather than being satisfied with measures like the aforementioned president's suggestion to "drown the bunnies." Taking on the challenge to level the playing field would go a long way toward making higher education institutions more effective in serving the students who need them most.

Cultural and Social Capital

Summer bridge and other mentoring programs provide important support for low-income students because they address the issue of cultural capital. As mentioned in the context of creating a sense of belonging, low-income students sometimes face challenges adjusting to campus life due to different cultural expectations. Mentors can play a vital role in softening the impacts of cultural disconnects, providing both information and emotional support as students learn to navigate the transition from high school to college.

It can be difficult for those raised in families and schools where college preparation was assumed to appreciate fully how much support a young person socialized with different expectations might need. There are so many aspects of college readiness that seem obvious to middle/upper-income, continuing generation students that may require translation and/or explanation for low-income, first generation students. Welton and Williams (2015) describe this challenge in the story of a research participant:

> For example, Kendra, a freshman enrolled in AP courses, had aspirations to attend an Ivy League college but said, "I don't study, like in class for me. I don't like homework or studying or anything like that, so if they give me homework or they say study, I study in class. That's the only time I do it . . ." Unfortunately, in conversation it was clear that Kendra was unaware that her "I don't do homework at home" rule did not match the studying stamina she would need to gain access to her ultimate goal, an Ivy League institution.
>
> *(p. 198)*

Kendra's story illustrates the importance of understanding more deeply and precisely the challenges low-income students often bring to their higher education experience. The good news in this situation is that these challenges can be overcome. The problem is not inside of Kendra; she simply needs guidance about what is often referred to as *habits of the mind*, those time management, focus, persistence, and other cognitive skills necessary to translate one's goals into actionable outcomes.

The first step for Kendra is likely mentorship from someone who understands these habits of the mind as skills that can be taught rather than traits students either naturally have or lack. Too often, educators conflate lack of preparation with lack of intelligence and/or drive. These educators are likely well intentioned; people generally enter education fields with good motivations. But the "you don't know what you don't know" proverb applies here.

For those raised in households and schools where the aforementioned habits of the mind were part of the fabric, it can be difficult to even see these habits as skills that need to be explained. They simply become part of the taken-for-granted assumptions that constitute some—but not all—students' reality. Without intentional attention paid to these skills, low-income students may fall through the cracks, especially at large institutions where personalized help is difficult to access. Worse yet, the students themselves may attribute these holes in their knowledge as evidence that they don't belong in college, internalizing a systemic problem as an intellectual or character defect.

Early scholarship on economically disenfranchised students tended to focus on their lack of cultural capital in the context of higher education. While it's true low-income and/or first generation students may not be as familiar with some of the cultural norms of college life, focusing exclusively on cultural capital tells a distorted story. As DeRosa and Dolby (2014) explain, "Framing the issue in this way fosters the tendency to adopt a deficit language in which poor student outcomes are attributed to the shortcoming of the student rather than the institution's role" (p. 3). It is therefore important to examine how social and cultural capital intersect in the experiences of low-income students.

Social capital refers to the networks people access as they progress toward their goals. Obvious forms of social capital may be relatives or friends with connections to employment opportunities. Subtler examples of social capital might include an older sibling who attended law school and can advise a student on the LSAT and application process, and provide information about programs. Social capital often exists even more amorphously in the form of knowledge that feels so intuitive to a person they can hardly remember not knowing it. Not only is the knowledge itself a form of capital, but the confidence that comes from easily feeling part of the community of knowers provides a big advantage to those who enter a new environment armed with these resources.

Cultural and social capital work in concert. As Tierney (2013) explains, "The simple accumulation of instrumental pieces of knowledge—cultural capital—was insufficient without the networks to put those pieces of knowledge into play" (pp. 258–259). Middle- and upper-class students often enter college with social capital in the form of family and friends who can connect them to enrichment opportunities. As research on the intersection between social class and childrearing demonstrates, middle- and upper-class parents approach childrearing with what Lareau (2011) calls an emphasis on concerned cultivation. Concerned cultivation includes teaching children skills like how to talk to adults and self-advocate. As a result, these children grow up with a sense of comfort and ease in the networking skills that lead to an ever-expanding social capital.

Working-class parents, on the other hand, tend to raise their children in what Lareau termed the natural growth approach. Obedience to adults is more emphasized in this method, resulting in fewer opportunities to develop the networking skills that accompany the concerned cultivation approach more common in middle- and upper-class parenting. Both approaches have assets and liabilities. Concerned cultivation can result in both good networking and problematic entitlement; natural growth yields both resilience and unfamiliarity with some aspects of negotiating with adults.

One of the most positive outcomes in Lareau's and others' research on the ways social class and parenting intersect is that it has the power to correct assumptions about what we think all students should somehow know. Greater understanding and incorporation of this research could shape better, more informed university practices designed to help all students thrive.

Meritocracy

All that has been discussed to this point assumes low-income students make it to college in the first place. Given the considerable challenges these students experience, admission ought not be understood as a foregone conclusion. The politics of what can, should be, and/or is considered when admitting freshman classes to public universities—particularly flagship institutions—remains hotly contested. Class-based affirmative action seems like a fair solution. Poor and working-class students often overcome many barriers in graduating from underfunded secondary schools. We believe it is fair for admissions processes to acknowledge these students' resilience in the face of adversity.

Yet class-based affirmative action raises thorny issues due to its use by some politicians seeking to avoid affirmative action based on race. It seems intuitive that class-based affirmative action would achieve the goals of greater ethnic minority participation in higher education as well, given the overrepresentation of students of color in low-income schools. Yet studies have shown that class-based affirmative action does not solve the problem of achieving racial parity in colleges and universities (Reardon, Baker, & Klasik, 2012). Hence race and class need to be examined both where they intersect as well as where they diverge in the context of recruiting a truly diverse range of students.

The nuances of race and class-based affirmative action are important to consider, but too much emphasis on this specific issue can cause educational leaders to miss the bigger picture of what constitutes merit in the first place. In *The Tyranny of the Meritocracy: Democratizing Higher Education in America*, Lani Guinier (2015) posits competing visions of meritocracy. She terms the status quo version *testocracy*, a term she uses to describe merit based on test scores regardless of a student's character. She advocates a return to the original definition of merit as "earned by service" (Guinier, 2015, p. 4). She adds to the definition, arguing that merit worth striving toward includes qualities essential to advancing democratic aims.

Guinier presents the substantive problems that have resulted from the testocracy vision of merit in higher education. She traces the well-known histories of standardized tests as race and class biased, pointing out their relatively weak correlation with college success compared to their high correlation with family income (Guinier, 2015, p. 19). But even if the SAT and ACT were better at predicting college students' performance, would they still be worth using to measure merit?

No, Guinier argues, because this vision of merit reduces universities to sorting machines rather than places where people grow, develop, and apply their talents to working in collaboration with others to address the most important issues of our time. In response to Supreme Court Clarence Thomas's testocratic argument against affirmative action, Guinier states:

> If, as Justice Thomas argues, students must be only admitted to places that "evenly match" them, what responsibilities are left to higher education? In Justice Thomas's formulation, universities perform little more than sorting functions, cherry-picking students who have come up the escalator of excellence and arrive at their doorsteps presumably pre-packaged and pre-equipped with everything they need for success. This drift from a mission-driven to an admission-driven higher education system should give all of us pause.
>
> *(2015, p. 4)*

Guinier makes an important and powerful argument here, moving equity concerns from the periphery to the center of higher education's purpose. Universities lose relevance when the claim can be made that they simply reflect rather than change the status quo. The assertion that students learn, grow, and change in college is predicated on the assumption that they do not, in fact, arrive perfectly educated and socialized on Day One.

A related reason Guinier cautions against the testocratic notion of merit is its role in justifying the disproportionately high allocation of resources the elite enjoy. The difference between old money and new money is that the former often knew they experienced the luck of inheritance and thus felt compelled to give back through charity and service. New money feels earned though institutionally validated merit, which can eliminate the sense of responsibility to help others who may now be viewed as less able than less fortunate. She offers a similar example of a series of articles published in the *Harvard Crimson*, mocking women students for choosing majors in education and public service over finance. The effect is to blame women for the wage gap by reminding them of their choice to enter less lucrative fields. The reduction of merit to test scores and the salaries they can buy eliminates the need to confront social injustices.

For these reasons, we agree with both Guinier's assertion that the definition of merit is important and that it ought to be re-imagined as something which includes character. We recognize this is a controversial position, complicated by the potential competing ideologies about what constitutes character. But we believe the pendulum has swung too far toward the detached rationalism that pervades public university life these days. While institutions of higher education have evolved from their colonial college tradition of instilling religious values, the current overemphasis on personal gain over all else serves neither individual students nor the public at large.

Balance between religious indoctrination and academic Darwinism is possible. Re-inserting character and moral development as serious goals of a college education would serve as a potential corrective to the obsessive sorting and ranking that continually disadvantage socioeconomically disenfranchised students. In their research on the role of spirituality in faculty life, Lindholm and Astin (2011) discuss the consequences of failing to address the competing values in contemporary higher education:

> In recent years, these conflicts have been intensified by declining resources and public pressures for greater "accountability" and, at a more personal level, by the divisions and tensions that often emerge between personal and professional life. The resulting dynamic has potentially serious implication for the academic community, not only for those faculty and staff whose lives have become increasingly fragmented and disconnected, but also for their students.
>
> (p. 51)

The fragmentation and disconnection Lindholm and Astin identify are natural consequences of organizations that have lost their center. If we continue down the path of favoring rankings and growth to the exclusion of character development and service, it will become increasingly difficult for members of a university community to have any shared vision about the purpose of their work. What value do economically disenfranchised students have in organizations that define merit in terms of test scores and other markers of prestige? Re-defining excellence and merit in light of whom they include rather than exclude is fundamental to interrupting the cycle of inequality in higher education.

Ethic of Care

There is a pervasive theme in both higher education news and scholarship about universities conducting themselves more like businesses. Whether hailed as innovation or criticized as managerialism, there is strong agreement that higher education institutions increasingly parrot elements of for-profit organizations. This book and others critique some of the specific corporate practices, such as the mission creep that can result when students are treated as customers. While these are legitimate points, sometimes the big picture gets lost in the discussion about specific issues like consumerism, executive pay, and other concerns. These more detailed issues can start to sound like minor problems that might annoy certain academics, making the concern itself easy to dismiss as either nostalgia or resistance to change.

Yet the problem of universities running like businesses is more about substance than style. Managerialism runs counter to what educational philosopher, Nel Noddings, termed an *ethic of care*. Noddings (2013) articulates with clarity and precision what is at stake when educators choose institutional thinking over human connection:

> We establish funds, or institutions, or agencies in order to provide the caretaking we judge to be necessary. The original impulse is often the one associated with caring. It arises in individuals. But as groups of individuals discuss the perceived needs of another individual or group, the imperative changes from "I must do something" to "Something must be done." This change is accompanied by a shift from the nonrational and subjective to the rational and objective. What should be done? Who should do it? Why should the persons named do it? This sort of thinking is not in itself a mistake; it is needed. But it has buried within it the seed of major error. The danger is that caring, which is essentially nonrational in that it requires a constitutive engrossment and displacement of motivation, may gradually or abruptly be transformed into abstract problem solving. There is, then, a shift of focus from the cared-for to the "problem."
>
> (p. 25)

It would be difficult to argue that higher education has not experienced this phenomenon as a result of the pressure to function more like a business. Noddings' specific point about the "displacement of motivation" required to enact a true ethic of care warrants strong consideration. The value of great teachers is widely known in the K-12 education system, yet often underemphasized at the college level. Higher education scholars frequently reference the undervaluing of teaching in colleges and universities where the premium is placed on research, particularly of the sponsored variety.

The loss of full-time, tenured faculty in colleges and universities also limits the supply of caring teachers available for both the additional academic help and personal mentoring needed by many of the most vulnerable students in an institution. The research overwhelmingly demonstrates that meaningful interaction with faculty matters both intellectually and emotionally in students' development throughout their college years (Krumrei-Mancuso, Newton, Kim, & Wilcox, 2013). Adjunct and/or non-tenured faculty can and do support students as well, but are typically stretched thin as they juggle multiple gigs to make ends meet.

The practice of shifting from full-time tenured to part-time non-tenured faculty is a well-researched topic in the literature about the professoriate, but the connection to the student experience is not always clear. Generally implemented by administrators as a cost-saving measure, the loss of tenure lines creates its own, often hidden expenses. Slaughter and Rhoades (2004), for example, found a relationship between the decline in tenured faculty and student retention rates in universities. Given the correspondence between meaningful connection with faculty and student success, this should not be a shocking finding. Yet the same administrators who express concern about retention in the context of its impact on the financial bottom line often fail to make the connection between student success and practices that support quality undergraduate education.

Until undergraduate education gains prominence as a truly worthwhile way for faculty to spend their time, it requires near heroic levels of commitment for professors to give students their due diligence. This is particularly true for low-income students who may need additional feedback and mentorship due to the issues of college readiness discussed previously in this chapter. As we write, our own institution is considering more task forces, committees, staff positions, and funding to promote new diversity initiatives. While we have no doubt the intentions behind the new diversity initiatives are good, this approach echoes Noddings' caution about institutionalizing care. It seems that a better course of action would be to free faculty up from the various task forces and meetings that take time from students so we might offer a more personalized, accessible version of care.

Conclusion

Economist Dan Ariely (2008) offered an analogy that might be useful as a close to this chapter. In his book *Predictably Irrational*, he invited readers to imagine a lovely Thanksgiving dinner in their family's home. He wrote about the tasty food, pleasing ambiance, and warm company surrounding a happy tradition many of us have experienced. He then asked us to imagine offering our families cash payment at the end of the evening. Our families would likely be mortified because what they gave us was a labor of love, not a service sold on the open market.

Ariely's metaphor provides a powerful reminder of the limits of market-based thinking. While there is an appropriate economic element to higher education, the financial aspect ought to serve as a means rather than an end. As higher education leaders, we owe our students something closer to the Thanksgiving dinner than a Happy Meal.

There is a running joke at a state-wide conference I attend about a high level administrator who apparently refers to students as "tuition-bearing units." The joke is more of the "laugh to keep from crying" variety as no one with whom I interact at this conference actually finds the idea funny. Whether the analogy is bunnies or tuition bearing units, any line of thinking that dehumanizes, objectifies, or otherwise diminishes students as human beings has no place in education. Most people would agree with this statement, yet many fail to see how increasingly corporate mindsets lead to the kinds of organizational practices that undermine an ethic of care. In the next chapter, we will explore this theme in greater depth and offer alternative ways of leading more congruent with the humanistic tradition higher education at its best serves.

References

Ariely, D. (2008). *Predictably irrational, revised and expanded edition*. London, UK: Harper Collins.
Armstrong, E., & Hamilton, L. (2013). *Paying for the party: How college maintains inequality*. Cambridge, MA: Harvard University Press.
Barratt, W. (2011). *Social class on campus: Theories and manifestations*. Sterling, VA: Stylus Publishing.
Crossley, N. (2008). Social class. In M. Grenfell (Ed.), *Pierre Bourdieu: Key concepts*. Stocksfield, UK: Acumen.
DeRosa, E., & Dolby, N. (2014). "I don't think the university knows me": Institutional culture and lower-income, first-generation college students. *InterActions: UCLA Journal of Education and Information Studies, 10*(2).
DiGregorio, D., & Shane, S. (2003). Why do some universities generate more start-ups than others? *Research Policy, 32*(2), 209–227.
Espinoza, R. (2011). *Pivotal moments: How educators can put all students on the path to college*. Cambridge, MA: Harvard University Press.
Fischer, K. (2014, May 25). For some foreign students, US education is losing its attraction. *New York Times*. Retrieved from www.nytimes.com/2014/05/26/world/asia/for-some-foreign-students-us-education-is-losing-its-attraction.html?_r=0.
Guinier, L. (2015). *The tyranny of the meritocracy: Democratizing higher education in America*. Boston, MA: Beacon Press.
Holland, N. E., & Farmer-Hinton, R. L. (2009). Leave no schools behind: The importance of a college culture in urban public high schools. *High School Journal, 92*(3), 24–43.
Hundley, K. (2011, May 9). Billionaire's role in hiring decisions at Florida State University raises questions. *Tampa Bay Times*. Retrieved from www.tampabay.com/news/business/billionaires-role-in-hiring-decisions-at-florida-state-university-raises/1168680.
Jaschik, S. (2008, February 27). Buying a spot on the syllabus. *Inside Higher Ed*. Retrieved from insidehighered.com.
Jaschik, S. (2016, January 20). Furor at Mount St. Mary's over president's alleged plan to cull students. *Inside Higher Ed*. Retrieved from insidehighered.com.
Kasler, K. (2014, August 7). Ohio's constitutional update could eliminate school funding mandate. WKSU. Retrieved from www.wksu.org/news/story/40033.
Krumrei-Mancuso, E., Newton, F., Kim, E., & Wilcox, D. (2013). Psychosocial factors predicting first-year college student success. *Journal of College Student Development, 54*(3), 247–266.
Lareau, A. (2011). *Unequal childhoods: Class, race and family life* (2nd ed.). Berkeley, CA: University of California Press.
Lindholm, J., & Astin, H. (2011). Understanding the interior life of faculty: How important is spirituality? In M. D. Waggoner (Ed.), *Sacred and secular tensions in higher education: Connecting parallel universities* (pp. 41–71). New York, NY: Taylor & Francis.
Noddings, N. (2013). *Caring: A relational approach to ethics and moral education*. Oakland, CA: University of California Press.
Pascarella, E., Pierson, C., Wolniak, G., & Terenzini, P. (2004). First generation college students: Additional evidence on college experiences and outcomes. *Journal of Higher Education, 75*(3), 249–284.
Reardon, S., Baker, R., & Klasik, D. (2012). *Race, income, and enrollment patterns in highly selective colleges, 1982–2004*. Stanford, CA: Center for Education Policy Analysis Stanford University. Retrieved from http://cepa.stanford.edu/sites/default/files/race%20income%20%26%20selective%20college%20enrollment%20august%203%202012.pdf.

Roth, M. (2014). *Beyond the university: Why liberal education matters.* New Haven, CT: Yale University Press.

Slaughter, S., & Rhoades, G. (2004). *Academic capitalism and the new economy: Markets, State, and higher education* [Kindle version]. Baltimore, MD: Johns Hopkins University Press.

Soria, K., & Bultmann, M. (2014). Supporting working-class students in higher education. *NACADA Journal, 34*(2), 51–62.

Strauss, V. (2014, March 28). The Koch brothers' influence on college campuses is spreading. *Washington Post.* Retrieved from www.washingtonpost.com/news/answer-sheet/wp/2014/03/28/the-koch-brothers-influence-on-college-campus-is-spreading.

Tierney, W. G. (2013). Life history and identity. *Review of Higher Education, 36*(2), 255–282.

Welton, A., & Williams, M. (2015). Accountability strain, college readiness drain: Sociopolitical Tensions involved in maintaining a college-going culture in a high "minority," high poverty, Texas High School. *High School Journal, 98*(2), 181–204.

Wolverton, B., Hallman, B., Shifflett, S., & Kambhampati, S. (2015). Sports at any cost: How college students are bankrolling the athletics arms race. *Huffington Post & The Chronicle of Higher Education.* Retrieved from http://projects.huffingtonpost.com/ncaa/sports-at-any-cost.

Yan, K., & Berliner, D. C. (2013). Chinese international students' personal and sociocultural stressors in the United States. *Journal of College Student Development, 54*(1), 62–84.

3
THE ROLE OF DIMINISHED PUBLIC FUNDING IN CLASS INEQUALITY

In Chapter 2, we identified problematic practices resulting from the diminishment of public funding for higher education. In this chapter, we recover a not so distant time when public financing of higher education was fairly uncontroversial as the populace understood higher education as the "tide that lifted all boats." The citizenry looked to university presidents as intellectual leaders and viewed higher education institutions as beneficial to the public through their research, teaching, and service functions. However, contemporary higher education is experiencing decreased public support which contributes to funding practices that are disproportionately consequential for low SES students. We will analyze problematic and cyclical relationships among declining public support, privatization, tuition increases, reliance on alternate funding sources, and growing class inequality in higher education.

The Complicated Issue of Higher Education's Cost

In recent years, cost has become the main story in higher education. More specifically, the rising cost of higher education appears as a theme in outlets ranging from scholarly articles to political candidates' speeches. Characterized as *alarming* and *astronomical,* the cost of higher education raises ire among students, parents, politicians, and the public at large. Despite being pummeled with news coverage of this issue, it is actually difficult to ascertain when the cost crisis began, what the culprit(s) might be, and how we might change course.

Is There a Cost Crisis?

To complicate matters, there is no consensus about whether there is a cost crisis in higher education. While most of the stories on this topic argue or assume higher education costs are spiraling out of control, some contain evidence that contradicts conventional wisdom. According to the College Board's most recent data, higher education costs rose at a rate of 3 percent in 2015, which is above the current inflation rate (less than 1 percent), but not markedly so (College Board, 2015). Interestingly, the net price has actually decreased in recent years due to discounting on the part of institutions. So while sticker prices have increased at rates that sound the alarm about cost, what students and their families actually pay after all the financial aid packages are factored in has declined.

Still, those sticker prices grab headlines and rightfully so. I (Laura) teach at the institution where I completed my undergraduate degree. I'm 25 years older than first year students at my university, who pay about $10,000 per year in tuition expenses (in-state) according the Ohio University Fact Book. When I was an undergraduate in the mid-1990s, tuition at our institution was approximately $2,000 per year, making the increase from then to now about 400 percent.

How Did College Get So Expensive?

Conversations about higher education's rising cost often ignore the aforementioned caveats about sticker price versus net cost, which are considerable and worth noting. Yet it would be difficult to argue against the general notion that college is expensive and many families struggle to pay for it. The reasons for this challenge are more complex than they might appear on the surface. While politicians have built careers on blaming higher education for its purported inefficiencies, the cost story is more complicated. The sometimes intricate and difficult to understand financial aid system adds a significant layer of complexity to the cost story. Another related and significant factor is the issue of student debt.

Student debt is one indicator that suggests students and families struggle to pay for higher education. Data indicate students now borrow larger amounts of money to pay for college than they did previously. Fry (2014) reports that in 1990–91 annual borrowing per full-time equivalent student was $2,485. However, by 2012–13, that annual borrowing figure had nearly tripled to $6,928. Fry also reports that the typical student borrower in the class of 2011–12 owed about $26,900 in student debt upon graduation. But the typical student borrower in the graduating class of 1992–93 owed $12,400, which is less than half the amount of the 2012–13 students.

In addition to an increase in the borrowing amounts, the percentage of college students who borrow money to pay for their education has increased. This means debt has increasingly become a reality for graduating college students. In 2011–12, seven out of ten students (69 percent) borrowed money for college compared to 20 years earlier when just less than half (49 percent) of students did (Fry, 2014).

Higher education institutions bear some responsibility for the cost issue, which we will discuss in greater depth at this chapter's close. Yet it's also true that higher education is simply an expensive enterprise even when budgets are managed responsibly. Quality teaching, research, and student support services require serious investment in personnel and facilities. Until fairly recently, there was a social contract between higher education and the public wherein citizens agreed to invest in colleges and universities because the benefits were clear. Higher education was still expensive in the past, but state and federal subsidies reduced the cost to the student.

While those working in higher education express acute awareness of this point, declining public support is often the missing link in national conversations about higher education's rising cost to students and their families. It can appear that college is simply getting more expensive when it would be more accurate to say college is getting more expensive for the students because they are paying a greater share of the bill. According to Douglas-Gabriel (2015), tuition replaced public funding as the largest source of university revenue in 2012. To understand the significance of this shift, consider that state and federal government funding accounted for 75 percent of the cost required to educate a public university student in 1975.

How Public Divestment from Higher Education Happened

When did things change in public financing for higher education and what were the causes? California served as a trendsetter in public divestment from higher education, with Governor Ronald Reagan attacking the California public university system in the 1960s. The Reagan administration called for an end to the highly revered free tuition policy for state residents, cut budgets by 20 percent annually, reduced construction expenditures, and fired the successful and able University of California President, Clark Kerr (Clabaugh, 2004). Reagan made these moves despite the significant role California's public university system played in building its robust economy. These radical policy shifts make little sense until one considers the broader political context in the case of Reagan and the University of California in the 1960s.

Culture Wars

While politicians nearly universally claim to support the goal of achieving a large middle class, this idea threatens the status quo in ways that make those in power ambivalent at best in actually supporting policies that truly level the playing field. Hence California's then-governor launched a culture war in the middle of the state's widening access to higher education and prosperity. Using the unrest at the University of California-Berkeley as a pretext, Reagan effectively positioned decent, hardworking Americans against the "small minority of hippies, radicals, and filthy speech advocates . . . that should be taken by the scruff of the neck and thrown off campus—permanently" (Turner, 1966, p. 14).

In his later years as president, Reagan would use similar dichotomies to attack racial progress, invoking the "welfare queen" image to demonize beneficiaries of social programs (Hancock, 2004). Both rhetorical strategies achieved their intended aim to cast aspersions on those who were making progress toward greater enfranchisement in the democratic system. These images allowed Reagan and others the possibility of substantively attacking democracy without the political consequences of doing so openly.

The effects of this rhetoric for higher education have been both highly consequential and mightily underappreciated. Newfield (2008) made this case brilliantly in his aptly titled book, *Unmaking the Public University*. Long treated as a sideshow in higher education politics, the culture wars must be understood as integral to higher education's defunding; this is at the heart of Newfield's argument. While the shift from sideshow to main production may seem like a negligible difference, Newfield's argument exposes the false confusion created by the dominant discourse about higher education funding.

The mainstream narrative positions vague fiscal crises as the cause of declining public funding, despite the fact that attacks on higher education began at a time of relative prosperity in the US. Newfield argues that public higher education was not the unfortunate and unintended victim of economic woes, but a calculated choice on the part of an elite defending its position against a movement that could upend its privilege:

> The unmistakable trend on college campuses [in the 1960s] and in college communities was toward increased self-organization of political activity. Some of the ethnic barriers that had blocked alliances around common issues were becoming less important, suggesting that collaborative organization could spread. All of this was bad news for a traditional version of US democracy in which little power sharing took place, and where racial divisions made the social majority relatively disorganized and controllable.
>
> *(2008, p. 33)*

Contemporary politicians sometimes carry out Reagan's legacy of characterizing universities as hotbeds of radical politics. The state of Arizona's attempt to ban ethnic studies on the basis of its "victim rhetoric" and "anti-Americanism" provides one of many recent examples.

The culture wars continue to present problems for higher education in terms of garnering public support. Those threatened by higher education's potential to upset the social order also seize on issues like the ethnic studies curriculum in order to characterize colleges and universities as wasteful government bureaucracies where people have nothing better to do than argue about esoteric issues. The liberal arts have suffered enormously as a result of policies driven by this mentality, with humanities and social science departments being heavily downsized on many campuses in favor of business and engineering programs.

The conventional wisdom these days is that education is about knowledge transmission; students should learn marketable skills from experts without much debate about the nature of knowledge or what is worth learning. While this argument is generally made in an economic framework, it has origins in the culture wars as well. Universities focused on career development and job placement tend to be more docile places than those where students wrestle with the bigger questions about critical thought and challenge intellectual authority.

Overstated Financial Strain

While the culture wars continue to some extent, the more recent impediment in garnering support for public higher education is the misconception that there is a scarcity of money. The problem with this line of reasoning is that financial constraint can be used as an excuse to avoid any kind of public investment. Until very recently, vague claims about economic hardship preempted any serious discussion of a national healthcare system. It took an enormous amount of research, benchmarking with other countries, and political will to achieve the Affordable Care Act. This work resulted in changing the national discourse regarding healthcare and we believe these same efforts can inspire re-investment in higher education, too.

As Babones (2012) states simply and precisely, "The problem isn't a lack of money. The problem is where the money is going" (para. 5). Part of his assertion comes from Pollin and Garrett-Peltier's (2011) findings indicating that $1 billion investments in clean energy, education, and healthcare all create substantially more jobs than investing that same billion dollar in military spending. Hence a rational response to true economic hardship would be to invest more, not less, in education spending.

While there are widespread misconceptions about the costs and benefits of higher education to the public, it is fairly easy to debunk these notions. Research demonstrates higher education's public benefits. Trostel (2015) demonstrated that extra tax revenues from college graduates are more than six times the gross government cost per college degree. Not only do college graduates contribute more in extra tax revenues, but there are also less government expenditures on college graduates. Simply stated, the public benefits from college graduates more than it contributes to college graduates. Conservatively, Trostel suggests that the government's return on investment in college students is 10.3 percent. Hence if college were a stock, our financial advisors would strongly recommend it.

There are public benefits in addition to the extra tax revenues contributed by college graduates. For example, philanthropy and civic engagement both increase with college attainment. In synthesizing the expansive research demonstrating the public benefits of education, Trostel (2015) states that college graduates volunteer, and engage in not-for-profit employment more often than high school graduates. College graduates also make more charitable contributions than high school graduates. In addition, Trostel details findings of college graduates' increased political participation, political awareness, and community involvement compared to high school graduates. Although the private benefits of college to each student receives much attention, research clearly demonstrates that our society benefits in numerous ways from college graduates as well.

If higher education is indeed worth the investment, why is it such an easy target for elected officials seeking to cut university budgets? As Spring (2015) observes, "Blaming education for economic problems is a safe path for politicians" (p. 146). Universities suffer from an image problem, frequently characterized as bureaucratic and inefficient despite their longevity compared with most private sector institutions. Wisconsin Governor Scott Walker used his "tough on academics" policies to enter the national political scene during the 2016 Republican Presidential primary. Politicians are now building careers by painting a picture of snobby academics working a few hours a week and getting rich at the expense of struggling families toiling ever harder to pay ever increasing tuition costs.

This is a disingenuous political strategy because politicians almost never point out the connection between their defunding policies and the rising cost of tuition. Yet one can trace the connection between declining public support and increased cost to students and families over the years. Although there are multiple factors associated with tuition increases, declines in public support in the form of state appropriations have been a central factor (National Conference of State Legislatures, 2015). Unlike mandated state appropriations (such as primary and secondary education, and Medicaid), higher education appropriations tend to be one of the most discretionary items in a state budget. This means in recessionary times the state's spending on higher education tends to decrease. Colleges then offset the reductions in state support by increasing tuition.

Between 2008 and 2013, states cut their higher education spending by 28 percent on average (Oliff, Palacios, Johnson, & Leachman, 2013). However, 28 percent is the average; states like Arizona and New Hampshire have cut their per-student spending on higher education in half (Oliff, Palacios, Johnson, & Leachman, 2013). During this same time period (2007–08 to 2013) the published tuition at four-year public colleges increased on average 27 percent (Oliff, Palacios, Johnson, & Leachman, 2013). While there may be tuition increases at specific institutions that are only partially tied to reductions in state spending on higher education, these data suggest a compelling argument: when states disinvest in higher education, the students will experience increases in tuition.

Politicians like Scott Walker count on the public not making the connection between defunding and rising tuition. They would prefer that citizens attribute higher education's cost increase to its organizational ineptness. To be fair, anyone working in academia knows an uninspiring professor or a committee that has been spinning its wheels without producing results. Universities are complex organizations with employees performing at a wide range of levels from excellent to terrible. Annual reviews, merit pay, and other measures exist to incentivize good performance and promote improvement when people fall short. There is a difference between advocating accountability and demonizing an entire sector for political gain.

Privatization

The narrative of lazy faculty and hapless bureaucrats driving up the cost of tuition for working families sets the stage for policies built on privatization. This conflation of *public* and *inefficient* is a bigger story than higher education; the demonization of all things public and sanctification of all things private permeates the organizational discourse more generally. It is an inaccurate and unfortunate characterization, one that allows Wall Street to continue its destructive ways without adequate oversight while public institutions suffer under excessive accountability measures. In educational contexts, this unbalanced view of public and private manifests in particularly insidious ways.

Jamie Vollmer's famous blueberry story captures the issue clearly and powerfully. Vollmer (2010) writes of being one of the countless reformers convinced he could solve education's real or perceived woes by running schools more like businesses. He tells the story of speaking to a group of teachers, suggesting they model their classrooms on his success in the ice cream business. A teacher begins asking him questions about how he selects his ingredients, luring him into hearty agreement that he only uses the freshest and highest quality blueberries. The story builds to a crescendo of her announcing that public schools must work with all blueberries, the bruised and neglected ones as well as the pristine ones. Success in education is not predicated on screening out imperfect products, hence efficiency and accountability must take on more complex meanings in the public sector.

To his credit, Vollmer discusses being humbled and changed by both this story as well as by spending some time in actual classrooms and witnessing first hand the extraordinary talent and empathy it takes to work effectively with all the proverbial blueberries. While some public higher education institutions are not as truly open access as their K-12 counterparts, community colleges and less elite four-year institutions do, in fact, strive to provide quality higher education to all students regardless of their preparation level. Due diligence to a truly diverse set of students requires time, attention, mentoring—all activities that can be stubbornly inefficient. Further, these practices prove difficult to measure.

Assessment-obsessed, "what gets measured gets done" organizational climates produce perverse incentives. For example, many colleges and universities employ the market-driven practice of investing heavily in branding campaigns both to boost enrollment and solicit alumni donations. Unfortunately, this allocation of human and financial resources skews toward prospective students and graduates without enough attention devoted to people during their actual student experience.

Admissions, enrollment, and development departments receive institutional resources while cuts are made to teaching, advising, and counseling functions. There is surprise when these practices result in decreased retention and increased mental health issues, as if there is no correlation between service support and student success. Indeed, privatization proponents work hard to de-emphasize the connection between financial investment and school performance, arguing that factors like class size and faculty workload do not impact teaching quality. Yet the same people frequently emulate the Ivy League in terms of increasing both selectivity and rankings while failing to account for the reasonably-sized classes and generous faculty-workload policies that allow these institutions to achieve such excellence in the first place.

Anti-intellectualism

Perhaps the cruelest irony in the drive to make public education more like the Ivy League is the anti-intellectualism both created and reflected in the process. If there is a single quality that defines the elite college experience, it is what is variously called intellectual curiosity, life of the mind, and learning for learning's sake. Having worked most of my adult career at Stanford University, I (Laura) speak from a wealth of experience living and working in one of the most academically enriching environments that exists. Students, faculty, and staff enjoy great latitude in pursuing intellectual work without the pressure of immediate, measurable results. Creativity and independence are highly valued in this environment where people routinely laud the virtues of decentralization. If Stanford is the kind of organization to which one aspires, micromanagement and bean counting should be understood an antithetical to the goal.

Unfortunately, it seems the goal is not actually to emulate the substantive qualities of excellent universities, but instead to attain their more shallow assets like money, prestige, and power. This ambivalence sometimes results in bizarre institutional behavior wherein colleges seek money, prestige, and power at the expense of their academic mission. Hocking College, a community college located in an impoverished part of rural Ohio, offers an illustration of this phenomenon. According to the *Columbus Dispatch*, Hocking's enrollment has declined nearly 50 percent in the last five years (Lane, 2014). The upper administration has reacted by cutting core academic programs, laying off faculty, and eliminating services to students (Hawley, 2015). The college has prioritized one new initiative, however: the creation of a football team. Despite college athletics' dismal record in generating revenue (Matheson, O'Connor, & Herberger, 2012), Hocking College now has a football team to support during this time of economic hardship.

We will not argue there was once a Golden Age for higher education to which we long to return. Like all institutions, colleges and universities both create and reflect the societies in which they exist. Students of color, women, LGBT, and other marginalized groups continue to struggle for full enfranchisement in all sectors of society, including higher education institutions. At the same time, colleges and universities often lead the way on social justice issues, serving as incubators for progressive social change on issues ranging from more inclusive curricula to clean energy.

The recent Volkswagen emissions scandal illustrates this point. Publicized as environmental news, the Volkswagen case should also be understood as a higher education story. It was a professor and a group of engineering students at West Virginia University working on a government grant who exposed the company for installing a component designed to cheat emissions tests (Glinton, 2015). This is the kind of public good higher education at its best achieves, yet the dominant narrative restricts citizens' imagination of college to a largely private commodity.

Until we understand higher education's role as something that benefits the public regardless of whether we or our children are in college at a given moment, it is nearly impossible to garner public funding. While private dollars are attractive and probably necessary, they cannot replace the important role of public money in promoting financially disinterested research. It's hard to imagine, for example, that West Virginia University's lab would have cracked the Volkswagen case had it been sponsored by the company.

The widely reported conflicts of interest that arise with pharmaceutical industry sponsored research in university labs illustrate the problems that occur when scholarship is not conducted in a financially disinterested manner for the public good. Even when the issue is not an overt ethical breach, researchers are encouraged to study more potentially lucrative areas rather than acting in the public interest. This practice diminishes higher education's legitimacy as a public good, potentially reducing the public's inclination to fund it.

The close relationship between public universities and the private sector did not always exist. It's difficult to imagine now, but there was a time when universities were safeguarded against the very co-opting just discussed. It was not a particularly radical idea that public institutions ought to act in the interest of the public, which, in turn, justified the case for public funding. The situation was not perfect; in fact, much of what government leaders decided was in the public good turned out to be defense research. But the idea that public colleges and universities existed for the benefit of the citizenry was an uncontroversial one, providing a convincing rationale for public support.

Three Questions to Resolve in Building the Case for Public Support

Fortunately, the problem is not that colleges and universities fail to contribute to the public good. The problem is that those of us within higher education lost control of the discourse and allowed it to skew toward being uncritically negative. Whether that happened during Reagan's epic culture wars with the

University of California system in the 1960s or more recently in the current economic downturn matters less than what we do about it today. In Chapter 7, we discuss in greater depth our recommendations for revitalizing public commitment to funding higher education. We posit the resolution of the following questions as important context for these recommendations.

1. Is College a Right or a Privilege?

The American Council on Education (2015) published a study showing a 10 percent decline in low-income students' college enrollment rates over the past decade. Several people noted in the comments section that this wasn't a higher education problem, arguing that poor K-12 education was the culprit. The growing literature on college readiness sometimes takes this position. Colleges and universities used to accept remediation as part of their role, but financial pressures due to loss of public funding have caused many institutions to cut remedial programs.

Remediation is labor intensive, requiring considerable faculty and staff resources dedicated to helping students get up to speed. Further, pressures to increase standing in college rankings have caused some institutions to invest more resources in competing with other schools for high achieving students rather than assisting those who are struggling. As one higher education leader interviewed for the film *Declining by Degrees* stated, "With our financial aid today, we are helping people God already helped" (McClenney in Hersh, Merrow, & Wolfe, 2005).

Of course, not all low-income students need remediation. Many high-achieving/low-income students fail to enroll in college simply due to lack of funds. As a society, we decided long ago that this lack of equal opportunity was unfair and created policies to ameliorate the situation. In 1965, President Lyndon Johnson signed the Higher Education Act as part of his larger Great Society domestic agenda designed to address race and class injustice. The Higher Education Act expanded low-income students' access to postsecondary education through a variety of grants, including the wildly popular and successful Pell Grant.

Unfortunately, these programs have come under attack in recent years, most notably by Speaker of the House of Representatives Paul Ryan, whose 2015 budget plan called for a 10 year freeze on the Pell Grant and eliminating it entirely for students who attend college at less than half time. The erosion of programs designed to mitigate class inequality occur in the spirit of Reagan's successful attempt to undo the progress made by the Great Society.

In a *Chicago Tribune* article about Reagan's war on welfare, Clarence Page (1985) invoked responses to Richard Nixon's Family Assistance plan as historical background about wealthy peoples' responses to social programs. Page posited full employment at decent jobs as the only substantive solution to poverty, but argued those in power were ambivalent at best about this plan. He quoted a man identified only as a Southern congressman who asked in response to the idea of a fully and gainfully employed populace, "who will iron my shirts and rake the yard?" (para. 18).

While we may disregard the congressman's question as distasteful, it reflects a widely held sentiment admittedly expressed more often with greater subtlety. But the fact of the matter is that we have not really decided as a society whether higher education is a right or a privilege. "College isn't for everyone" is a platitude most people have heard more than once, but people generally don't mean their own children when they say it.

In *Our Kids: The American Dream in Crisis*, author Robert D. Putnam (2015) argues that there was a time when our ethos reflected a greater dedication to equal opportunity than it does now. Careful not to romanticize the past (especially with regard to racial and gender discrimination), Putnam argues compellingly that we have been on a downward trajectory in terms of providing wide access to the American dream over the past few decades. Possibly because the statistics about the wealth gap have become well-known and therefore lose their ability to shock, the author frames his argument in terms of his own graduating high school class in Port Clinton, Ohio.

Putnam juxtaposes his own peers' upward mobility (75 percent obtaining more education than their parents) with their descendants' lack of progress (0 percent obtaining more education than their parents). Coupled with the description of his hometown's descent from a thriving middle-class community to a place where people struggle to make ends meet, Putnam paints a grim picture of life without strong policies that mitigate class inequality.

Part of the power of Putnam's work comes from its title and central metaphor, *Our Kids*. He advocates for a renewed commitment to conceptualizing opportunity beyond what's good for me and mine. Whether we agree it should be the case or not, some sort of postsecondary education is now required for nearly all jobs that pay a living wage. Hence, we take the position that higher education ought to be understood as a right for those willing to do the work necessary to achieve its promise.

2. What are the Most Pressing Issues of Our Time and How is Higher Education Addressing Them?

In addition to its necessity for career advancement, higher education plays a vital role perhaps now more than ever in inculcating the critical thinking skills citizens need to be able to participate meaningfully in a democracy. As we write, the nation's campuses are erupting with students protesting racism. University of Missouri students demanded the firing of President Timothy M. Wolfe over the college's inadequate response to racist hate crimes (Wolfe did resign after a high-profile walkout of the university's football team). Hundreds of students also demonstrated at Ithaca College in protest of racial insensitivity on campus, including an alumni speaker who used the term *savage* in reference to a black alumna. At Princeton University, students staged a sit-in in the president's office with the goal of the university removing Woodrow Wilson's name from places of honor based on his support of racist policies.

It's not an accident that university campuses are the sites where communities are working out the hard questions about racism in this country. The issues are complex and universities provide an important space for this conversation, especially in a post-Ferguson society. Whether the issue is racism, sexual assault, climate change, or one of a host of other issues with which our society is grappling in a given moment, universities must position themselves as leaders in cultivating public discourse.

Unfortunately, the current corporate climate pervading many campuses proves inhospitable to voices of dissent. Image conscious executives generally seek to quell rather than encourage debate, particularly on issues that might highlight the gap between their privilege and other peoples' marginalization. It feels safer to avoid difficult conversations on controversial topics and aim for pleasant campus environments where teaching and learning occur with as much neutrality as possible.

The first problem with this approach is that neutrality is largely an illusion. Even in fields where it seems one might be able to teach something devoid of politics, ideology occurs even in what is omitted. For example, one can teach coding without discussing the digital divide, but that lack of conversation reflects a political sensibility as much as the discussion itself would. Hence the more honest approach is to deal with the ideological facets of knowledge as clearly and directly as possible.

Not only is it more authentic to welcome the discussion of ideological tensions, it makes higher education much more relevant when we do so. Students and faculty who engage with the most pressing issues of our day raise the profile of the institutions they represent. When Ohio State University professor Michelle Alexander published *The New Jim Crow: Mass Incarceration in the Age of Color Blindness* in 2010, people talked about the institution in reference to something other than football. The public needs to see those in higher education institutions demonstrating leadership on serious problems in order to feel motivated to continue investing in them.

3. What is the Purpose of Higher Education and How Can We Articulate it Clearly, Concisely, and in a Way that is Relevant to the Public?

This is a question about which higher education institutions must achieve clarity if they are to regain public support. Alexander's aforementioned book provides a case in point. While her book was wildly successful and relevant to the broader public, faculty reward structures typically privilege journal articles over books and other more accessible forms of publication. Hence it is more advantageous for tenure and merit increases to write for a small, niche audience rather than the general public. This reward system seems at odds with the goal of promoting higher education's relevance to the public to which it is beholden for support.

The faculty reward system is just one example of a policy that reflects confusion about the purpose of higher education, particularly in its relationship to the public at large. While most institutional mission statements still claim adherence to common good notions of citizenship, some have shifted away from the public and toward the private. For example, Washington State Community College in Marietta, Ohio recently celebrated its 40th anniversary; part of the celebration included sending updated strategic plans to its alumni. One of my doctoral students analyzed these documents in contrast to the institution's original mission. She found significant discrepancy between the historical documents' emphasis on serving the local community and the contemporary strategic plan's focus on enhancing students' ability to compete in the global marketplace.

We acknowledge universities' important role in preparing students for the job market. This role does not have to exist in opposition to higher education's public mission; in fact, these purposes ought to function in congruence with one another. Chambers (2005) writes of the inseparable nature of higher education's private and public roles:

> Simply put, the world does not work in discrete boxes. Like every other part of life, who receives benefits and how they receive them is multicontextual. Private benefits contribute to public benefits and vice versa. The same is true for economic and social benefits. Private economic and social benefits often translate into public economies and social benefits.
>
> (p. 11)

The public and private sectors ought to co-exist in balanced and reasonable ways. Private entities provide goods, services, and jobs that enrich both individuals in the form of paychecks and communities in the form of tax revenues. Public services provide the roads, utilities, law enforcement, and other key provisions necessary to run businesses. The key is for the private and public sectors to exist in healthy tension with neither eclipsing the other.

Reinvigorating Public Support

The aforementioned tension between higher education's public and private costs and benefits exists at the heart of the public funding issue. Generally speaking, those on the left tend to gravitate toward arguments about higher education as a public good, emphasizing critical thinking, citizenship, and the liberal arts. Conversely, those on the right highlight higher education's role as a private commodity, favoring vocationalism, employment, and applied fields. Neither narrative solves the problem of how to garner public support. The left's story is vulnerable to criticism, such as the following remark from Governor Rick Scott of Florida:

> If I'm going to take money from a citizen to put into education then I'm going to take that money to create jobs. So I want that money to go to degrees where people can get jobs in this state. Is it a vital interest of the state, to have more anthropologists? I don't think so.
>
> *(as cited in Anderson, 2011, para. 6)*

Higher education insiders generally oppose arguments like the governor's. We tend to frame our points in the language of critical thinking, taking up the anthropologists' transferrable skills and enhanced ability to engage as informed citizens in a democracy. We may love these concepts, but we need to do a better job of operationalizing them and making them accessible if they are going to resonate with the public.

I (Laura) saw *The Big Short* when it was released in theaters; this movie gave me a chance to reflect on the gift of my English and Women's Studies degrees (subjects I assume Governor Scott would find as useless as anthropology). *The Big Short* is a film about the housing bubble bust of 2008. I purchased a home in the San Francisco Bay Area at the height of the housing mania in 2002, so I recall the constant enticement of adjustable rate mortgages with no down payment necessary. Real estate agents and mortgage brokers talked many clients into purchasing homes they couldn't afford based on the fiction that their properties would appreciate indefinitely. While the fantasy seems all too clear in hindsight, it would be difficult to overstate how vehemently and successfully those in the housing and financial sectors argued their case in the early 2000s.

I have never taken a course in finance and claim no brilliance in these matters, but I was able to ask some basic questions that allowed me to avoid the crash that left many people with homes they couldn't afford once their teaser rates expired and their interest rates increased. Even when presented with seemingly expert advice from well-dressed people wielding impressive spreadsheets of the California housing market's glory, the story felt wrong to me. My English and Women's Studies courses taught me how to look behind the power suits and question the potential bias in the evidence that was presented to me. One agent mocked my reticence about adjustable rate mortgages, accusing me of thinking like a scared old person afraid of change.

It was my liberal arts education that empowered me to resist intimidation and walk out of that person's office rather than signing on the dotted line. We need to do a better job of identifying and communicating these situations as public benefits of higher education. But even when we do make the case compellingly, the left's arguments do not conform neatly to sound bites, making them difficult to register in an already oversimplified story about why the public should or should not support higher education.

The right's higher education story of commodification seems on the surface less susceptible to critique, which is perhaps why so many colleges and universities have succumbed to it. Marketability of one's college education is the dominant theme in virtually every piece of media used to sell higher education today. The College Scorecard offers one such example, advertising the difference in income between high school and college graduates in many places on a website that purportedly exists to help students and families compare costs between institutions. Similarly, individual universities emphasize the value of a college degree in a variety of contexts including justifying the cost of tuition as well as providing a cautionary tale about being doomed to poverty should a young person not seek postsecondary education.

These strategies seem bulletproof because the data is consistent about the value of a college degree in terms of income enhancement over the course of a graduate's lifetime. For the last 40 years (1970–2013), data shows workers with bachelor's degrees on average earned 56 percent more than workers with a high school diploma (Abel & Deitz, 2014). Not only does a college degree yield higher earnings, but those with college degrees also have lower unemployment rates (Canon & Gascon, 2012). With higher earnings and lower unemployment, during their working lives those with bachelor's degrees earn over $1 million more than workers with high school diplomas (Abel & Deitz, 2014).

The problem with this argument, however, is that the public rightfully asks why it should subsidize something that has essentially become a private good. As renowned author and cultural critic, Wendell Berry (2010) warned:

> But the land-grant universities, in espousing the economic determinism of the industrialists, have caught themselves in a logical absurdity that they may finally discover to be dangerous to themselves. If competitiveness is the economic norm, and the "competitive edge" the only recognized social goal, then how can these institutions justify public support?
>
> *(p. 135)*

If higher education is truly a private commodity only useful for one's own personal employment, then why should the public be compelled to pay for it? Our answer is that the public should not be expected to finance something that exists solely for private consumption. Of course, we argue with equal conviction that higher education does serve a vital public good and is therefore worthy of public support.

Conclusion

Public funding is key to reversing the trend of socioeconomic class polarization in higher education. When the public divests from higher education, universities raise tuition to cover their expenses. Those least able to pay suffer the greatest consequences as the result of this practice. Though framed as an economic problem, divestment is actually more of a political issue that can be addressed through correcting misleading stories about both the costs and benefits of higher education.

Even sympathetic scholars treat public divestment as a foregone conclusion, arguing as higher education writer Goldie Blumenstyk (2014) has, "Colleges hoping for some big new infusion of government support will surely be disappointed" (p. 152). We respectfully disagree with this approach, believing that giving up on public funding would essentially be the same as accepting the current disenfranchisement of low-income students. In the absence of public funding, universities have compensated with market-based policies and practices that have largely exacerbated rather than mitigated class inequality.

References

Abel, J., & Deitz, R. (2014). Do the benefits of college still outweigh the costs? *Federal Reserve Bank of New York: Current Issues in Economics and Finance, 20*(3), 1–12. Retrieved from www.newyorkfed.org/medialibrary/media/research/current_issues/ci20-3.pdf.

Alexander, M. (2010). *The new Jim Crow: Mass incarceration in the age of color blindness*. New York, NY: New Press.

American Council on Education. (2015). Where have all the low-income students gone? *Higher Education Today*. Retrieved from https://higheredtoday.org/2015/11/25/where-have-all-the-low-income-students-gone.

Anderson, Z. (2011, October 10). Rick Scott wants to shift university funding away from some degrees. *Herald Tribune*. Retrieved from http://politics.heraldtribune.com/2011/10/10/rick-scott-wants-to-shift-university-funding-away-from-some-majors.

Babones, S. (2012, August 21). To end the jobs recession, invest an extra $20 billion in public education. *Truthout*. Retrieved from www.truth-out.org/opinion/item/11031-to-end-the-jobs-recession-invest-an-extra-$20-billion-in-public-education.

Berry, W. (2010). *What are people for?: Essays*. New York, NY: Counterpoint Press.

Blumenstyk, G. (2014). *American higher education in crisis?: What everyone needs to know*. Oxford, UK: Oxford University Press.

Canon, M., & Gascon, C. (2012). College degrees: Why aren't more people making the investment? *Regional Economist, 18*, 4–9. Retrieved from www.stlouisfed.org/~/media/Files/PDFs/publications/pub_assets/pdf/re/2012/b/college_degrees.pdf.

Chambers, T. (2005). The special role of higher education in society: As a public good for the public good. In A. J. Kezar, A. C. Chambers, & J. Burkhardt (Eds), *Higher education for the public good: Emerging voices from a national movement* (pp. 3–22). San Francisco, CA: Jossey-Bass.

Clabaugh, G. K. (2004). The educational legacy of Ronald Reagan. *Educational Horizons, 82*, 256–259.

College Board. (2015). *Trends in college pricing*. New York, NY: College Board. Retrieved from https://trends.collegeboard.org/sites/default/files/trends-college-pricing-web-final-508-2.pdf.

Douglas-Gabriel, D. (2015, January 5). Students now pay more of their public university tuition than state governments. *Washington Post*. Retrieved from www.washingtonpost.com/news/get-there/wp/2015/01/05/students-cover-more-of-their-public-university-tuition-now-than-state-governments.

Fry, R. (2014). *The changing profile of student borrowers: Biggest increase in borrowing has been among more affluent students*. Pew Research Center. Retrieved from www.pewsocialtrends.org/2014/10/07/the-changing-profile-of-student-borrowers.

Glinton, S. (2015, September 24). How a little lab in West Virginia caught Volkswagen's big cheat. NPR Morning Edition. Retrieved from www.npr.org/2015/09/24/443053672/how-a-little-lab-in-west-virginia-caught-volkswagens-big-cheat.

Hancock, A. M. (2004). *The politics of disgust: The public identity of the welfare queen*. New York, NY: New York University Press.

Hawley, S. (2015, January 11). Hocking College saving $1.34 million with position cuts. *Athens Messenger*. Retrieved from www.athensmessenger.com/news/hocking-college-saving-million-with-position-cuts/article_83ddd93a-26f3-5b6c-995f-258219681d32.html.

Hersh, R., Merrow, J., & Wolfe, T. (2005). *Declining by degrees: Higher education at risk* [DVD]. Retrieved from www.youtube.com/watch?v=BcxDVYo2wH8.

Lane, M. (2014, October 20). Budget, enrollment, leadership problems rack Hocking College. *Columbus Dispatch*. Retrieved from www.dispatch.com/content/stories/local/2014/10/20/budget-enrollment-leadership-problems-rack-hocking-college.html.

Matheson, V., O'Connor, D., & Herberger, J. (2012). The bottom line: Accounting for revenues and expenditures in intercollegiate athletics. *International Journal of Sport Finance*, 7, 30–45.

National Conference of State Legislatures. (2015). *Tuition policy*. Washington, DC: National Conference of State Legislatures. Retrieved from www.ncsl.org/research/education/tuition-policy.aspx.

Newfield, C. (2008). *Unmaking the public university: The forty-year assault on the middle class*. Cambridge, MA: Harvard University Press.

Oliff, P., Palacios, V., Johnson, I., & Leachman, M. (2013). *Recent deep state higher education cuts may harm students and the economy for years to come*. Washington, DC: Center on Budget and Policy Priorities. Retrieved from www.cbpp.org/research/recent-deep-state-higher-education-cuts-may-harm-students-and-the-economy-for-years-to-come.

Page, C. (1985, October 13). Wealth, power, and welfare. *Chicago Tribune*. Retrieved from http://articles.chicagotribune.com/1985-10-13/news/8503090864_1_corporate-subsidies-comic-relief-working.

Pollin, R., & Garrett-Peltier, H. (2011). *The US employment effects of military and domestic spending priorities*. Political Economy Research Institute. Amherst, MA: University of Massachusetts Amherst. Retrieved from www.comw.org/pda/fulltext/Pollin-Garrett-Peltier.pdf.

Putnam, R. (2015). *Our kids: The American dream in crisis*. New York, NY: Simon & Schuster.

Spring, J. (2015). *Economization of education*. New York, NY: Taylor & Francis.

Trostel, P. (2015). *It's not just the money: The benefits of college education to individuals and to society*. Margaret Chase Smith Policy Center & School of Economics Lumina Issue Paper. Retrieved from www.luminafoundation.org/resources/its-not-just-the-money.

Turner, W. (1966, May 14). Reagan demands Berkeley inquiry; "Beatniks" and "Radicals" scored at GOP rally (special dispatch). *New York Times*.

Vollmer, J. (2010). *Schools cannot do it alone: Building public support for America's public schools*. Fairfield, IA: Enlightenment Press.

4
CLASS INEQUALITY AS A HIGHER EDUCATION LEADERSHIP PROBLEM

I (Laura) recently learned of new research findings about the link between money and poverty. As it turns out, money tends to lift people out of poverty (Doucleff, 2015). As I contemplated the study, I found myself wondering how out of touch we must be if this research finding came as a surprise to anyone. Are attitudes about poor people so negative that we assume they squander money and therefore feel shocked that an influx of cash would help them? Or are we so unaware of the systems and structures that lead to vastly inequitable wealth distribution that any potential solution seems like a mystery? As I listened to the story, it struck me that poverty is not so much a research problem as it is an ethical one. Rather than conducting more research on a problem for which we already know the answer, perhaps that intellectual energy might be better spent figuring out why we lack the political will to deem poverty unacceptable and therefore do something about it.

Class inequality in higher education presents a similar disconnect between topic and tool. There are many good, important, and useful books on the financing of colleges and universities. Major themes in these works include the public defunding of higher education and strategies for replacing those funds. The books vary in terms of what strategies they advocate; some focus on cutting costs while others highlight alternative revenue streams like grants and corporate partnerships. What is harder to find is a clear analysis of how and why public support declined in the first place. When did it become acceptable to essentially privatize higher education, shifting the burden from state and federal governments to students and families?

To understand and address class inequality in higher education, we must move away from what Heifetz, Grashow, and Linsky (2009) called the "technical" perspective and begin to embrace the "adaptive" alternative. Technical solutions are those that tackle the surface level of a problem. We are making this mistake in our approach to class inequality in higher education by trying to apply band-aid fixes rather than understanding the problem more deeply so that we might change course in a truly fundamental way. The result is what Senge (1990) called a systems problem: a circular pattern of disease and cure that doesn't really fix the disease because the cure itself becomes part of the problem.

Take the issue of universities replacing state and federal budget allocations with grant funding as discussed in Chapter 2. From a simple, linear, short-term perspective, this seems like a pretty good idea. The problem is that technical fixes often fail to account for unintended consequences over the long haul. Replacing public funds with grant dollars requires grant writers as well as staff to oversee and file the considerable paperwork most grants demand. New administrative costs are generated and now more money is needed to pay for those costs. In addition, these kinds of technical fixes tend to shift institutional priorities, often creating mission creep. As grants gain prominence, faculty are encouraged to allocate a greater percentage of their time to research projects likely to generate more funding. As many scholars have pointed out, teaching becomes a lower priority and is often not given much weight in tenure, promotion, and reward structures. Hence, a circular problem has been created, requiring ever more money, staff positions, and faculty time to keep the operation afloat.

Circular problems abound in many higher education institutions today as they struggle to make up for budget shortfalls caused by reduced state and federal funding. The "facilities arms race" provides another example of this phenomenon. Because greater percentages of university budgets are now driven by tuition, institutions feel pressured to compete for student-customers by featuring luxury dorms and state-of-the-art workout facilities, complete with the infamous "lazy rivers" frequently maligned in news outlets. The facilities arms race creates a systems problem in that a university may lure more student-consumers with its lazy river, but it has now created an expectation that will require even more money to maintain. Using facilities to compete for students also causes administrators at peer institutions to feel the need to build lazy rivers or something even better, feeding an already expensive arms race few can really afford. Mission creep occurs in this circular pattern, too, as institutions increasingly treat students like customers. It's difficult to maintain academic rigor, for example, when faculty are told to maintain enrollment and not stimulate parent complaints about grades.

In this chapter, we examine economic inequality in higher education using Heifetz, Grashow, and Linsky's (2009) concepts of technical versus adaptive leadership. Economic inequality in higher education presents what these authors call an *adaptive* challenge. An adaptive challenge is one that requires uncovering the systems, structures, and cultures that result in the challenge at hand. The authors define adaptive challenge in contrast to *technical* problems, which can often be solved by straightforward, short-term fixes. An example used in the text is a 95-year-old person whose car is frequently marred with dents and scratches.

The technical solution would be to take the car to the body shop for repairs. In contrast, an adaptive approach might involve examining whether it is safe for the person to continue driving as well as what driving means to the elderly person in terms of convenience, self-concept, etc. Technical solutions are not always wrong, but they are too simplistic when deeper issues are involved.

While some of the distinction between adaptive and technical approaches seems intuitive, there is clearly a theory–practice gap given our penchant for quick, surface-level solutions. This leadership mistake is especially evident in contemporary higher education's managerial culture, which is particularly vulnerable to fads (Birnbaum, 2001). We argue that the lack of adaptive leadership in higher education's approach to class inequality accounts for the exacerbation of this problem in recent years.

The Limits of Technical Leadership

Technical leadership proves difficult to critique given the ubiquity of technological fixes for every problem. Indeed, technology provides remarkable conveniences and comforts, but our uncritical acceptance of it as the solution to every problem exacerbates our lack of progress on complex issues like class inequality. Kentaro Toyama (2015) provides an excellent analysis of this mistake in the introduction of his book, *Geek Heresy: Rescuing Social Change From the Cult of Technology*, where he describes trying to help underprivileged schoolchildren in India by providing more and better computer accessories. While his team's hearts were most certainly in the right place, they failed to consider longer-term challenges like how their games matched the curriculum, what maintenance the equipment would need, and where items would be stored in hot, over-crowded buildings.

Toyama's technology credentials are impressive, including a PhD in Computer Science from Yale and several research and development jobs with the University of California-Berkeley and Microsoft. Yet he describes himself as a "recovering technoholic," meaning he came to realize technology's limits as the solution to all problems. Reports of students mindlessly typing words into search engines without developing the cognitive and literacy skills necessary to research a topic effectively was just one of the data points that convinced him "technology never made up for a lack of good teachers or principals" (p. 6).

This is an important point to consider for those who laud technology's role in promoting active learning. This technical solution seems attractive and intuitive; it's easy to say kids are naturally curious and gravitate to creative play. Yet research consistently demonstrates that young people need guidance in order to integrate technology thoughtfully and intentionally into their learning (Koutropoulos, 2011; O'Neil, 2014). Otherwise, they generally play video games and look at Facebook like the rest of us.

Technical fixes do not always come in the form of technology. Obsession with numbers, measurement, and assessment constitutes another pervasive form of technical solutions in educational environments. Turner's (2015) story on the issue of high school drop-outs illustrates the limits of this approach. To summarize briefly, all public schools are required to report drop-outs in order to measure their success in retaining and graduating students. This practice seems like a good idea; schools should be held accountable for student achievement. However, the consequences of having too many drop-outs are so severe that some administrators have resorted to fudging the numbers and listing students as "home schooled" or "re-located" instead of accurately reporting them as drop-outs.

Some administrators are undoubtedly acting in bad faith and should face censure for essentially lying to the government about the fates of these young people. But other administrators are likely doing the best they can to help those who drop out and not lose funding for the students who remain. Their reasonable argument is that they cannot be held solely responsible for students dropping out when the school is just one variable among a constellation of other concerns like a student's home life, motivation, ability, etc.

It is this obsession with numbers over substance that Thomas Piketty (2014) confronts directly in *Capital in the Twenty-First Century*. It seems unlikely that a 700-page economics book would attain such popularity, but the book was #1 on Amazon, selling out at times shortly after its release. We believe part of its appeal is Piketty's divergence from his fellow economists, arguing,

> Economists are all too often preoccupied with petty mathematical problems of interest only to themselves. This obsession with mathematics is an easy way of acquiring the appearance of scientificity without having to answer the far more complex questions posed by the world we live in.
> *(2014, p. 32)*

In short, technical solutions can be useful for some, but not all problems. Our society places a premium on the immediate, action-oriented fix, which oversimplifies issues and causes us to choose efficiency over effectiveness too often.

Massification as Technical Solution

Unfortunately, higher education has taken a largely technical approach to class inequality. The massification of higher education illustrates this point. There are currently 150 million college students worldwide, a 53 percent increase in the past 10 years (Altbach, 2013). The massification of higher education seems like a positive development; world leaders routinely issue calls for greater proportions of their populations to be university educated. In his first address to Congress, President Obama stated his goal for the US to once again lead the world in college graduation rates by 2020 (White House, 2009). Attending and graduating college are different matters, however; unfortunately, the increases in college access do not translate into similarly high graduation rates.

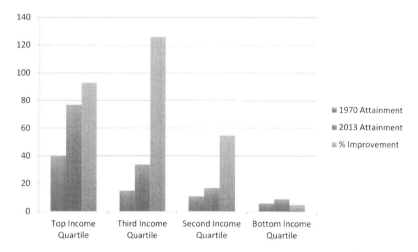

FIGURE 4.1 Percentage change 1970–2013 in bachelor's degree attainment by age 24 for dependent family numbers by family income quartile

Source: Adapted from *Indicators of Higher Education Equity in the United States: 45 Year Trend Report*, Pell Institute, 2015, p. 1.

The Pell Institute (2015) released a 45-year trend report detailing the changes in higher education attainment. When attainment numbers are broken out by SES, every income group has improved their attainment rate from 1970 to 2013. However, a closer look at the data show concerning disparities. Figure 4.1 contrasts the percentage change in bachelor's degree attainment by age 24 for dependent family members by family income quartile for 1970 and 2013.

Based on the Pell Institute (2015) data, Figure 4.1 shows that in 1970, 40 percent of top income students obtained a bachelor's degree. Forty-three years later, that number had grown to 77 percent. This represents a 93 percent improvement in attainment rates for the top income quartile students. The third income quartile students have experienced an even higher percentage attainment increase of 126 percent. But over the same time span, students in the two lowest income quartiles have experienced significantly smaller percentages of increase in bachelor's degree attainment. Attainment for the second quartile income students increased by 55 percent. The smallest improvement of any income quartile is found in the lowest income students at 50 percent. In 1970, 6 percent of the lowest income students attained a bachelor's degree, and by 2013 that number had only grown to 9 percent. So, while every student group increased their attainment percentage over the years, students in the bottom half of family income had much smaller increases in bachelor's degree attainment compared to the growth that the students in the top half experienced.

Why hasn't expanded access to higher education produced proportional graduation rates? The proverbial low hanging fruit answers have been widely discussed in the scholarly literature on the topic. First, college used to be an elitist enterprise, accepting only the most academically prepared. This is still true for Ivy League institutions; their students have high "inputs," meaning they come to college with so much knowledge that it can be difficult to measure institutional effects on their learning. As a result, high selectivity and high graduation rates correlate nearly perfectly for elite colleges and universities.

The majority of students attend institutions with lower selectivity and lower graduation rates than those at the top. This wide (and widening) disparity in institutional quality and resources accounts for the disproportional access and graduation rates. Levy (1986) coined the term "demand-absorbing" to describe the proliferation of institutions capitalizing on higher education's increasing popularity, but delivering very little in terms of quality learning. While Levy used the term mostly in the context of private schools in Latin America, a more subtle version of this phenomenon can be seen in the increasing stratification of the US higher education sector.

These two explanations—inputs at Ivies and stratification in other institutions—shed light on the disparity between access and graduation in higher education. There is another, deeper explanation that must be considered; namely, access has been used as a technical solution to class inequality when a more adaptive approach is needed. On the surface, it appears that the simple solution to low- and middle-income students' participation in higher education is to increase access. The problem, however, is that this technical solution leaves the systemic, structural, and cultural assumptions undergirding class inequality firmly in place.

As a result, wealthy students continue to enjoy quality higher education and the high graduation rates that correspond with excellent schools. Yet low- and middle-income students continue to suffer because while they may have access, they do not necessarily have the reasonably sized classes, faculty interaction, and all of the other factors demonstrated through empirical research to contribute to student learning.

Rent-seeking

Rent-seeking offers another example of a technical approach to the financial challenges facing higher education. Stiglitz (2012) defines rent-seeking as creating wealth without adding value. There are a host of activities that can fall under the rent-seeking umbrella including forming monopolies, exploiting asymmetries of information, and predatory lending. Unfortunately, some colleges and universities have engaged in practices inspired by the rent-seeking ethos in an attempt to create quick fixes to budget cuts. The University of Akron, for instance, received negative publicity for its attempt to add fees for upper-level courses (Armon, 2015a). This fee was to serve as a technical solution to the state's tuition freeze as well as the university's own attempt to lure new students with the promise of introductory courses at $50 per credit hour. Outcry against the fee has already caused it to be rescinded (Armon, 2015b).

Our own university faced similar criticism for its guaranteed tuition initiative, which allows students to lock in their freshman year price for all four years. The "tuition guarantee" is sold on its promise of "no surprises" to unsuspecting students and parents who wonder how much tuition will increase every year. Yet the tuition guarantee simply shifts the burden of four years of college to the first two years as students pay more upfront for the security of paying less later.

Senge (1990) discusses "shifting the burden" as a way organizations avoid the hard work and potentially difficult politics that true systemic change requires. The University of Akron's recasting of tuition increases as fees and Ohio University's guaranteed tuition plan may offer short-term relief, but they do not address the harder issue of declining support for public higher education. These technical solutions may, in fact, exacerbate the problem by reducing their respective institution's credibility when the public feels bamboozled by gimmicks.

Adaptive solutions require organizational leaders to consider the long-term consequences of their decisions beyond the 24-hour news cycle. This is particularly challenging in a sector increasingly dominated by executives who "institution hop" from one university to another. Not only is the average length of service decreasing among college presidents (American Council on Education, 2012), but there is also a burgeoning industry built on turning over presidents. There has been a sharp increase in the use of search consultants to recruit college presidents (American Council on Education, 2012) and search firms can make money by essentially "recycling" presidents. Questionable practices of search firms, such as "poaching" recently placed presidents, prompted Curris (2014) to advocate the adoption of ethical standards for colleges engaged in executive searches. However, in the absence of established ethical standards, the increased trend of using search firms for presidential hiring perpetuates presidential institution hopping.

Institution hopping tends to promote short-term thinking as leaders strive to make a name for themselves, then move onto something bigger and better without really investing in their current organization. In *The Road to Character*, Brooks (2015) takes an unpopular stance in defending the role of long-term commitment to preserving institutions as a vital part of substantive leadership:

> Life is not like navigating through an open field. It is committing oneself to one of the few institutions that were embedded on the ground before you were born and will be here after you die. It is accepting the gifts of the dead, taking on the responsibility of preserving an institution and then transmitting that institution, better, on to the next generation.
>
> *(p. 115)*

Brooks contrasts the shortcomings of the current start-up culture with this deeper commitment to dedicating one's career to something larger than oneself. Leaders who jump from one institution to another rarely build the kind of trust necessary to convince an already wary public that their decisions are driven by what is best for the organization. One can easily intuit that it's easier to make ethical compromises when leaders do not stay around long enough to be held accountable for the consequences of those acts.

The presidency of Michael Young at the University of Washington (UW) provides an example to consider. Just four years into his presidency, Young surprised everyone at UW by announcing that he had accepted the presidency at Texas A&M. The move to Texas A&M yielded Young a hefty pay increase. Instead of the $622k salary at UW, Young received $1 million annually, a $200k housing allowance, and $800k up front for signing on with Texas A&M (Peshek, 2015). The sting for UW was made stronger because Young replaced Mark Emmert, who had left one year into his five-year contract extension. After just six years, Emmert left UW for the highly paid leadership role at the National Collegiate Athletic Association. Stripling (2015) reports that at UW "the fatigue with leadership turnover is palpable" (p. 1). Stripling continues that "Professors, alumni, and local business leaders say they have simply had enough of what seems to be today's typical college president, whom they view as overly opportunistic, increasingly corporate-minded, and downright greedy" (p. 1). Each new president prioritizes initiatives differently, and now UW will begin learning and reacting to their new president's focus. While Young and Emmert are enjoying significant personal salary increases, it is UW that seems to be paying a steep price.

Rent-seeking represents the worst of technical leadership. The recent closing of the Corinthian Colleges provides perhaps the sharpest picture of the harm an organization driven by rent-seeking can inflict on tens of thousands of students. These institutions preyed on the most economically vulnerable members of society, promising them high quality education at low cost and delivering just the opposite. While for-profit institutions are not a focus of this book, we mention them here because we have observed non-profit universities mimicking some of the for-profits' unsavory practices. We hope to encourage non-profit institutions to eschew these forms of technical solutions and move toward the adaptive leadership necessary to effect substantive and sustainable change.

Diagnostic Challenges

Moving toward the more adaptive solutions needed to address class inequality requires a more sophisticated diagnosis of the problem. Technical solutions result from oversimplification at the diagnosis stage. Perhaps the most significant feature of adaptive leadership is its heavy focus on diagnosis as the key to addressing challenges in ways that are truly substantive and sustainable.

In terms of socioeconomic class issues, visibility is a confounding paradox in diagnosing problems and generating adaptive solutions. On the one hand, poor people are made hyper-visible in our society. The term *poverty porn* captures this idea well; this term refers mostly to media like reality television shows that sensationalize poor peoples' struggles as amusing entertainment.

There is another form of hyper-visibility that falls short of poverty porn, but has some of the same effects of reducing complex human experiences to the most extreme of class struggles. This is often referred to as varying forms of *objectification* by those who critique the power differential between those being studied and those doing the studying. Objectification occurs when those being researched are filtered through the lens of the researcher, whose privileged position can distort peoples' complex experiences in ways that are highly reductive.

Farmer-Hinton, Lewis, Patton, and Rivers (2013) expand on this theme of hyper-visibility in their narrative inquiry study about Jonathon Kozol's (1991) widely read *Savage Inequalities*. In *Savage Inequalities*, Kozol documents in vivid detail the deteriorating, violent, and underachieving aspects of the East St. Louis school system and surrounding community. This work is frequently used in urban education college classrooms to educate and sensitize future teachers about the conditions faced by the nation's poorest students.

In their counter-narrative, "Dear Mr. Kozol," Farmer-Hinton, Lewis, Patton, and Rivers acknowledge the positive aspects of Kozol drawing attention to the "savage inequalities" for which the book is named. But they also challenge the way his work uses what Delgado (1989) called "stock stories," instances where the storyteller's privilege to pick and choose flattens the complexity of the story. The authors of the counter-narrative agree with some of Kozol's characterizations, but add the positive aspects of their schools and communities as well. They wanted their experiences of helpful teachers, supportive parents, and vibrant church communities included, even if they complicated the story.

Distorted and/or reductive representations of the economically disadvantaged comprise one challenge in diagnosing the problem accurately. Paradoxically, the poor's invisibility in the higher education context presents an equally compelling problem. While there is a relatively strong spotlight on poor youth in the K-12 sector, they tend to disappear from the higher education discourse. Stuber's (2011) study on how students from different socioeconomic classes experience higher education illuminates this point. The high-income students in her study overwhelmingly failed to notice the low-income students, continually erasing them from their college experience. Stuber speculates that part of this erasure may be due to political correctness since students have likely learned that it is impolite to point out class differences. But even when asked directly, high-income students consistently minimized or even countered the reality that low-income students would attend their school.

Homophily

The students that the upper-class participants in Stuber's study did notice were those at even higher-class levels than themselves. They reported on the products, vacations, and professional contacts of these students in vivid detail. Stuber's findings make sense in the context of *homophily*, a term social scientists use to describe our tendency to relate to and associate with people like ourselves. Personal networks are homogeneous with regard to many characteristics (McPherson, Smith-Lovin, & Cook, 2001). Within our social networks, "birds of a feather" really do flock together (Curry & Dunbar, 2013). According to McPherson, Smith-Lovin, and Cook (2001), "Homophily limits people's social worlds in a way that has powerful implications for the information they receive, the attitudes they form, and the interactions they experience" (p. 415). Geography, or being from the same area, contributes greatly to our homophily. This is important to note because neighborhoods are highly segregated by socioeconomic class (Sharp & Iceland, 2013).

Homophily contributes to rich peoples' difficulty in empathizing with those of more modest means. In their meta-analysis of research on the wealthy, Kraus, Piff, and Keltner (2011) found that upper-class individuals demonstrate less empathy, less altruism, and generally more selfishness than those of lower-class status. Their findings are consistent with Grewal's (2012) synthesis of empirical studies on this topic for *Scientific American*. One of the studies highlighted was University of California-Berkeley psychologists Paul Piff and Dacher Keltner's study on drivers' behaviors. Luxury car owners were consistently more likely to try to speed past pedestrians in crosswalks and cut off other drivers than other motorists. Another study by Keltner involved examining the relationship between social class and agreement with statements like "I often notice people who need help" and "It is important to take care of people who are vulnerable." Findings indicate that affluent participants consistently reported less agreement with these kinds of assertions than their poorer counterparts.

The desire to identify with the wealthy can be a strong motivator. Veblen (1918) theorized that some items are purchased not for the item's intrinsic utility, but because it is a signal to others of wealth. Peng (2006) used Veblen's concepts of "invidious comparison" and "pecuniary emulation" to present an economic model: "Invidious Comparison refers to situations in which rich agents consume in order to be distinguished from poor agents, whereas Pecuniary Emulation refers to situations in which the poor agents consume in order to be identified as being rich" (p. 1). These concepts describe how identifying with the wealthy becomes a normative standard driving decisions.

Higher education institutions are also guilty of trying to emulate the affluent. Gardner (2010) describes these institutions as having a "striving culture" (p. 659). Through interviews with 38 faculty members and 60 doctoral students, Gardner researched the effects an institution's striving culture had on the faculty and students' experiences. Gardner contends that, from the faculty perspective, the quest for institutional prestige was never questioned. In fact, the faculty criticized the institution for not doing enough to improve the institutional prestige. However, the students in her research felt the efforts to build institutional and departmental prestige were entirely misguided. For example, students reported the striving culture was having a negative impact by increasing competitiveness between students (Gardner, 2010).

Simply stated, the striving culture of the institution to recruit and retain "higher quality" students (judged by entry qualifications), made the current students feel demeaned. And because these were doctoral students, their experience was providing a "model" of what academia is about. So, the "next generation" of academics is socialized to engage in the striving culture. The tendency toward "striving culture" shows how homophily creates the tendency to replicate class privilege.

In her year-long study of what can be understood as a striving institution, Stitch (2012) offered an analysis of how the notion of prestige works to perpetuate inequality:

> Weaker reputations built upon notions of inferiority and inadequacy are then buttressed by an arbitrary system of rank and privilege. Though reputation becomes embodied and personified, it is never tactile. Even if it passes freely into permeable space through these arbitrary systems and discursive practices that accumulate and converge over time to produce real social consequences, it cannot be moved or held, pushed away, or covered up. Reputation has endurance, the kind that leaves behind a long historical line of constructed social reality.
>
> *(pp. 32–22)*

Stitch (2012) helps explain why what would appear to be a positive push toward excellence can further alienate the most vulnerable students. She describes established faculty encouraging new faculty to lower their expectations of students, reasoning they are not the best and the brightest and are therefore unworthy of investment. Faculty time would be better spent investing in one's own research in hopes of advancing to a position at a more highly ranked institution. Helping students where they are at is a waste of time and energy if this is the ethos. Instead of interrupting the cycle of inequality, striving institutions too often prioritize prestige over parity, often in ways that are not readily apparent.

The Paradox of Rich People's (In)Visibility

This issue of visibility is an important one in identifying the often hidden systems perpetuating class inequality in higher education. On the one hand, wealth is hyper-visible as status symbols abound. It is well known that the rich are overrepresented in media, reifying the impression that class issues are minimal in the United States. Through analysis of newspaper articles and television entertainment programs, Kendall (2011) demonstrates how media contribute to the social construction of reality about class in the US. She argues that the media justifies superior positions of the upper-middle and upper classes and establishes them as entitled to their privileged position in the stratification system. Kendall contends:

> With regard to the portrayal of class in the media, all of this means that we are not receiving "raw" information or "mere" entertainment that accurately reflects the realities of life in different classes; in fact, audiences are receiving formulaic products that have been previously sanitized and schematized so that readers and viewers do not have to think for themselves or deal with the underlying problems of our society.
>
> *(2011, p. 6)*

Media frames of the wealthy are important to consider because they contribute to whether people see economic inequality resulting from individual circumstances or larger structural conditions in our society. The media frames can contribute to whether the economic inequities seem justified or are unpalatable. Kendall (2011) details six dominant media frames and their messages used in articles and story lines about the rich and famous. The dominant frames are:

> The consensus frame: the wealthy are like everyone else.
>
> The admiration frame: the wealthy are generous and caring people.
>
> The emulation frame: the wealthy personify the American Dream.
>
> The price-tag frame: the wealthy believe in the gospel of materialism.
>
> The sour-grapes frame: the wealthy are unhappy and dysfunctional.
>
> The bad-apple frame: some wealthy people are scoundrels.
>
> *(Kendall, 2011, p. 29)*

These frames show the conflicting messages the media constructs about the wealthy. On one hand the wealthy are to be admired and emulated for their philanthropic generosity and their hard working, self-made success; on the other hand, the wealthy are to be pitied for their dysfunctional, materialistic, and scoundrel-like lives. Either positively or negatively, discernable media frames contribute to our perception of the wealthy.

While wealthy people are over-exposed in some ways, the structures, systems, and cultural norms that support their privilege remain hidden from view. Their products and preferences may be common knowledge, but the structural privileges they enjoy are typically not part of the public discourse. As Atwood (2008) writes, "This is in fact what has happened over the long course of our history: those that won the wars wrote the laws, and the laws they wrote enshrined inequality by justifying hierarchical social formations with themselves at the top" (p. 21). This enshrining cloaks the processes by which the wealthy maintain their position; namely, by concealing active lobbying on behalf of the privileged as simply "how things are."

The Submerged State

Suzanne Mettler's (2011) construct of the *submerged state* demonstrates the practical consequences that result from the ability of those in power to hide the policies that benefit them from plain view. Mettler defines the submerged state as the collective incentives the government provides to private citizens, ostensibly for a public purpose. One example she highlights is the mortgage interest deduction, a huge subsidy that disproportionately benefits wealthier citizens with large home expenses.

Those homeowners with an income between $16,751 and $68,000 save about $3,600 in taxes while those at the top save nearly twice that, with the potential to save closer to $30,000 should they purchase a home in the million dollar range (Mettler, 2011, pp. 4–5). These discrepancies do not even address the poorest members of our society who do not benefit at all from this submerged state policy due to their inability to purchase a home in the first place. Renters, in essence, subsidize homeowners since they do not get the mortgage interest deduction and therefore pay a greater share of their income in taxes.

Mettler's work is important because she shines the light on the biased ways in which government subsidizes are framed. When you read the words, *government subsidy*, what images come to mind? Do you see the proverbial welfare queen buying steak for her excessive number of children at a store near their housing project or do you see a family of four smiling in front of their suburban home?

Even politically progressive people most likely conjure a picture closer to the former than the latter in the aforementioned exercise. Social constructionists explain the reason for this bias in terms of our tendency to confuse the status quo with objective reality. Even though both welfare recipients and homeowners can accurately be said to receive a government subsidy, our minds tend to associate the first group more closely with this term due to how marginalized groups are "othered." The seemingly objective, but most definitely biased way language is used to describe different segments of society provides clear insight into how some groups are marked while others are understood as simply normal. Think of "marriage" versus "same sex marriage" or "unarmed African American teenager" versus "thug" and you begin to see how language simultaneously reflects and creates the biases embedded in our society.

The result of mistaking a socially constructed reality for an objective one is a skewed understanding of class bias. This prejudice allows the suburban family to go unnoticed as a beneficiary of a government subsidy, hiding them from our view and therefore our scrutiny. They are simply normal and therefore unworthy of comment. To correct this bias, we must—to borrow Nader's (1972) term—"study up." In the next section, we examine this idea and discuss its role in providing a more sophisticated diagnosis of the problem of class inequality in higher education.

Studying Up

Over four decades ago, Nader (1972) made a compelling point about the importance of "studying up"; that is, shifting the focus of inquiry from those at the bottom to those at the top of a society's power structure. By constantly making the poor, colonized, or otherwise marginalized population the subject of study, we allow the rich, colonizers, or otherwise privileged segment of society to remain hidden from scrutiny.

Nader's assertion remains relevant today as well-intentioned higher education leaders aim to increase access without examining how those at the top adapt in order to maintain their status. One can look at generational differences with regard to education to gain a rough understanding of how this works. For example, finishing high school would have been prestigious in our grandparents' time. For our parents to achieve distinction, they needed to complete college. For our generation, a graduate degree is often required to rise to the top of a competitive pool for many positions.

Bastedo and Jaquette's (2011) study on gains in academic achievement illustrates this point. In this research, students at all socioeconomic class levels earned higher test scores. On the surface, this appears to be good news as increased scores often translate into greater access to quality higher education institutions. The problem, however, is that the wealthiest students made disproportionately higher gains, thus pulling the proverbial ladder up behind them. So while the poor students made strides, they were still left behind.

Without shifting the focus of inquiry from the disenfranchised to the privileged, it can be difficult to ascertain why the bar keeps shifting. This conundrum relates back to the access issue; it can appear that the problem of class inequality would be solved by greater participation in higher education when scholars focus on helping the marginalized rather than challenging the privileged. Hence, a vicious circle results. Those at the top aim to secure their status by reducing a credential's availability. The lower- and middle-class populations are taught to emulate the wealthy, so they seek access to the credential they believe will open doors. Once they gain access, the wealthy raise the stakes, often by demanding either a higher credential or a degree from a more prestigious institution.

A problematic result of not "studying up" is that the disproportionately high focus on the disenfranchised allows the workings of those in power to carry on with relatively little scrutiny. The privileged rely on this anonymity to recast the status quo as simply normal, therefore unremarkable and in no need of study. As Nader writes:

> The most usual obstacle is phrased in terms of access. The powerful are out of reach on a number of different planes: they don't want to be studied; it is dangerous to study the powerful; they are busy people; they are not all in one place, etc. As some of our students found out in their studies of corporate use of the courts there are problems of secrecy and confidentiality.
> *(1972, p. 18)*

Thus, any movement from technical to adaptive leadership on class inequality in higher education must include a more sophisticated diagnosis of the problem that is focused on those in power. There have been many worthy studies about the economically disenfranchised and their experiences in colleges and universities. Yet poor people did not create higher education's economic inequality problem, so researching them paints an incomplete picture of the issue. In the next section, we turn our attention to higher education's leaders and examine their role in both problems and solutions.

The Promise of Adaptive Leadership

Despite its necessity in addressing complex challenges like economic inequality in higher education, people resist adaptive leadership for several reasons. As Heifetz, Grashow, and Linsky (2009) point out, leaders receive mandates from employers and face opposition when they try to deviate from the status quo. If, for example, leaders call out contradictions between espoused values and theories-in-use, the system pushes back as it attempts to continue business as usual without implementing real change. The creation of powerless committees and task forces provides an example of how an organization might passively resist change by giving the appearance of doing something about an issue without the necessary follow through. Sometimes, systems push back more actively through scapegoating or other forms of organizational bullying.

If a leader thoughtfully examines the challenge, reads the political climate, and forms the necessary relationships, however, adaptive leadership proves possible. Perhaps the best feature of adaptive leadership is its intelligent balance of change and preservation. As opposed to fads that evoke a "destroy and start over" mentality, adaptive leadership takes the more realistic position that at least some parts of an organization are probably working well. The following insight demonstrates the wisdom of an approach modeled on creative evolution rather than destructive colonization:

> More than 98 percent of our current DNA is the same as that of a chimpanzee: it took less than a 2 percent change of our evolutionary predecessors' genetic blueprint to give humans extraordinary range and ability. A challenge for adaptive leadership, then, is to engage people in distinguishing what is essential to preserve from their organization's heritage from what is expendable. Successful adaptations are thus both conservative *and* progressive.
> *(Heifetz, Grashow, & Linsky, 2009, p. 15).*

To reverse the trend toward greater class polarization, higher education will need to engage this kind of evolutionary adaptation. It's a specific kind of evolutionary adaptation we posit, one built on the understanding of organizations as ecosystems with each part existing in interdependence with the whole. We join the many scholars who argue we have reached the end of the Industrial Era approach to leadership as constant extraction for individual gain. As we approach the conclusion of this chapter, we provide examples of the kind of twenty-first-century leadership needed to help colleges and universities provide a quality education to all students regardless of class.

From Good to Great

Jim Collins, one of the top leadership scholars in the US, made the case for leadership as interdependence many years ago in his widely read and referenced book *Good to Great* (2001). He created a hierarchy of leadership based on his research of over 1,400 organizations; the ability to sacrifice individual gain for the common good is the distinguishing variable between "good" and "great" leaders. As Collins (2005) explained:

> My preliminary hypothesis is that there are two categories of people: those who don't have the Level 5 seed within them and those who do. The first category consists of people who could never in a million years bring themselves to subjugate their own needs to the greater ambition of something larger and more lasting than themselves. For those people, work will always be first and foremost about what they get—the fame, fortune, power, adulation, and so on. Work will never be about what they build, create, and contribute. The great irony is that the animus and personal ambition that often drives people to become a Level 4 leader stands at odds with the humility required to rise to Level 5.
>
> *(para. 46)*

The former University of Cincinnati President Santo Ono exemplified this idea when he made headlines by returning his bonus and refusing a raise in response to the challenging economic climate for higher education. From a technical perspective, his action might be considered ineffective as those at the top like to make the excuse that their salaries do not make that much of a difference in the overall budget. While it is often the case that colleges spend a very small percentage of their overall budgets on their presidents, the salaries are perhaps better contextualized using different comparative figures. For example, among public colleges, the median presidential pay was 50 times the median student tuition but it ranged as high as 112.27 times the student tuition (Kambhampai & O'Leary, 2015). Also, Wood and Erwin (2014) assert that between fiscal years 2006 and 2012 among the 25 state universities with the highest paid presidents, the tuition and fees increased on average 50 percent and those same institutions also increased their use of low-wage adjunct faculty 27 percent. So, at a time when student debt is climbing (Almanac of Higher Education, 2014) and the number of living-wage earning positions for faculty are decreasing (Edmonds, 2015), high presidential salaries are extremely consequential.

Hence, there is a technical argument against the significance of President Ono's refusal of a bonus and salary increase. The adaptive perspective, however, is perhaps even more important here. President Ono chose to sacrifice short-term personal gain in favor of long-term public trust. In this practice of Level 5 leadership, President Ono's built credibility, possibly generating some of the public goodwill needed to work toward stopping the defunding of higher education.

I/Thou

Some might argue President Ono may have won some publicity points, but acting against one's own self-interest is actually impractical and detrimental most of the time. Useem (2015) addressed this issue in a recent *Atlantic* article, provocatively titled, "Why it Pays to be a Jerk." Weaving together the results of several research studies, Useem ultimately argues it does pay to be a jerk (generally defined as pushing an agenda forcefully), but only on behalf of one's team. Those organizational "jerks" whom others perceived as forcing their own agendas were left hanging when they needed the support of the group.

Philosopher Martin Buber (1958) created the famous construct, *I/Thou* to describe this idea of existing in relation to others. Elegant in its simplicity, I/Thou exists in contrast to I/It, which reflects a relationship of extraction and objectification. For too long, leadership has been associated with this I/It, might makes right, ruthless competition for short-term gain. Born of the Industrial Era, this kind of leadership reduces organizations to machines that can be exploited for their various parts (Morgan, 2006). Leadership theories based on an understanding of organizations as interdependent ecosystems have been around for approximately 50 years, yet our practices have not always kept up with our theories.

We can no longer afford to keep practicing the antiquated, I/It approach to leadership in higher education if we are to garner the public trust needed to educate all students in a fair and equitable manner. Fortunately, there are leaders other than President Ono thinking and acting like adaptive leaders in the spirit of an I/Thou relationship with both students and the public. One such leader is Harvard University professor James Anderson, who was one of the first people within higher education to lead a campaign calling for university endowment divestment from fossil fuels. While many faculty have engaged in environmental activism, this push for financial accountability represents a harder hitting approach.

Part of why Anderson has been so effective is that he frames the argument in terms of the young people he teaches, advocating for moral courage in a way that is difficult to oppose. If universities claim to care about young people and their futures, it stands to reason that we must include addressing the very real threats to their physical environment as part of our responsibility as higher education leaders. Further, Anderson acts as an adaptive leader in applying his teaching and research skills to something relevant and important in promoting the public good. While news reports of politicians mocking supposedly useless majors like gender studies (Dewitt, 2013) ought to be challenged on their short-sightedness, we also need to provide counter-stories about higher education's leadership on issues clearly relevant to public health.

Conclusion

Leadership premised on quick-fix, technical solutions to socioeconomic inequality will continue to feed the cycle of inequality. The systemic and cultural assumptions that perpetuate class inequality will not go away until we do the work of adaptive leadership. When we resist oversimplifications and misrepresentations in the diagnosis stage of adaptive leadership, we can begin to expose and dismantle what keeps us in a cyclical production of class inequality. Interrupting the cycle of class inequality requires leadership practices that bring about lasting improvements. Real change will be spearheaded by leaders who can embrace the importance of existing in relation to others. Rather than succumbing to homophily, extraction, or objectification, our leadership efforts can be premised on adaptation and relationships that treat all parties as ends, not means.

References

Almanac of Higher Education. (2014). Average total debt levels of bachelor's degree recipients at public 4-year colleges, 2001–2 to 2011–12. *Chronicle of Higher Education.* Retrieved from http://chronicle.com/article/Average-Total-Debt-Levels-of/147309/.

Altbach, P. G. (Ed.). (2013). *The international imperative in higher education.* Rotterdam, Netherlands: Sense Publishers

American Council on Education. (2012, March 12). *Leading demographic portrait of college presidents reveals ongoing challenges in diversity, aging.* Retrieved from www.acenet.edu/news-room/Pages/ACPS-Release-2012.aspx.

Armon, R. (2015a, July 13). State lawmaker criticizes University of Akron's new $50-per-credit-hour fee. *Akron Beacon Journal.* Retrieved from www.ohio.com/news/break-news/state-lawmaker-criticizes-university-of-akron-s-new-50-per-credit-hour-fee-1.607740.

Armon, R. (2015b, July 21). University of Akron to rescind $50-per-credit-hour fee. *Akron Beacon Journal.* Retrieved from www.ohio.com/news/break-news/university-of-akron-to-rescind-50-per-credit-hour-fee-1.609579.

Atwood, M. (2008). *Payback: Debt and the shadow side of wealth.* Berkley, CA: Publishers Group West.

Bastedo, M. N., & Jaquette, O. (2011). Running in place: Low-income students and the dynamics of higher education stratification. *Educational Evaluation and Policy Analysis, 33*(3), 318–339.

Birnbaum, R. (2001). *Management fads in higher education: Where they come from, what they do, why they fail.* San Francisco, CA: Jossey-Bass.

Brooks, D. (2015). *The road to character*. New York, NY: Random House.

Buber, M. (1958). *I and thou*. New York, NY: Charles Scribner's Sons.

Collins, J. C. (2001). *Good to great: Why some companies make the leap . . . and others don't*. New York, NY: Random House.

Collins, J. C. (2005, July/August). Level 5 leadership: The triumph of humility and fierce resolve. *Harvard Business Review*. Retrieved from https://hbr.org/2005/07/level-5-leadership-the-triumph-of-humility-and-fierce-resolve.

Curris, C. (2014). Ethical standards for executive searches. *Trusteeship Magazine*. Association of Governing Boards of Universities and Colleges. Retrieved from http://agb.org/trusteeship/2014/7/ethical-standards-executive-searches.

Curry, O., & Dunbar, R. (2013). Do birds of a feather flock together? The relationship between similarity and altruism in social networks. *Human Nature, 24*, 336–347.

Delgado, R. (1989). Storytelling for oppositionists and others: A plea for narrative. *Michigan Law Review, 87*(8), 2411–2441.

Dewitt, D. (2013, January 29). McCrory wants to tie university funding to jobs. *WUNC*. Retrieved from http://wunc.org/post/mccrory-wants-tie-university-funding-jobs

Doucleff, M. (2015, May 15). What it takes to lift families out of poverty. *National Public Radio*. Retrieved from www.npr.org/templates/story/story.php?storyId=406757551.

Edmonds, D. (2015, May 28). More than half of college faculty are adjuncts: Should you care? *Forbes*. Retrieved from www.forbes.com/sites/noodleeducation/2015/05/28/more-than-half-of-college-faculty-are-adjuncts-should-you-care/.

Farmer-Hinton, R., Lewis, J., Patton, L., & Rivers, I. (2013, May). Dear Mr. Kozol . . . four African American women scholars and the re-authoring of Savage Inequalities. *Teachers College Record, 115*(5), 1–38.

Gardner, S. (2010). Keeping up with the Joneses: Socialization and culture in doctoral education at one striving university. *Journal of Higher Education, 8*(6), 658–679.

Grewal, D. (2012, April 10). How wealth reduces compassion: As riches grow, empathy for others seems to decline. *Scientific American*. Retrieved from www.scientificamerican.com/article/how-wealth-reduces-compassion/.

Heifetz, R. A., Grashow, A., & Linsky, M. (2009). *The practice of adaptive leadership: Tools and tactics for changing your organization and the world*. Cambridge, MA: Harvard Business Press.

Kambhampai, S., & O'Leary, B. (2015, June 8). Executive compensation at public and private colleges. *Chronicle of Higher Education*. Retrieved from http://chronicle.com/factfile/ec-2015/#id=table_public_2014.

Kendall, D. (2011). *Framing class: Media representations of wealth and poverty in America* (2nd ed.). Lanham, MD: Rowman & Littlefield Publishers.

Koutropoulos, A. (2011). Digital natives: Ten years after. *MERLOT Journal of Online Learning and Teaching, 7*(4). Retrieved from http://jolt.merlot.org/vol7no4/koutropoulos_1211.htm.

Kozol, J. (1991). *Savage inequalities: Children in America's schools*. New York, NY: Crown Publishing.

Kraus, M., Piff, P., & Keltner, D. (2011). Social class as culture: The convergence of resources and rank in the social realm. *Current Directions in Psychological Science, 20*(4), 246–250.

Levy, D. C. (1986). *Higher education and the state in Latin America: Private challenges to public dominance*. Chicago, IL: University of Chicago Press.

McPherson, M., Smith-Lovin, L., & Cook, J. (2001). Birds of a feather: Homophily in social networks. *Annual Review of Sociology, 27*(1), 415–444.

Mettler, S. (2011). *The submerged state: How invisible government policies undermine American democracy*. Chicago, IL: University of Chicago Press.

Morgan, G. (2006). *Images of organization*: Thousand Oaks, CA: Sage.

Nader, L. (1972). Up the anthropologist: Perspectives gained from studying up. In D. Hymes (Ed.), *Reinventing anthropology* (pp. 284–311). New York, NY: Pantheon Books.

O'Neil, M. (2014). Confronting the myth of the "digital native." *Chronicle of Higher Education*. Retrieved from http://chronicle.com/article/Confronting-the-Myth-of-the/145949/.

Pell Institute. (2015). *Indicators of higher education equity in the United States: 45 year trend report*. Retrieved from www.pellinstitute.org/downloads/publications-Indicators_of_Higher_Education_Equity_in_the_US_45_Year_Trend_Report.pdf.

Peng, B. (2006). A model of Veblenian growth. *BE Journal of Macroeconomics: Topics in Macroeconomics, 6*(1), 1–25.

Peshek, S. (2015, March 10). Michael Young to sign contract that offers $1 million annually as Texas A&M's New President. *Theeagle.com*. Retrieved from www.theeagle.com/news/local/michael-young-to-sign-contract-that-offers-million-annually-as/article_9a69bc08-54f5-5ece-9efa-ab9cb0f7c658.html.

Piketty, T. (2014). *Capital in the twenty-first century*. Cambridge, MA: Harvard University Press.

Senge, P. M. (1990). *The fifth discipline: The art and practice of the learning organization*. New York, NY: Currency Doubleday.

Sharp, G., & Iceland, J. (2013). The residential segregation patterns of whites by socioeconomic status, 2000–2011. *Social Science Research, 42*, 1046–1060.

Stiglitz, J. (2012). *The price of inequality: How today's divided society endangers our future*. New York, NY: W.W. Norton & Co.

Stitch, A. (2012). *Access to inequality: Reconsidering class, knowledge, and capital in higher education*. Lanham, MD: Lexington Books.

Stripling, J. (2015, June 22). U. of Washington wants a president who will stick around, for a change. *Chronicle of Higher Education*. Retrieved from http://chronicle.com/article/U-of-Washington-Wants-a/231041/.

Stuber, J. M. (2011). *Inside the college gates: How class and culture matter in higher education*. Lanham, MD: Lexington Books.

Toyama, K. (2015). *Geek heresy: Rescuing social change from the cult of technology*. New York, NY: Public Affairs.

Turner, C. (2015, June 10). *Raising graduation rates with questionable quick fixes*. Retrieved from www.npr.org/sections/ed/2015/06/10/412240568/raising-graduation-rates-with-questionable-quick-fixes.

Useem, J. (2015, June). Why it pays to be a jerk. *Atlantic Monthly, 315*(5), 48–59.

Veblen, T. (1918). *The theory of the leisure class; an economic study of institutions*. New York, NY: B. W. Heubsch.

White House. (2009, February 24). *Remarks of President Barack Obama: Address to joint session of Congress*. Retrieved from www.whitehouse.gov/the-press-office/remarks-president-barack-obama-address-joint-session-congress.

Wood, M., & Erwin, A. (2014, May 21). The one percent at state u. *Institute for Policy Studies*. Retrieved from www.ips-dc.org/one_percent_universities/.

PART II
Forging the Solutions

5
LEADING COLLABORATIVELY

The Flint water contamination crisis became one of the biggest news stories in 2016. One of the heroes in this story was a Virginia Tech professor named Marc Edwards, who responded to Flint resident Lee-Ann Walters' call to test the water in her community. Walters' family had experienced rashes, hair loss, and pain that she suspected were connected to the foul smelling water coming from the taps in her house. While city and state officials ignored her requests for help, Edwards brought a team of researchers to the city, spending $150,000 of his own money to do so (Kozlowski, 2016). His research marked the beginning of the end of the contamination cover-up, forcing political leaders to take action to remedy the situation.

Kozlowski quoted Walters' describing her experience working with Edwards, "Nobody else was listening, nobody else cared, nobody else was taking this seriously . . . but Marc was listening and he was interested and concerned about what was happening. Without him, I don't think we would be where we are with this" (para. 8). Marc Edwards' role in the Flint story represents the best of what is possible when people translate their most deeply held values into actionable outcomes that benefit the common good.

In Chapter 2, we referenced Nel Noddings' warning about institutional thinking threatening human beings' capacity to both care and act from that care. While Edwards, his research team, and Walters were the heroes in this case, the city and state officials played the role of villain. Hamstrung by bureaucratic layers that allowed for buck passing, no one took responsibility for addressing the problem. Officials ignored Walters' pleas for help because she had no power within the organizational hierarchy and could therefore be dismissed.

Edwards could have chosen to ignore Walters as well. He not only cared, but was able to translate that care into actionable outcomes. It would be easy to chalk up the difference between Walters and the city officials to differences in individuals' values or character, but that may be an oversimplification. It's unlikely that every person working in city and state government felt cravenly indifferent to the Flint citizens' need for clean water. It's more likely that at least some people did care, but were stuck in a system that made them feel powerless to act.

In this chapter, we examine how institutional leaders can create systems and structures that empower people to behave more like Walters and less like Flint's officials. As promised, the second half of this book focuses less on problems and more on paths forward in interrupting the cycle of class inequality in higher education. To achieve this goal, we need a fresh way of looking at organizations so that we might start to get unstuck from the stale thinking that makes it difficult to generate truly innovative ideas.

Critical Management Studies

At its essence, Critical Management Studies (CMS) can be defined as "a movement that questions the authority and relevance of mainstream thinking and practice" in organizations (Alvesson, Bridgman, & Willmott, 2009, p. 1). This seems simple and perhaps like something most of us do fairly regularly. The reality is that questioning our taken-for-granted assumptions proves easier said than done because power relations are often hidden from plain sight. We may see manifestations of power like different positions on organizational charts, but we're trained to accept the thinking behind the organizational chart itself as the background noise we don't generally notice or challenge.

As a result, we're primed to understand power relations fairly shallowly without the tools to unpack the underlying systems and structures we accept as background noise. As Pusser (2015) explains,

> the ultimate mobilization of bias occurs when norms and understandings of power are instantiated to such a degree that many forms of contest and resistance are inconceivable and thus are never put forth in political decision making. In essence, they become "non-decisions" that legitimize existing norms within the status quo.
>
> (p. 65)

In the following sections, we posit competition, human capital, and Darwinian budgeting as three current "non-decisions" exacerbating inequality in higher education. Though taken for granted as "the ways things are" or "business as usual," these underlying assumptions can be unpacked and contested. We propose this process as fundamental to helping universities abandon some of the most harmful organizational practices that contribute to the cycle of class inequality. Fortunately, these practices have alternatives, which we present alongside the problems.

Competition versus Collaboration

Competition and collaboration are notions ripe for a CMS lens. Competition is a fairly uncontested mainstream principle, but it came from somewhere and thus should not be understood as a law of nature that cannot be changed. Even if one uses competition in the natural world as a basis to support the idea, there are plenty of examples of collaboration and even self-sacrifice for the greater good in nature. So how did competition become the foundation on which we build and understand organizations?

Fredrick Winslow Taylor is widely accepted as the father of what organizational scholars call the *classical approach* to management or *Taylorism*. The main idea of this philosophy is to maximize efficiency through hierarchy, insularity, and reductive mechanization. Although largely discredited in the literature as outdated and unsavory, it would be difficult to argue that these ideas do not continue to dominate in most contemporary organizational practice. Even as these classical management vestiges are covered by kinder, gentler human resource language, hierarchy, insularity, and reductive mechanization still characterize most institutions, including universities. It is therefore worth elaborating on these characteristics.

Taylor was a product of the Industrial Revolution, a time of rapid change requiring massive numbers of people to transition from small farms to large organizations. People used to doing several different kinds of jobs within a relatively small community had to adapt to functioning as cogs in a machine. In fact, organizational scholars use the machine as a metaphor to describe Taylor's vision for organizations (Morgan, 2007). The cold, impersonal, non-communicative nature of the machine embodied the ideal organization under Taylorism.

In his classic text *The Principles of Scientific Management*, Taylor (1911) identifies the first step in achieving organizational efficiency as the "deliberate gathering together of the great mass of traditional knowledge which, in the past, has been in the hands of the workmen, recording it, tabulating it, reducing it in most cases to rules, laws, and in many cases to mathematical formulae" (p. 65). These rules, laws, and mathematical formulae, in turn, became the basis for the famous time–motion studies of the era. Management subjected workers to constant scrutiny and pressure to produce more products in less time. Blatant disregard for the environment and workers' health resulted from this relentless obsession with efficiency. These factors were reframed as externalities under Taylorism; management defined productivity in an insular way that ignored the broader impact of their decisions.

Taylor's writings generally seem amoral, or sometimes even morally responsible since he did address the mutual responsibility between workers and managers. One of the most basic problems with scientific management, however, is that structure cannot be separated from morality. Efficiency for efficiency's sake produces situations like the famous Good Samaritan Experiment where 90 percent of seminary students ignored a stranger's request for help because they were told they were running late to deliver their sermons on the Biblical story of the Good Samaritan (Darley & Batson, 1973). The study is often told as an amusing tale, but it illustrates the meaningful consequences of letting the more trivial aspects of a task override the important ones.

At its most extreme, single-minded focus on efficiency contributes to the "just following orders" mentality associated with regular people carrying out atrocities. In their aptly titled work, *Unmasking Administrative Evil*, Adams and Balfour (2014) analyze the administration of the Holocaust. The majority of people who actually carried out the work of this horrible event were not hate-filled ideologues, but ordinary functionaries "just doing their jobs." This dynamic can be observed in real and experimental examples like the Milgram Experiment, the Stanford Prison Experiment, and the Abu Ghraib prison scandal.

Relentless pursuit of efficiency at all cost leads to cutthroat competition that requires, by definition, winners and losers. In a context like a sporting event, competition is appropriate because the stakes are relatively low. Coaches, athletes, and fans may feel passionately about the game, but the costs and benefits of winning and losing are fairly limited. In complex organizations, competition often produces less positive results as individuals and departments feel pressured to compete rather than collaborate.

Competition may work when there is a singularity of purpose and a relatively simple organizational dynamic with which to contend. In a complex organization, however, competition can create divisions working at cross purposes, and actually reduce organizational efficiency by replicating functions. Perhaps more importantly, competition tends to distort the broader mission, changing the terms of the work itself as the means become the end. In the section that follows, we will examine this distortion in terms of the most fundamental goal of universities: developing human capital or developing humans?

Human Capital versus Human Development

Economists use the term *human capital* to describe the knowledge people have that contributes to their economic productivity. While both the term and underlying concept are now widely accepted by academics and laypersons like, this was not always the case. Tan (2014) provides a brief history of human capital, highlighting the conflicted relationship scholars have expressed about the idea. While formally introduced into the economic lexicon by University of Chicago economists Theodore Schultz and Gary Becker in the 1950s, academics criticized the term for its connotation of slavery. Tan invokes John Stuart Mill's (1909) distinction between humans and wealth, defining the latter as existing for the former.

We take Mill's position that the notion of human capital carries within it the potential for nefarious use. Human capital is based in rational choice theory, which is the idea that humans act in their own self-interest. As Tan (2014) explains, "it tells us what we ought to do to reach our goals. It does not, however, tell us what our goals ought to be" (p. 415). Hence, rational choice theory is a values-free enterprise supporting the idea of *Homo economicus*, a "purposeful, labor-aversive, and self-interested utility maximizer" (p. 417).

Taken together, human capital and rational choice theory echo Taylor's understanding of people as essentially animals that need to be controlled through carrots and sticks. These notions are used in tandem to justify rigid organizational hierarchies and lack of democratic process. It stands to reason that if people are only motivated by raw self-interest, Darwinian competition for domination must be the driving force in institutions. We do not generally talk about this idea so directly, but it is ubiquitous in how success is measured (ladder climbing, bigger office, etc.) We exist in an odd political moment. On the one hand, it's rude to lord our titles, salaries, entry to elite institutions, and other goodies over one another, yet it's also unusual to question the value of the victory in which these things are spoils.

Human capital's ubiquity makes it difficult to see and therefore difficult to question. Fortunately, some scholars not only challenge human capital, but also imagine alternatives. World-renowned philosopher Martha Nussbaum (2011) argues for what she calls the *human development* approach, the idea that people should be able to develop their full capacity. Nussbaum grounds her work in economist Amartya Sen's capability approach, defined by "its choice of focus upon the moral significance of individuals' capability of achieving the kind of lives they have reason to value" (para. 1).

Nussbaum does not conceptualize human beings as animals whose main right is the ability to compete with others for domination. She advocates for an understanding of policy choices that put people "in a position to function effectively in a wide range of areas fundamental to a fully human life" (p. 4). As a result, she rejects measures like GDP as appropriate metrics of economic health, arguing they are too reductive because a country can be rich, but still fail to develop the capacities of its citizens. She also points out nuances like that which Sen calls *adaptive preferences*, meaning the ways in which economically disenfranchised people lower their expectations to avoid disappointment. Adaptive preferences maintain the status quo as disillusioned people refrain from registering their discontent, resigning themselves instead to systemic marginalization.

Nussbaum's and Sen's alternative to human capital provides for a re-imagining of prosperity. No longer reduced to GDP or the proverbial corner office, success must now be measured in terms of a moral economy. People are not welcome to treat others as a means to an end in the service of their own self-interest. Success becomes defined by collaboration rather than competition.

How might this paradigm shift look in a contemporary organization? The Broadway United Methodist Church in Indianapolis offers an example. Pastor Mike Mather uses the human development approach to build partnerships between the church and local community. Mather explains that he does not believe in charity because it often widens the chasm between givers and receivers. Charity can serve as a kinder, but still problematic extension of human capital in reinforcing the capital of one human group while diminishing the other. Instead, Mather focuses on true collaboration between equals in his approach to working with the community. Mather described for me how he came to this idea:

> I kept noticing the same problems not getting fixed through charity. So I started walking around the neighborhood asking people what they were good at. One woman told me she was good at cooking for large groups of people. Fine. So the next time someone called to reserve space in the church, I told them, "Okay, we have a caterer for you, too."
> *(personal communication, March 16, 2016)*

This spirit of human development has afforded Mather much credibility in a community that continues to face economic challenges. There is even a "roving listener" position at the church; this person's job is not to talk at, but rather listen to the community, and identify assets, contributions, and collaboration opportunities. The church and community solve problems in the context of organizational policies and practices built on the basic principle of equality.

The reader might dismiss this example because it involves a church, not a university. Yet higher education leaders routinely look to the business world for organizational guidance, so why should other kinds of organizations be excluded as potential models? This particular church is engaged in a collaborative relationship with the Indiana University–Purdue University Indianapolis (IUPUI). Tamara Leech, Associate Professor of Public Health at IUPUI, works with Mather and the surrounding community on participatory action research projects that promote health in urban communities.

One such project Leech described to me (Laura) in an interview involved researching how teen pregnancy impacted the neighborhood. Leech trained community members to participate as co-researchers in the project. She emphasized that neither the research nor corresponding program that came from the research involved experts giving contraception or parenting classes. Instead, researchers and participants engaged as equals. The result was a State Department of Health grant to facilitate exchanges between young and mature women discussing healthy families. Years after the program implementation, the young participants were less likely to have additional children in their teenage years than those who had not participated in the program (personal communication, April 28, 2016).

The Broadway church–IUPUI partnership offers an example of what is routinely referred to as a *town–gown* relationship. Town–gown describes the relationship between local communities and universities, and they are notoriously difficult for both parties to navigate. Community leaders often resent the strain thousands of young people put on a town, especially at "party schools" that necessitate increased police and fire services. Well-meaning university affiliates conduct research and lead service projects intending to help the community, but often fail to do so on the egalitarian terms Mather's approach exemplifies. Hence finding models that build on the assets of everyone involved is an essential part of effective collaboration.

Managerialism versus Shared Governance

Much of the scholarship critiquing the corporatization of higher education references the idea of *managerialism*. Critics maintain that universities' expansion into market behaviors has tipped the balance of power away from faculty and toward an executive class of managers. As Bleiklie (2005) explained more than a decade ago, managerialism refers to "the more formal mechanisms of management control and the rise of stronger administrative apparatuses nationally as well as within institutions" (p. 20).

Managerialism impedes shared governance, an academic tradition that has served universities well. There is no consensus on what exactly constitutes shared governance, but the term generally refers to a balance of power and accountability in university decision-making (Olson, 2009). Many higher education leaders understand there can be a healthy tension between the administrators and faculty. Hence the ideal situation is governance that is truly shared in a spirit of mutual respect for the pressures each side experiences as well as the expertise both groups bring to the table.

Unfortunately, the healthy tension afforded by shared governance has been lost in recent years. As Bousquet (2008) explains, "the decades of the late nineteenth and early twentieth century saw the successful imposition of Taylorist management practices on aspects of the faculty work process" (p. 123). The result has been a decided shift from an educational to a business mindset. For example, the sheer growth in administrators compared to faculty (Desrochers & Kirshstein, 2014) illustrates this shift in values. Similarly, the salary differentials between administrators and faculty also provide evidence of how unbalanced the power dynamic has become (Flaherty, 2014).

The replacement of tenure lines with contingent faculty also speaks to the new managerialism as adjuncts hold less power in institutions than their tenured counterparts. This practice also sends an unmistakable message about the value of the work if leaders believe it can be essentially outsourced. Even though some have argued it actually makes more sense to outsource administrative work since it does not require the specialized knowledge of faculty, this is not a common practice in universities (Rank, 2016).

Undervaluing teaching may appear to be a separate issue from economic inequality in higher education, but it is actually highly relevant. Due to gross inequalities in K-12 education, low-income students often need high quality teaching the most. Hence, it matters most to them whether their faculty are empowered to spend time teaching or whether they are being micromanaged with endless meetings and reports. This is why Nelson (2011) asserts "unless shared governance includes a faculty role in defining institutional mission, everything else about the educational environment is at risk" (p. 42).

Managerialism's defenders claim that shared governance may have been a good idea when universities enjoyed ample funding, but that today's economic volatility requires an organizational system that can respond quickly to change. Basically, the idea is that the democratic process takes too long, so those at the top should not have to bother with consulting faculty, students, and other stakeholders. This claim has some merit. There are indeed daily decisions in the life of a complex organization that must be made and wide consultation is not always possible. But, again, a healthier balance is possible.

An even more important notion to examine in the aforementioned argument is the assumption that action is always good and passivity is always bad. As is the situation with shared governance, one of the critiques of CMS is its perceived impracticality. King and Learmonth (2014) took on this issue, explaining "In other words, to continue doing the same thing would be the real inaction. Stopping doing it—becoming paralyzed by critique—is actually what enables some kind of genuine change as it forces one to engage in deeper questioning and transformation" (p. 26).

Non-participation in at least some activities that perpetuate the status quo may be a first step in unpacking the current system and imagining a better one. Teelken (2012) studied faculty experiences of increasingly corporate campus environments and found they employed a variety of coping strategies. Faculty engaged in various forms of strategic noncompliance to keep doing the work they loved with minimal interference. While many of the pro-business perspective criticize faculty as "resistant to change," the actual behavior might be more accurately described as simple resistance to a system where their opinion is not truly valued.

Hence a break in the frenetic activity that characterizes most universities might not be a bad thing. Interrupting this cycle might provide an opportunity to ask the important question of whether we are doing the right things as opposed to how many things we're doing. Moving quickly gives the appearance of decisiveness, proactivity, and many of the other terms considered positive in the business lexicon. Yet it's easy to confuse efficiency with effectiveness, so we must first consider the direction of the movement before aiming for a particular pace.

The issue of managerialism versus shared governance matters for creating and implementing important decisions in universities. The issue goes beyond structures and processes though, as those mechanisms can only do so much to support sound decision-making. As prolific organizational scholar William Tierney (2008) explains,

> ultimately, an academic community needs to foment active involvement so that individuals are talking and thinking about the issues that confront the organization rather than the process one might use to discuss those issues. A successful governance process is one in which multiple constituencies have been involved in the main problems that confront the college or university. An unsuccessful campus is one where structures exist, but because of angst or alienation, no one participates or the dialogue focuses on the structures rather than the issues and problems.
>
> *(pp. 170–171).*

In other words, it's the people, not the structures that lead universities at the end of the day. There can be forums, meetings, evaluations, and many other opportunities for input, but people will not participate in these activities if they do not believe their voice will be heard.

People in organizations find out about "the real meeting before the meeting" and other sorts of deals cut behind closed doors. If university leaders do not evoke trust and transparency in how they actually do their work, the organization suffers from the loss in knowledge, expertise, and dedication fully committed members of a community bring to the table. Given the enormity of the challenges higher education faces with regard to economic inequality, public universities need the full participation of all members of their communities in problem solving and creating continual improvement.

Darwinism versus Academic Community in University Budgeting

Co-existing in any kind of community requires commitment and work. Perhaps this is why hierarchy is so attractive; it seems simply easier and more efficient to consult a chain of command rather than engage in any sort of collective decision-making. Yet for reasons discussed previously in this chapter, community yields many benefits in organizations. Membership in a community mitigates raw self-interest, allowing individuals to work together toward a common goal rather than against each other in a Darwinian struggle for survival.

Hierarchical management practices encourage competition over community in universities. As Giroux (2015) explained,

> grounded in the culture of hierarchical power relations, post-Fordist managerial principles, competitiveness, and bottom-line interests, corporate time reworks faculty loyalties, transforming educators into dispensable labor with little or no power over the basic decisions that structure academic work. Faculty interaction is structured less around collective solidarities built upon practices that offer a productive relationship to public life than around corporate-imposed rituals of competition.
>
> *(p. 122)*

The recent economic downturns in higher education have created a sense of scarcity that encourages a bunker mentality. While most people would probably agree with the concept of community as an ideal to which to aspire, fear holds many of us back.

Nowhere are fear and competitiveness more apparent in universities than in their budgeting processes. University budgets are complex and a full-scale investigation of the strengths and weaknesses of all the various models is beyond the scope of this work. We do, however, believe it necessary to identify the ways in which budgeting can mitigate or exacerbate class inequality. Budgets appear neutral, possibly because they involve spreadsheets and numbers and therefore seem boring to most people. This quality lulls many of us into complacency about the fiery ideological debates behind the seemingly objective way money gets allocated in university systems.

Consider the popular Responsibility Centered Management (RCM) approach to university budgeting. Though its earliest proponents believed RCM only worked in simple organizations (Hirshleifer, 1956), RCM is popular in today's corporate-style university. RCM has many facets and iterations, but the main one we examine is the competition it creates between university departments to enroll greater numbers of students. In this model, budgets are allocated according to the proverbial "butts in seats," with more butts translating into more money for the department. On the surface, this seems like a good idea: why shouldn't departments with more students receive more funding?

In the chapter titled "Kafka was an optimist," David Kirp (2003) detailed the decidedly non-fiction story of RCM's rise and fall at the University of Southern California. He described the shift from an academic community to a "Hobbesian war of all against all" (p. 118) as departments dumbed down requirements, encouraged faculty to enroll in classes to boost enrollments, and advocated budget cuts for campus-wide services such as the library and counseling center. Each college within the university demanded its own general education courses, career centers, and any other entity it believed would lead to revenue generation. We have seen the results of duplication of services in contemporary universities, which only adds to the high cost already being paid by students who feel increasingly squeezed out of the enterprise in the first place.

Before RCM, most universities practiced something close to what scholars refer to as centralized budgeting. Budgets were allocated based on need with some understanding that lucrative departments like Engineering in effect subsidized poorer departments like Philosophy. There was something like a social contract operating within universities, acknowledging that Philosophy departments had value in producing well-rounded students. Humanities fields may lack easy access to corporate and governmental partnerships, but they serve a vital function in university communities.

Kirp quotes Morton Schapiro, a former University of South California dean, who explained the problem succinctly, "RCM is a wonderful accounting system. But if you don't have a vision it becomes your vision" (p. 122). Fortunately, some higher education leaders have a different vision. They are working to create both academic and financial structures that correspond more closely to the values of collaboration over competition.

A Vision for Academic Community

We began this chapter with a discussion of Taylorism and the destructive nature of its reduction of knowledge to rules, laws, and formulas. In complex systems like universities, organizational effectiveness requires the collective wisdom of all its members. The goal cannot be dominance of one group over another or even unity of voice; creative tension is absolutely necessary in making the best possible decisions in the complicated world of universities. The insularity of Taylor's time is also not functional today as universities must be connected to the broader world in order to maintain relevance, viability, and equity. In the sections that follow, we identify adaptive organizational trends for moving universities forward in ways that interrupt the cycle of inequality.

Student Participation in Governance

Universities ostensibly exist to serve students, yet students' role in the power structure is unclear at best. Student demand for participation in university decision-making has ebbed and flowed throughout the history of higher education. The Baby Boomers' legendary overthrow of *in loco parentis* during their college years in the 1960s was until recently perhaps the only significant push back universities experienced from their students. The authors' generation (Generation X) was known for its political apathy and was bemoaned by many university leaders as too complacent. Today's campuses have witnessed a resurgence in activism as students protest issues ranging from tuition hikes to unsatisfactory campus responses to sexual assault.

Pundits tend to characterize generational differences as if there were qualities in the people themselves that account for their differences in behavior. We argue the distinctions are better explained by the conditions in which each generation experiences higher education. The Baby Boomers attended college at a time when the Civil Rights, Women's Rights, and other liberation movements dominated the national discourse. They also faced the fear of being drafted to serve in the Vietnam War. Hence their demands tended to center around a host of issues, many not directly tied to university policy (*in loco parentis* being the exception). Even students' demand for an end to *in loco parentis* was connected to the broader context of arguments like "old enough to die in war, old enough to be an adult."

In the post-Civil Rights, post-Vietnam War era, Generation X engaged in less visible forms of activism. The previous generation impacted change around national problems like race and sex discrimination as well as higher education specific issues like *in loco parentis*. Though less inclined to coalesce around big picture issues reminiscent of the Civil Rights era, Generation X students were more inspired to work on smaller, more tangible projects. Arthur Levine and Jeanette Cureton's 1998 book *When Hopes and Fears Collide: A Portrait of Today's College Students* provides much insight into this generation. The authors provide several accounts of students who felt disconnected from the political system broadly, but empowered to act locally to impact positive change. The metaphor for this generation is the student who may not vote, but would sign up for a local pond clean-up.

In addition to some degree of apathy regarding national politics, Generation X students demanded little in the way of participation in university governance. Tuition was still fairly affordable for students attending public universities in the 1980s and 1990s, so student debt had not emerged as an issue to galvanize this generation. This has changed in recent years as students have suffered significant financial hardship in their quest to earn a college degree. Millennial students have connected the dots between paying more for their education and expecting a meaningful role in university governance. However, as Ordorika and Lloyd (2015) explain, higher education leaders are generally not heeding these students' call for greater participation:

> The nature of student participation—once a fundamental part of university power dynamics—has changed dramatically in the globalized era. In most countries, students are expected to shoulder an increasing financial burden but are largely excluded from institutional decision-making. This is particularly true in the case of online degree programs, in which students have little contact with their professors and even less with university administrators.
>
> *(p. 143)*

It is important at this point to draw a distinction between customer service and having a meaningful voice in institutional decision-making. The increase in tuition has caused universities to be more responsive to student demands in the customer or consumer paradigm. At times, this might be useful and appropriate, but often the consumer model has actually hurt students in substantive ways. Grade inflation, for example, is an issue exacerbated by the pressure to placate and please student-customers lest their parents call the president's office to complain about faculty. Grade inflation and general lack of rigor hurt students in the end, allowing them to graduate without the knowledge and skills necessary to thrive in their post-college lives. Hence we do not advocate the greater participation of students as customers in university systems.

We do, however, argue students should be the most important and empowered constituency in the public university. We acknowledge the reality of what former University of California Chancellor Clark Kerr termed the *multiversity*; that is, a complex organization defined by sometimes competing constituencies that must be attended to. Students are not the sole constituents in university systems, nor should they be. We also do not advocate turning the proverbial keys over to young students who often lack the knowledge and experience necessary to run a large organization. Yet we must strive for some sort of balance because the current system fails to prioritize students in the endless quest for research grants, fundraising, and related activities. Universities need these things to survive, but we cannot afford to lose sight of educating students as our primary purpose.

Advocating as One Voice

The contemporary multiversity Kerr theorized contains many interest groups competing with one another for human and financial resources. As discussed previously in this chapter, funding models like RCM often serve to intensify that competition. While competition may have utility as a model in some organizations, we argue it has largely outlived its purpose where public universities are concerned. We have reached a point where the duplication of effort, replication of systems, and sheer selfishness competition inculcates are no longer adaptive. If public universities are to thrive in our current moment, they are going to need to learn to re-imagine themselves around the principles of community so they leverage the power of the group and advocate as one voice.

One of the reasons institutional solidarity is so important is that state governments have created processes that hinder universities' advocacy efforts. An example is the creation of consolidated governing boards, which Tandberg (2013) studied in relation to the state appropriation process, finding that

> with the institutions funneling their appropriations through the consolidated governing board and the governing board serving as the chief, and perhaps sole, advocate for and representative of the institution, the sum lobbying effort may be significantly less than if every institution was able to advocate for themselves.
>
> *(p. 515)*

Based on Tandberg's findings, the ideal situation would be for public universities within a given state to be able to function in a spirit of community when advocating for resources and perhaps that should be the end goal. But in the meantime, academic communities can no longer afford the fragmentation that occurs when each individual unit competes with others for an increasingly small piece of the pie.

It may seem impossible to overcome the divisive political and budgeting practices that lead to destructive competition, but it can be done. In their book *Organizing Higher Education for Collaboration*, Kezar and Lester (2009) describe budgeting processes where each unit has input on all units' budgets, thus creating transparency and buy-in for the whole process. The authors acknowledge this kind of process does not eliminate all competition, but it does inspire people to advocate on behalf of other units when they believe it's the right thing to do. Given that everyone understands their budget will also be up for collective review, a collaborative spirit carries practical implications as well.

Earlham College's famous consensus-based approach to decision-making also provides an example of how collaboration can be achieved. Rooted in Quakerism, the college encourages all members to attend meetings to discuss how to respond to issues that arise in the community. Earlham even occasionally cancels class to do so, indicating a high level of commitment to making it possible for everyone to participate in the dialogue.

Quick to admit the process is both slow and not perfect, Earlham's leaders assert consensus does provide more opportunities for more voices to be heard on the most important issues impacting the community (Earlham College, 2004). Many express concern about the slowness point, but our earlier assertion about faster being better must be noted again here. Speed is only good if the organization is going in the right direction. The consensus idea is that more voices will yield better decisions, an assertion that seems at least anecdotally true given the Quakers' historical success in being early and on the right side of abolition, Civil Rights, and other movements many others only recognized either late or in hindsight.

While not practiced as a fully participatory democratic process at Earlham, the consensus-based approach to dialogue nonetheless creates the possibility for those not at the top of the hierarchy to have some voice. This greater (if not full) inclusion of students' voices has the potential to interrupt the cycle of inequality because it breaks up the insularity of homophily and empowers people to engage across statuses. There is the possibility for wholeness when formerly fragmented groups can function together, even if the process is messy. We posit that a similar model is needed for academic disciplines.

Higher education leaders sometimes tout the merits of an interdisciplinary ethos, but rarely is this kind of work valued and supported, especially in the RCM environment. Yet interdisciplinary work is a vital part of interrupting the cycle of inequality. Most specifically, the interdisciplinary field of Poverty Studies is an important site both for generating new knowledge on the issue of inequality and attracting scholars whose lives have been impacted by the issue.

The promising practice of cluster hires has the potential to both increase underrepresented scholars' access to academic jobs and promote interdisciplinarity. Cluster hiring refers to hiring multiple scholars across disciplines based on shared research interests. According to a study of faculty and administrators at ten public research universities, cluster hiring increased faculty diversity and increased interdisciplinary collaboration (Severin, 2013). This is the kind of practice universities ought to promote, especially given its position in making the case for public funding. As Severin (2013) explains, despite budget cuts, governmental agencies, nonprofits, and businesses are looking to higher education to help them solve the "big problems," such as global climate change, food insecurity, health care, political instability, and new-age literacy. Cluster hiring would seem to move us forward into this new, more urgently collaborative world.

(para. 2)

"Urgently collaborative" strikes us as the right way to characterize what needs to happen to move higher education forward, particularly in terms of class inequality. We can no longer afford the disciplinary silos created by competition rather than collaboration. The problems higher education must address are too complicated for a single discipline; new collaborative practices must both accompany and drive universities' progress in fulfilling their public mission.

Justice as Organizing Principle

In the essay "Modeling justice in higher education," Kelly (2015) makes a compelling case for justice as the right organizing principle around which higher education leaders should govern universities. While few would argue against justice as a good idea, what makes Kelly's argument so convincing is how she uses economic development, business, and scholarcentric models as foils for justice. Although aspects of these models have their place in higher education, each fails as a central purpose. Economic development requires adhering to an economic system measured by GDP, an indicator that does not account for the ethical dimension. The business model, too, is limited because for-profit entities serve, rather than shape clients' desires. Universities should challenge and stretch students, not simply pander to their whims. Finally, Kelly argues against the scholarcentric model, pointing out the selfishness that can come with faculty intellectual autonomy not tempered by the responsibility to study things that benefit humankind.

Kelly does a great service to those of us seeking to understand the cycle of inequality in higher education. First, she surfaces the taken-for-granted assumptions inherent in the economic development, business, and scholarcentric models operating in higher education today. Second, rather than getting stuck in the same old fight between the first two models and last one, she shows how they all lead to the current situation of higher education institutions floundering without a clear sense of purpose. It's easy to dismiss purpose and vision conversations as esoteric, but clarity of mission is the essential foundation on which everything else is built. Without it, people and systems work at cross-purposes, hamstringing institutional progress on important issues like addressing inequality.

One argument Kelly makes in the case for justice as the right organizing principle is that of public support. The public has little compelling reason to support higher education based on the business or scholarcentric models, since those are easily criticized as self-serving. Sometimes the public buys the economic development model because politicians push it so hard, but even that model fails to stand up when people look beyond the surface. One reason for this is that the public is increasingly skeptical of the current economic system. The 2016 presidential election illustrates this point. While Bernie Sanders ultimately lost the primary, he greatly exceeded expectations by voicing dissent against economic inequality. Donald Trump expressed a similar message, actually winning the election by harnessing voter disenfranchisement with the current economic system. In light of the national mood, universities selling themselves as appendages to that system may not have the most effective strategy for garnering public support.

Recognizing that justice depends on cultural context, Kelly frames the concept more specifically in the notion of fair opportunity. The *fair* qualification serves as a preemptive strike against the argument that class-bound SAT scores suffice as signals of opportunity. Kelly argues that fair opportunity is perhaps the only organizing principle that can justify public support for higher education:

> College education is costly, and if that cost is to be shared collectively, its value needs a convincing public justification. Hopeful proclamations about the value of higher education to the further democratization of American political culture do not suffice. On the other hand, a personal fulfillment rationale for universal college education is also unlikely to survive scrutiny in a pluralistic society. A compelling basis for staking a fair-opportunity requirement is the actual social function of universities in regulating the production and distribution of wealth, opportunity, and social goods such as knowledge, innovation, and culture.
>
> *(2015, pp. 140–141)*

Kelly makes an important point about the conditions under which the public bears responsibility for an institution; namely, its benefit to the common good. It's not enough to have a mission statement extolling a public benefit. Universities ought to model justice in their own organizational structures, starting with admissions practices that honor the idea of fair opportunity.

Fair opportunity has significance beyond the lives of the individual students admitted under more equitable admissions policies and practices. Fair opportunity ensures those "regulating the production and distribution of wealth, opportunity, and social goods" represent the citizens of this nation (Kelly, 2015, p. 141). Without equitable representation, the cycle of inequality is strengthened as the rich continue to create the structures and systems that shape our lives.

Nguyen's (2016) research on the overrepresentation of wealthy individuals in the doctoral student population illustrates this point. Recent cuts to graduate student financial aid have created a situation where today's graduate students rely more heavily on family support than previous generations. Given that low-income families are less likely to be able to continue funding adult offspring, high-income individuals constitute a greater percentage of today's doctoral students.

If we think about where university presidents come from, the doctoral population is a very solid pipeline. Restricting talented low-income students' access to graduate education moves universities in the exact opposite direction of where they need to be if the cycle of inequality in higher education is to be interrupted. Re-centering the work of higher education around a model of justice could provide an important first step in addressing this and the many other policies and practices that ought to mitigate rather than exacerbate class inequality.

Conclusion

How universities conduct their daily operations impacts whether they promote or impede progress on socioeconomic class issues. As Kezar (2011) explains, we must "understand the broader hidden or obscured practices and policies that become practiced norms that create barriers for certain classes to advance. The focus is on the larger structure or system as determining and shaping human behavior, rather than seeing class distinctions as only a result of individual actions or behavior" (p. 10).

University structures can promote or impede the collaborative work required to address issues like class inequality effectively. The aforementioned story of Tamara Leech and Mike Mather's campus–community partnership provides a powerful example. In my (Laura's) interview with Leech, she described challenges in getting the university to recognize her work as research rather than service. While we would argue research and service should be equally valued, this is rarely the case in universities so the distinction matters in terms of Leech's standing with her department. Leech also faced issues with listing community members as co-authors in a system that values single-authored scholarship more highly than collaborative works.

Leech's and Mather's work embodied the collaboration grant agencies like to see, making them successful in winning multiple grants based on their demonstrated track record of success. Leech described her institution as both supportive of the grant success as well as the ideals of community engagement. Yet she still experienced problems both administratively and in terms of having her work recognized. She attributed this disconnect to the marginalization of service learning and other forms of truly participatory policies and practices in institutions of higher education. Until work like Leech's moves from the periphery to the center of universities, institutions of higher education will fail to realize their full potential as change agents in the communities they exist to serve.

Who is at the proverbial table, how decisions get made, and what defines success are important considerations that drive institutions' ability to address inequality. If low-income students are unintentionally, but systematically kept out of the decision-making processes of institutions, leaders must change the systems themselves. Part of this process requires recasting success as a collective rather than individual endeavor. Taylorism and its modern manifestation in Human Capital Theory may have had a place in the Industrial Era, but we have reached a point in human history when our fates are interconnected. Climate change, poverty, diseases, and other large-scale problems necessitate the human capacity of all the world's people, not just the elite.

References

Adams, G., & Balfour, D. (2014). *Unmasking administrative evil*. New York, NY: Routledge.
Alvesson, M., Bridgman, T., & Willmott, H. (2009). *The Oxford handbook of critical management studies*. Oxford: Oxford University Press.
Bleiklie, I. (2005). Organizing higher education in a knowledge society. *Higher Education*, *49*(1–2), 31–59.
Bousquet, M. (2008). *How the university works: Higher education and the low-wage nation*. New York, NY: New York University Press.
Darley, J. M., & Batson, C. D. (1973). "From Jerusalem to Jericho": A study of situational and dispositional variables in helping behavior. *Journal of Personality and Social Psychology*, *27*(1), 100.
Desrochers, D. M., & Kirshstein, R. (2014). *Labor intensive or labor expensive? Changing staffing and compensation patterns in higher education*. Issue brief. Delta Cost Project at American Institutes for Research. Retrieved from www.deltacostproject.org/sites/default/files/products/DeltaCostAIR_Staffing_Brief_2_3_14.pdf.
Earlham College. (2004). *Governance manual: Introduction*. Retrieved from www.earlham.edu/policies-and-handbooks/handbooks/governance-manual/.
Flaherty, C. (2014, April 7). Professor pay up 2.2%. *Inside Higher Ed*. Retrieved from www.insidehighered.com/news/2014/04/07/faculty-salaries-are-22-report-sees-many-financial-issues-facing-professors.
Giroux, H. A. (2015). *University in chains: Confronting the military-industrial-academic complex*. New York, NY: Routledge.
Hirshleifer, J. (1956). On the economics of transfer pricing. *Journal of Business*, *29*(3), 172–184.
Kelly, E. (2015). Modeling justice in higher education. In H. Brighouse & M. McPherson (Eds), *The aims of higher education: Problems of morality and justice* (pp. 135–155). Chicago, IL: University of Chicago Press.
Kezar, A. (Ed.). (2011). *Recognizing and serving low-income students in higher education: An examination of institutional policies, practices, and culture*. New York, NY: Routledge.
Kezar, A., & Lester, J. (2009). *Organizing higher education for collaboration: A guide for campus leaders*. Hoboken, NJ: John Wiley & Sons.
King, D., & Learmonth, M. (2014). Can critical management studies ever be "practical"? A case study in engaged scholarship. *Human Relations*. doi:10.1177/0018726714528254.
Kirp, D. (2003). *Shakespeare, Einstein, and the bottom line*. Cambridge, MA: Harvard University Press.
Kozlowski, K. (2016, January 24). Virginia tech expert helped expose Flint water crisis. *Detroit News*. Retrieved from www.detroitnews.com/story/news/politics/2016/01/23/virginia-tech-expert-helped-expose-flint-water-crisis/79251004/.
Levine, A., & Cureton, J. (1998). *When hopes and fears collide: A portrait of today's college students*. San Francisco, CA: Jossey-Bass.

Mill, J. S. (1909). *Principles of political economy*. New York, NY: Longmans, Green & Co.
Morgan, G. (2007). *Images of organization*. Thousand Oaks, CA: Sage.
Nelson, C. (2011). *No university is an island: Saving academic freedom*. New York, NY: New York University Press.
Nguyen, D. J. (2016). *Exploring financial considerations role in shaping doctoral student socialization*. Unpublished doctoral dissertation. Michigan State University, East Lansing, MI.
Nussbaum, M. (2011). *Creating capabilities: The human development approach*. Cambridge, MA: Belknap Press of Harvard University Press.
Olson, G. A. (2009, July 23). Exactly what is "shared governance"? *Chronicle of Higher Education*. Retrieved from www.chronicle.com/article/Exactly-What-Is-Shared/47065/.
Ordorika, I., & Lloyd, M. (2015). The state and contest in higher education in the globalized era. In A. M. Martínez-Alemán, B. Pusser, & E. M. Bensimon (Eds), *Critical approaches to the study of higher education: A practical introduction*. Baltimore, MD: Johns Hopkins University Press.
Pusser, A. (2015). Critical approach to power in higher education. In A. M. Martínez-Alemán, B. Pusser, & E. M. Bensimon (Eds), *Critical approaches to the study of higher education: A practical introduction*. Baltimore, MD: Johns Hopkins University Press.
Rank, S. (2016). Why not adjunct administrators instead of adjunct instructors? It makes far more sense. *Scholarpreneur*. Retrieved from http://thescholarpreneur.com/not-adjunct-administrators-instead-adjunct-instructors-makes-far-sense/.
Severin, L. (2013, September 30). Doing "cluster hiring" right. *Inside Higher Education*. Retrieved from www.insidehighered.com/advice/2013/09/30/essay-how-colleges-can-engage-cluster-hiring.
Tan, E. (2014). Human capital theory a holistic criticism. *Review of Educational Research*, *84*(3), 411–445.
Tandberg, D. (2013). The conditioning role of state higher education governance structures. *Journal of Higher Education*, *84*(4), 506–543.
Taylor, F. (1911). *The principles of scientific management*. New York, NY: Harper & Brothers.
Teelken, C. (2012). Compliance or pragmatism: How do academics deal with managerialism in higher education? A comparative study in three countries. *Studies in Higher Education*, *37*(3), 271–290.
Tierney, W. (2008). *The impact of culture on organizational decision-making: Theory and practice in higher education*. Sterling, VA: Stylus Publishing, LLC.

6
TELLING A BETTER STORY

When an issue is highly entrenched, as we suggest class inequity has become in higher education, the introduction of a new narrative is crucial for advancing understanding and change. Narratives that are consciously created to improve the framing of socioeconomically diverse students can bring about much needed policy changes at the federal, state, and institutional levels. This chapter considers why better narratives are needed, what it is about higher education that narratives need to change, and who needs to change the narratives. This chapter is intended to promote solution-based thinking by encouraging narratives that frame higher education class inequality in a changeable rather than entrenched way.

Why Better Narratives Are Needed

Higher education needs better narratives for at least three reasons. One reason is because narratives influence how phenomenon are socially created. In its current socially created form, higher education reproduces socioeconomic privilege. A second reason is because narratives can change underlying beliefs. Changing underlying beliefs can then ignite behavioral and policy changes to foster a higher education system that serves diverse SES students. A third reason is because narratives frame incentives for change. Incentives can encourage higher education changes that create a more equitable system for students of all socioeconomic levels. Each of the three reasons for creating better narratives will be discussed in greater depth.

Narratives Impact Social Construction

Understanding that higher education has been, and continues to be, a product of social construction is an important step in improving the educational achievement of economically diverse students. As we have tried to impress throughout this book, the design of higher education in the US is not an example of natural law. Higher education as we now know it has evolved through leaders and decision makers crafting policies and practices. Originally, conceptions of higher education in the US were gleaned from other countries (Brubacher & Rudy, 2008). However, when early American higher education leaders found the designs from other countries did not satisfy their needs, they changed the designs for better ends. These and countless other evolutionary examples exist within the American higher education system. We contend addressing the ability to serve economically diverse students is the next evolutionary frontier, and we can better influence the evolution if we acknowledge higher education as a social construction.

Understanding higher education as a social construction allows us to stop accepting excuses like the status quo "just is what it is," or "that is just how the system works." The higher education system is the way it is as a result of individuals and groups of individuals making it that way. If we acknowledge higher education as a social construction, that acknowledgement opens opportunities for change. As a social construction, higher education can be viewed as malleable. With effort and decision, changes can be made.

Also, understanding higher education as a social construction illuminates some keys to improvement. Socially constructed phenomenon involve beliefs, motives, and actions of both individuals and groups of individuals inside organizations. Thus, beliefs, motives, and actions of both individuals and groups of individuals can be viewed as basic building blocks of larger systems like higher education. These basic building blocks are influenced by narratives. Therefore, it is the very nature of higher education as a social construction that suggests narratives will be paramount in influencing changes.

Consider how narratives can be used to alter the social construction of low SES higher education students in a way that affects policy making. In Chapter 1, we discussed three of the five propositions provided by the policy framework known as Social Construction of Target Populations (Schneider & Ingram, 1993). The final two propositions of the framework are appropriate for this chapter because they suggest how the social construction of target groups can change.

The fourth proposition of the Social Construction of Target Populations Framework suggests that "social constructions of target groups can change, and public policy design is an important, though certainly not singular, force for change" (Schneider, Ingram, & deLeon, 2014, p. 124). However, while social constructions of target groups can change, they are inherently resistant to change. This means that without strategic effort, the social construction of low SES students will remain the same.

An encouraging illustration of how social construction is changeable comes from the lesbian, gay, bisexual, and transgender (LGBT) community. In a relatively short period of time (compared to persisting social inequalities), the LGBT community has experienced a changed social construction. A negative social construction that limited personal rights has been changed to a positive social construction and helped contribute to milestone legal decisions such as the constitutionally protected same-sex marriage law (see Obergefell v Hodges, 2015).

In discussing the changed social construction of the LGBT community, Schneider, Ingram, and deLeon (2014) explain that

> the speed of this change may be partially due to the higher income and education status of GLBT individuals, enabling them to mobilize. Also, GLBT people are not ghettoized and over time have become far more visible, which enables almost everyone to know someone who is GLBT and to reject negative stereotypes based on personal experiences.
>
> *(p. 126)*

The change in LGBT social construction then spotlights several influential factors for changing social construction. In the LGBT policy example, as the social construction of target groups framework predicts, change occurred when a group was able to utilize financial strength, mobilization, and belief changes.

The lessons from the changed LGBT social construction are (1) that change is possible and (2) that means other than those used by the LGBT community will need to contribute to changing the social construction of low SES college students. Low SES students do not currently have financial or political strength, resources for mobilization, or positive public beliefs to leverage for change. According to Schneider, Ingram, and deLeon (2014),

> new conditions may emerge from unintended consequences of previous policy that alter perceptions of a group's deservedness, the actions of a moral entrepreneur, or a group's power and behavior. Only when such forces move to rearrange a group's social construction do we find a condition of political conflict and possible change.
>
> *(p. 128)*

Therefore, to affect the social construction of low SES college students, we argue that narrative can be used to meet the change requirements proposed by Schneider, Ingram, and deLeon. Narrative can draw attention to the negative consequences for low SES students that are the result of previous higher education policy decisions. Narrative is also a powerful tool for moral entrepreneurs to help improve how higher education meets the needs of socioeconomically diverse students. Additionally, narrative is also a tool to change the power and behavior of students who are currently disserved by public higher education.

The final proposition of the Social Construction Framework also suggests the importance of narrative. The fifth proposition suggests that "Types and patterns of policy change vary depending on the social construction and power of target groups" (Schneider, Ingram, & deLeon, 2014, p. 129). What this proposition provides is an understanding that in situations where the target population (in our case, low SES college students) does not have a particularly positive social construction or political power, the likelihood that research evidence and expert opinion will be influential in changing policy is very small. Instead, something has to change the social construction or the power of the target group. Narrative could be a tool to accomplish both because researchers have demonstrated the narrative frame given to particular social groups influences public opinion and the policy benefits awarded or denied the group (i.e., McAuliffe Straus, 2004).

The impact of a negative narrative frame for low SES individuals is wide reaching and influences many policy initiatives, not just higher education. Wines and Hamilton (2008) describe that in the "extreme version of the American Dream myth, there are no sick days, no non-traditional family groups, no mentally ill or totally disabled people; just folks who are too lazy to earn their way in the bounty that is America" (p. 437). Consider how that narrative constrains efforts to change the higher education system to better address the needs of low SES students. Without advancing narratives that positively frame socioeconomically diverse students, change to the status quo is not likely.

Narratives Can Change Beliefs

Higher education also needs better narratives because narratives can change beliefs about issues. Narratives structure and restrain understanding and beliefs. When narratives change, they can open people to change their beliefs. On the individual level, narrative therapy is a process counselors use to encourage (re)consideration of limiting narratives. Narrative therapy, first proposed by White and Epston (1990), encourages therapists to help individuals separate their problematic life narrative from their individual identity. By considering the narrative separately from the individual, the individual can claim ownership and authorship of less problem-centered narratives and new self-representations (Seo, Kang, Lee, & Chae, 2015). In this way, authoring new narratives can help individuals change their beliefs.

Because the way we story ourselves affects what we believe and do, (re)consideration of our story can then open our minds to the idea of believing in and being guided by a more helpful narrative. For example, people with depression may tend to "overly identify with problematic life narratives" (Seo, Kang, Lee, & Chae, 2015, p. 380). However, narrative therapy encourages the individual to re-author more positive life narratives. Drawing from the idea of narrative therapy, we suggest there is benefit to each of us as students or higher education professionals in examining our higher education narratives.

As higher education professionals (current or future), each of us may hold higher education narratives that are, or could be, limiting our ability to make changes in our sphere of influence. If each of us reconsiders our own limiting higher education narratives, we can begin to craft improved policies and practices and reduce socioeconomic inequality in higher education. Through a series of question prompts that follow, we invite you to consider your own higher education narrative and ways in which that narrative could limit understanding of socioeconomic inequality in higher education.

First, ask yourself, "What was my higher education access and success story?" Usually, a question like that would be rhetorical, but it is an important question for each higher education scholar to consider. There is value in the retrospective analysis of whether one's journey is similar to other students' journeys or unique, because our experiences have informed our opinions of how "easy" or "hard" it is to access and succeed in higher education. In turn, those opinions could affect the policies and narratives that we create as educational leaders.

Begin the reflection with your baccalaureate degree. Ask yourself, "How likely was I to earn a bachelor's degree?" Of freshmen entering college, 30 percent are the first in their families to attend higher education (Ramsey & Peale, 2010). A first generation college student may not have an understanding of the college entry process, what it takes to apply and attend higher education (Stebelton & Soria, 2012). However, if you had parents who attended college, your access to higher education was drastically increased compared to first generation students. And having parents and grandparents who attended college did not just improve your odds of entering college, it also greatly increased your odds of graduating. If you were not first generation, you were 39 percent more likely to graduate (Bowen, Chingos, & McPherson, 2009).

Like 47 percent of college students in 2012 (Radwin, Wine, Siegel, & Bryan, 2013), did you use loans to pay for college? Did you have financial support from parents and therefore not experience a financial barrier to college attendance? Seventy-one percent of students who drop out of college indicate that having to work to pay for college was a factor in their stopping (Ashburn, 2010). Not having to work to earn the next semester's tuition or money for books affords the opportunity to fully experience a residential university's offerings. It allows participation in many campus programs. A high level of engagement at university is reflective of financial circumstance and it also increases odds of college graduation (McClenney, Marti, & Adkins, 2012).

Next, reflect on your graduate school access and success story. How accessible was graduate school for you? At the graduate stage of education, access is a cumulative result of earlier access. For example, in 2012, 90 percent of individuals aged 25–29 had graduated from high school (NCES, 2013). Of this age cohort, 33 percent received their bachelor's degree, and only 7 percent their master's degree or higher (NCES, 2013). An individual must succeed at each level of education in order to gain access to the subsequent level.

Now, ask yourself, "What does my higher education narrative reveal or conceal?" When I (Monica) (re)examined my higher education narrative, it was an enlightening process. On the whole, my odds of gaining access and succeeding at each stage of my educational journey were higher than other students. Under the myth of meritocracy, or other limiting higher education narratives, my belief could be that I was given the same opportunity to get a bachelor's degree as my entire age cohort. My belief could be that I worked harder than students who entered but did not graduate college. But those are not my beliefs. I could claim a personal narrative that skips over the countless benefits awarded me. But I am under no illusion that I was, or am, significantly more intelligent than others who shared my goal of educational achievement. Reflection on my educational journey reveals that what increased my odds of success the most is what previous generations in my family were able to attain educationally and financially. This awareness informs my perspective on policy making.

The purpose then of considering our individual higher education narratives is to reveal underlying beliefs. Through a process inspired by narrative therapy, asking questions to identify our higher education narratives provides an opportunity to consider how our narratives might contribute to our beliefs. Understanding our own beliefs is of paramount importance because the desire to make social systems more equitable is first and foremost a struggle within each person. Nussbaum (2010) powerfully writes:

> What is it about human life that makes it so hard to sustain democratic institutions based on equal respect and the equal protection of the laws, and so easy to lapse into hierarchies of various types—or, even worse, projects of violent group animosity? What forces make powerful groups seek control and domination? What makes majorities try, so ubiquitously, to denigrate or stigmatize minorities? Whatever these forces are, it is ultimately against them that true education for responsible national and global citizenship must fight. And it must fight using whatever resources the human personality contains that help democracy prevail against hierarchy.
>
> *(p. 28)*

The hierarchy that exists in higher education suggests that important work remains undone. Exploring narratives at the individual level can help change beliefs that may interfere with desires to create equitable social systems.

Narratives Frame Incentives

A third reason higher education needs better narratives is because narratives frame incentives that can promote changes in the higher education system to make it more equitable for students of all socioeconomic levels. Incentives encourage particular beliefs, decisions, and actions. Therefore, framing incentives for a higher education system that closes the gap between economic statuses is important for change efforts. Without effectively framed incentives, individuals and groups lack motivation to change the status quo.

Currently, the prominent frame for higher education is that it is a private good. The frame that positions higher education as a public good is now less common. It is important for individuals who are concerned by the systemic inequities to create a narrative frame that elevates the public good narrative of higher education above the private good narrative. It is easy for those of us who study inequality in higher education to assume what is obvious to us is equally obvious to others. However, we make this assumption unwisely. If we assume higher education leaders who are increasingly appointed from outside higher education (Cook, 2012) are deeply grounded in the higher education as public good perspective, we miss a critical need to educate. To avoid such assumptions here, we provide some detail of how higher education can be framed as a public good and thereby communicate incentives for changing systemic inequities.

Labaree (2016) makes a compelling argument that perception of higher education as a public good was actually only in fashion for a comparably brief period of time in the US. At its origin, American higher education was viewed as a private good as evidenced by the exclusively private institutions that emerged. Labaree contends that it was the advent of World War II that first produced the view of American universities serving a national interest by helping to win a war. Then, the Cold War sustained the view of universities serving a public good. According to Labaree, the perception of American higher education as a public good did not emerge until the mid-twentieth century and only lasted roughly 30 years.

However, there is a concerning limitation in the evidence Labaree (2016) uses to suggest that American higher education was only seen as a public good for a brief period of time. Labaree uses overall trends in state and federal financial investments to support the argument that for the majority of its existence American higher education has been viewed as a private good.

Without state and federal investments, Labaree contends American higher education was market-driven. He writes that "The state was too weak and too poor to provide strong support for higher education, and there was no obvious state interest that argued for doing so" (Labaree, 2016, p. 26). Later, as a result of the world wars and then the Cold War, colleges experienced "what seemed like an endless flow of public funds and funded students" (Labaree, 2016, p. 31). We suggest that using state and/or federal policy maker investments in higher education as the proxy for viewing something as a public good omits the reality suggested by the social construction of target populations framework.

State and federal policy makers' investments in higher education are an inaccurate proxy for what is considered a public good. As the social construction of target groups framework suggests, policy makers award benefits to the most politically powerful and those deemed most deserving with only rhetorical benefits awarded those seen as system dependents with little political power. We contend there is an important distinction between how policy makers currently distribute resources versus what the American population considers a public good worthy of investment.

Seventy percent of Americans say a postsecondary education is "very important" according to the latest Gallup-Lumina Foundation poll on American's higher education opinions (Jones, 2016). However, the same research poll shows only 24 percent believe higher education is affordable for everyone (Gallup-Lumina Foundation, 2016). So, 70 percent of Americans think higher education is very important, and only 24 percent think it is affordable. While at the same time, 44 out of 50 states have decreased their per student support to public institutions (Prueter, 2014). The point is that framing higher education as a public good has to be independent of policy maker spending. Otherwise, it is an insular definition cycle unrelated to the voices of the larger population. Higher education has been a demonstrated public good for more than the 30 years when it received substantial public funding. It just has not always been framed in such a way.

Framing higher education as a public good provides incentive to create a system of higher education that works for students of all socioeconomic levels. To be clear, we are not arguing that students do not receive private benefit from college. They do. We are arguing that the narrative frame focusing exclusively on the private benefits has distorted the perception of higher education away from a public good. We encourage a narrative that includes the abundant evidence that the public benefits more from a student's higher education than the singular student benefits. This public benefit is additionally magnified when we consider the negative consequences of having ever-widening economic gaps in the US that could be addressed through a higher education system that serves lower SES students.

While the public benefits derived from college graduates are multiple, many of the greater good benefits from higher education are overlooked or underestimated (McMahon, 2009). As a result of extensive analysis, McMahon concludes that 52 percent of higher education's total benefits are realized as social benefits. McMahon argues that if people better understood the benefits of higher education to the greater good, they would be more supportive of it.

In his book, *Higher Learning, Greater Good*, McMahon (2009) provides a thorough examination of the diverse private and social benefits of higher education to help policy makers consider appropriate levels of public support. Indirect benefits and externalities are often overlooked in the estimates of higher education's social benefits. McMahon (2009) defines indirect benefits of higher education as those that influence another variable. Some indirect benefits of higher education that influence the often used measure of private earnings are

> lower crime rates, better health, better child education and cognitive achievement, lower fertility rates leading to lower per capita poverty, better civic institutions and greater political stability, and the more difficult to measure contribution of higher education to the diffusion of technology in all fields.
>
> *(McMahon, 2009, p. 52)*

These indirect benefits are obscured if the narrative is exclusively focused on the private earnings differential of college graduates compared to high school graduates.

Positive externalities are benefits from higher education that go to others in the society; they are the benefits realized by an individual that are a result of the education of others. For example, higher education prepares researchers who play a key role in the creation of new knowledge and then that knowledge is embodied and disseminated through the human capital of graduates. To illustrate, my nephew is just completing his bachelor's degree in industrial design. Through his course of study, his professors emphasized attention to safety issues in design. Now, as he enters the workplace, his product designs can reflect this education and, over time, the products in the marketplace become safer for everyone. Advances in safety are an example of externalities.

There are numerous positive higher education externalities. Some externalities of higher education that are experienced by our society are democratic behaviors like volunteering, charitable giving, and civic participation. Society also benefits from externalities in the form of human rights behaviors like decreases in unquestioned acceptance of authority and increases in tolerance of other races. Additional higher education externalities that benefit our society are political stability, increased life expectancy, reduced crime rates, and lower welfare, medical, and prison costs for states. Some positive externalities also have global impact. For example, higher education is associated with environmental improvements like reduced deforestation and air pollution. Higher education also has substantial effects on happiness via development of social capital. Social capital is measured by things like social cohesion, networking, club participation, community work, and workplace trust-climate.

As McMahon (2009) writes,

> what is probably the largest and most important social benefit of higher education is the benefit to the broader society from the dissemination of new knowledge. This includes skills in adapting the newly created knowledge and new technologies in all academic fields.
>
> *(p. 224)*

However, prevalent higher education narratives do not focus on the social good. Instead, the common frame is that higher education is a private good that should be the financial responsibility of the individual student. New narratives focused on the public good of higher education frame the incentives to change the systemic contributors to socioeconomic inequality.

What Needs to Be Changed in the Narratives

After exploring why new narratives are needed, it is now helpful to consider examples of specific narrative components that need to be changed. The following are examples of narrative components, but there are certainly additional components that need to be addressed. Use the following examples to raise your critical awareness of the higher education narrative components, then consider additional problematic narrative components from your own institution or system. By changing narrative components, you contribute to the disruption of the cycle of inequity perpetuated in the current system of public higher education.

Ranking

The quest for top rankings in higher education drives many decisions that feed an inequitable system. Competitive narratives that propel some institutions run counter to narratives that promote a higher education system that serves diverse SES students well. Selingo (2015) asserts that we tend to judge quality in American higher education by selectivity, wealth, and research. Each of these institutional quality criteria seem at odds with the goal of a more equitable system of higher education.

Ranking an institution highly because it is selective actually rewards the perpetuation of socioeconomic inequality. Selective colleges, Selingo (2015) writes, "receive the most attention only because they reject most of their applicants. Their education must be good if so few people can access it" (para. 3). But as we have repeatedly identified in this book, selectivity in admissions privileges wealthy students. Thus praising institutions that have the most exclusionary design encourages systemic inequality.

Ranking an institution highly because it is wealthy is based on the premise that if a school has a lot of money it can spend that money on the best faculty, facilities, and research practices. However, due to the highly selective exclusionary admissions process, the wealthiest schools tend to enroll few students from the lowest income brackets. Praising institutions for wealth accumulated through a century of engagement with practices that exclude low SES students in favor of wealthy students runs counter to a narrative that identifies neglect of students who need financial assistance. Rather than a narrative that praises institutions perched upon enormous endowments, a counter-narrative could critique the lack of stewardship toward a mission of helping diverse SES students achieve educational success.

The third quality criterion used for ranking institutions is research. As Selingo (2015) writes, "universities don't just teach, they help discover the next frontier of knowledge. So in our mind, those institutions that attract the most dollars to do research and hire top scholars must be the best" (para. 5). However, prioritizing dollars spent on elite researchers and research programs disincentives spending on student supports helpful for low SES students. Instead of a narrative that frames elitism in research programs as a clear indicator of quality, a counter-narrative could instead frame the notion that diverse backgrounds better contribute to the novel problem solving research necessary for today's societal concerns.

Financial Aid Contradictions

Prevalent financial aid narratives conceal contradictory propositions. As examples: while institutions proclaim concern for students with financial need, they increasingly award financial aid to students without financial need (Burd, 2015); while institutions publish one price for attending, they discount that price for some students (Gianneschi & Pingel, 2014); while institutions proclaim desires to serve the needs of their state, they strategically award financial aid to attract out-of-state students (Burd, 2015). Let us reflect on each of these contradictions in more detail.

Consider the contradiction of proclaiming concern for students with financial need, yet increasingly awarding financial aid to students without financial need. In the quest to raise their profile, institutions are increasingly awarding merit aid to attract top students. With finite financial aid resources to offer, merit-based aid means decreases in need-based aid. The competitive quest for elite status feeds a narrative that institutions are "better" if they are filled with high school students who fit a specific set of parameters. Unfortunately, most, if not all, of the parameters that are used to define student merit are highly affected by family SES. Therefore, because the metrics used to measure merit primarily reflect family SES, then merit-based aid exists in opposition to need-based aid.

Exclusive, competitive, institutional narratives perpetuate the awarding of financial aid on the basis of economically influenced merit measures rather than the student's financial need. In the past, institutions dispersed their financial aid to make college more affordable and accessible for students with the greatest financial need. This was particularly the case at state schools that were generally founded on the mission of providing affordable and accessible higher education for their state's students.

However, NCES data shows that between 1996 and 2012 public colleges and universities have steadily reduced the share of grants awarded to low-income students but increased the percentage of grants awarded to students in the highest income quartile (Burd, 2015). The trend of four-year state schools reducing aid to low-income students has resulted in a reduction in the number of Pell Grant recipients educated at these institutions (Wang, 2013). So, while institutional financial aid is increasingly going to students without financial need, low-income students are increasingly unable to afford to attend state four-year schools.

Consider the contradiction of institutions publishing one price of attendance, but then discounting the price for some students. This practice is referred to as tuition discounting. Gianneschi and Pingel (2014) assert that "tuition discounting is a form of price discrimination. Price discrimination occurs when producers (in this case, colleges and universities) charge different prices to different consumers (students)" (para. 8). Tuition discounting is intended to entice desirable students who are capable of paying with the incentive of a discount.

However, for institutions to be able to discount their price for some desirable students, they raise their published "sticker" price. This practice is akin to a department store first raising prices on their merchandise prior to a sale. The difference for colleges and universities is that the "sale" is not for all students. The tuition discount is only offered to desirable students. Again, the desirability of students is measured by metrics that are affected by economics.

Tuition discounting negatively impacts low SES students in an additional way. Low SES and minority students have heightened sensitivity to changes in published prices (Heller, 1997). By raising the published price of attendance, universities communicate to the most price sensitive students that higher education is not accessible.

Next, consider the contradiction of institutions proclaiming desires to serve the needs of their state, while they strategically award financial aid to attract out-of-state students. Campuses are strategically increasing their enrollment of out-of-state students because out-of-state students can have a sticker price three times that of in-state students (McKenna, 2015). Prestige and money seeking goals contribute to the practice of using financial aid to entice out-of-state students.

Burd (2015) conducted research at 424 public four-year colleges and universities to examine use of non-need-based aid. His research reveals a relationship between merit-based aid and out-of-state student enrollment. Burd explains that

> at high merit schools (those that provide merit aid to 25 percent or more of their freshmen), the freshman class is made up, on average, of 69 percent in-state students and 28 percent out-of-state students. In comparison, at low merit aid schools (those that provide merit aid to 5 percent or less of their freshmen), the freshman class consists of, on average, 87 percent in-state students and only 10 percent out-of-state students.
>
> *(2015, p. 16)*

These findings reveal a contradiction between public institutions proclaiming missions of serving the students of their states and the reality that their enrollments are increasingly made up of out-of-state students.

Additionally, the increase in out-of-state enrollment is negatively related to enrollment of low-income students (Jaquette, Curs, & Posselt, 2015). Jaquette, Curs, and Posselt revealed that the negative relationship was even stronger at prestigious universities and at universities in high poverty states. So, as public institutions seek prestige and money, the enrollment of out-of-state students increases. For example, at the Alabama state flagship, University of Alabama, in 2014 only 36 percent of new freshmen were Alabama residents (Anderson & Douglas-Gabriel, 2016).

This out-of-state enrollment trend requires understanding and scrutiny. Public four-year colleges and universities are seeking money to compensate for reductions in state contributions. If institutions do not get adequate state funding, then the institutions turn to student tuition for revenue. At the same time, institutions are also seeking prestige from ranking systems because high ranks can be parlayed into increased enrollment interest from top level students. Top level students bring not only increased prestige, but also increased graduation numbers. Increased graduation numbers are important as states utilize performance funding structures (National Conference on State Legislatures, 2015). Enrollment managers are then challenged to secure the students who can help the institution achieve the goals of increased revenue, prestige, and completion rates. Which students are most likely to contribute to these revenue, prestige, and completion goals? Simply stated: wealthy out-of-state students.

As institutions seek increased revenue, prestige, and completion rates, they distribute the finite amount of institutional financial aid they have in alignment with these goals. For example, instead of spending $20,000 to support one low-income student's attendance, institutions are giving four wealthy out-of-state students $5,000 each to entice them to attend and pay the remaining $15,000 tuition. The institution then collects $60,000, increases prestige from the students' high test scores (which the wealthy students are more likely to have as a result of the correlation between wealth and high test scores), and increases graduation rates (research suggests wealthy students are more likely to graduate [Bowen, Chingos, & McPherson, 2009]). The goals of the institution are arguably satisfied by this strategy. The problem is this does little to correct the growing gap between the income opportunity of wealthy and poor individuals and also does little to fulfill the public mission of state institutions.

The contradictions between the pursuit of increased revenue and prestige and the pursuit of a public mission are important to reflect in newly created narratives about higher education. These trends suggest the question Lambert (2015) rightly raises: What does it mean to be a public university?

Victims and Heroes

How higher education narratives frame heroes and victims is important in changing policy. The Narrative Policy Framework (NPF) (Jones & McBeth, 2010) is an evolving framework of the policy process that considers the role of narratives in the development, design, and implementation of public policy. Drawing from narrative policy analysis, which was first introduced by Roe (1994), the NPF supports the structural analysis of policy narratives. Structural analysis of narratives means determining the structural elements used in construction of the narrative. For example, narrative structural analysis identifies heroes, villains, victims, and story types. By analyzing policy narratives, scholars can not only determine how certain narratives are structured, but can also build knowledge about how narratives influence the policy process.

Researchers utilizing the NPF are beginning to build knowledge of policy narrative structures and the importance of narratives in the policy process (Jones, Shanahan, & McBeth, 2014). For example, researchers found that when it comes to persuading an audience, heroes are the key elements of a policy narrative (Jones, 2014; Shanahan, Jones, McBeth, & Lane, 2013). Researchers have also identified that when the victims of a policy issue are socially constructed in a positive light, the policy outcome tends to favor that group (Schneider, Ingram, & deLeon, 2014). These findings suggest the importance of considering the heroes and victims of higher education narratives.

Higher education reform narratives that identify low SES students as the victims of systemic inequality have proven ineffectual for change. As the social construction of target populations framework suggests, when policy victims are low-power dependents, policy changes do not award benefits to the group. A narrative that could encourage significant change to the higher education treatment of low SES students would frame the true victims of a system that perpetuates economic inequality as every person in the US who is concerned about the economic and democratic welfare of our country.

The victim of a higher education system that does not improve the SES of low-income citizens is more arguably the entire US population than it is one student group. Higher education was historically heralded as a mechanism of upward mobility. Without higher education functioning in this way, there is no mechanism supporting the upward mobility of low-income students. Those who are poor remain poor and those who are wealthy remain wealthy.

Historically, the promise of the America system was that a person could make something of themselves, could lift their station in this land of opportunity. Unlike other countries, America disapproved of privilege as a birthright. The caste system of other countries drew our criticism and pride in our democratic system grew.

Disparate educational opportunities for low-income students hurts more than just the low-income students themselves. They create a system that is unable to develop the human potential of our population. All the social benefits gained from higher education graduates detailed earlier in this chapter are left unattained. Instead of experiencing the benefits, we experience the societal problems linked to a populous without higher education. We suggest that low-income groups, high-income groups, and everyone in between are victims when we have a higher education system that perpetuates socioeconomic inequality.

Just as centering the victim narrative on low-income students is ineffective for change, it is also ineffective to create a hero narrative centered on a singular hero. There is no singular benevolent individual that can change the higher education system. Instead, the collective hero that can create an educational system that provides for all SES students is democracy. The reciprocal relationship between democracy and higher education has long been argued (for example, Dewey, 1916).

One of the reasons the public viewed higher education as a public good after the world wars and during the Cold War era was because it demonstrated the strength of democracy over communism (Labaree, 2016). Our nation's democratic commitment to education for all was a testimony to the world of the benefits of democratic philosophy. Labaree (2016) contends that during the Cold War, in higher education,

> we needed to provide high-level human capital in order to promote economic growth and demonstrate the economic superiority of capitalism over communism. And we needed to provide educational opportunity for our own racial minorities and lower classes in order to show that our system is not only effective but also fair and equitable. This would be a powerful weapon in the effort to win over the third world with the attractions of the American Way.
>
> *(p. 29)*

Thus, our nation's commitment to equitable higher education reinforced democratic ideals.

Democratic society is held together by shared values and beliefs. When individuals become exclusively self-concerned, the strength of our society weakens. The benefits of a higher education system that serves all SES students are felt throughout our society in myriad ways. Under the current system that excludes low SES students, the victim is not simply the excluded students, it is our entire populous. Accordingly, the hero of a higher education system that provides equity of access and success is a democracy that values the well-being of the greater society.

Who Changes the Narratives

After considering why new higher education narratives are needed and examples of specific narrative elements that need to be changed, we now turn to identifying who is responsible for changing the narratives. Narratives exist on multiple levels, and therefore changing the status quo of higher education as a mechanism of socioeconomic inequality requires addressing narratives on multiple levels. Here, we suggest that changing narratives on both the individual and organizational levels could promote overall change in higher education.

Individuals

Because narratives both reflect and create our realities, consideration of our personal narratives is important. Earlier in this chapter, we suggested the importance of narrative therapy inspired techniques in considering the limiting nature of personal narratives. It is also important to consider how unacknowledged social closure may be reflected in our individual narratives.

Drawing from Weber, Murphy (1988) defines social closure as a "process of subordination whereby one group monopolizes advantages by closing off opportunities to another group of outsiders beneath it which it defines as inferior and ineligible" (p. 8). Alon (2009) further refined the understanding of social closure by discovering how exclusion and adaptation work together to perpetuate inequality in higher education. Exclusion in higher education occurs through mechanisms like escalated tuition costs; adaptation occurs through practices such as inflated emphasis on standardized test scores. These social closures work to keep out so called "outsiders."

Exclusions are fairly straightforward; however, adaptations are more complex mechanisms. Alon (2009) specifically considered the adaptation to increased emphasis on standardized test scores in the admissions process. As higher education institutions raised their test score requirements, wealthy families adapted by using their resources to help their children meet the new requirements. Low-income families did not have equal resources to help their children, thus the new test score requirements became barriers for their children. Over time, as low-income students also adapt to the increased requirements, the threshold rises. The nature of the moving target is what closes certain groups out.

Karabel (2005) explored social closure at the elite private institutions of Harvard, Yale, and Princeton. He detailed how the definitions of "merit" have changed over the last 100 years, and thus demonstrates the social closure process. As Swartz (2008) summarizes, "No definition of 'merit' is neutral, for a particular definition always advantages some groups while disadvantaging others" (p. 415). However, as we have discussed in prior chapters, the definition of merit, like other mechanisms of social closure, is set by those in power so the definition will "reflect power relations among major social groups and the organizational interests of the schools" (Swartz, 2008, p. 411). Although Karabel's research draws attention to social closure at elite private institutions, we argue that public institutions are exhibiting similar closure techniques. Instead of social closure just being part of the elite, private institutional narrative, it is increasingly descriptive of the public institutions' narratives.

It is emotionally difficult to claim social closure as part of our individual narratives. It is certainly not comfortable to acknowledge participation in social closure behaviors. And rather than acknowledge our participation, we often cling to defensiveness and rationalizations because we feel guilt. Guilt is a strong human emotion and it is important to consider because narratives are a way of structuring our perceptions of an issue in a way that lessens our guilt.

Guilt even influences up the chain of command. Experiments conducted by Oc, Bashshur, and Moore (2015) suggest that candid disapproving feedback from subordinates to power holders lowered how self-interested the power holders' allocations of resources were over time. The researchers contend that guilt mediates this relationship. These findings suggest that each person, whether subordinate or power holding, can have influence when guilt is evoked. But just as guilt can encourage change, it can also discourage individuals from considering and acknowledging social closure practices.

A starting point for changing the narratives that conceal social closure practices is at the individual level. Each person associated with higher education can examine the socioeconomic inequity that is perpetuated by the current policies and practices and raise awareness through new narratives. The fear of change and the guilt of inequity can be overcome. Temporary personal discomforts can give way to the long term benefits of having a higher education system that functions for all socioeconomic levels.

Organizations

Historically, family wealth was passed to the next generation through transfer of family businesses or farm ownership. As the number of large corporations has grown and private business and farm ownership have substantially declined, families no longer have the same control of their intergenerational fates. When more individuals owned businesses, passing that business on to one's children was a way to maintain the family's social position for the next generation. Now, if a parent is an accountant at a large corporation, she cannot guarantee her children can be accountants at that corporation in the future.

Karen (1990) contends that "in advanced industrial societies, social structure is reproduced at the level of large organizations" (p. 228). Because the social status transfer mechanisms have changed, and fewer people leave family businesses to their children, the large organizations now have a role in reproducing social status. As the modes of intergenerational social status transfer have become less personal and more structural, there is increased urgency to examine the way organizations reproduce social status. Narrative, we argue, is one of the ways that organizations contribute to reproduction of social status.

There is growing awareness of the roles narratives play in organizations and in leadership (Auvinen, Aaltio, & Blomqvist, 2013; Boal & Schultz, 2007; Collison & Mackenzie, 1999; Denning, 2006; Ford, Ford, & McNamara, 2001; Schedlitzki, Jarvis, & MacInnes, 2015; Wines & Hamilton, 2008). Also, narratives have specifically been considered for their contribution to change in organizations (Boal & Schultz, 2007; Ford, Ford, & McNamara, 2001; Wines & Hamilton, 2008). We argue the current narrative operating inside higher education prioritizes institutional profit and prestige. This narrative then provides de facto leadership steering decisions and behaviors of employees in the higher education institutions. While narrative can perpetuate the negative, narrative can also foster organizational change.

Organizations, as complex social constructs, are changeable. Key to these change efforts is strategic leadership. And strategic leaders harness the power of narratives (Boal & Schultz, 2007). Strategic leadership is distinct from supervisory or managerial leadership. Boal and Schultz (2007) summarize the distinction: "supervisory theories of leadership focus on leadership 'in' organizations" and strategic theories of leadership "focus on the leadership 'of' organizations" (p. 412). Strategic leadership therefore provides vision and promotes organizational evolution.

Boal and Schultz (2007) elucidate the strategic leader's role. They suggest that

> strategic leaders articulate their visions by telling stories and promoting dialogue in which an organization's past, present, and future coalesce: stories and dialogue about our history; stories and dialogue about who we are; stories and dialogue about what we can become. Storytelling allows individuals to share their explicit knowledge and their implicit understandings, and over time, builds up a cognitive consensuality that identifies and defines the organization as an entity with a history and future.
>
> *(p. 427)*

Without these stories, individuals within the organization miss opportunities for motivation and sense of self. Without these stories, individuals miss out on one of the markers of a good life. As Wines and Hamilton (2008) remind us, "A good life involves doing good work not just gaining wealth" (p. 435).

For public higher education institutions, it should be fairly straightforward to narratively connect the organization's past, present, and future. However, deviation from the public mission is increasingly occurring. In-state students are shut out. Thresholds are established of higher and higher test scores privileging students with socioeconomic means. The gap between what Pell Grants cover and the total cost of attendance eliminates access to students in need. Institutional financial aid is awarded in merit-based aid to attract students with the ability to pay. Serving the public needs of the respective state was central in the origin story of state colleges and universities. Now, the narrative depicts the quest for prestige and profit. Increasingly, the present narrative is not reflective of the past public narrative. Left unaddressed, this trend will certainly have a negative impact in the future.

Stories can become part of the organization ideology; or as Wines and Hamilton (2008) describe, stories become part of the "reflexive, subconscious application of values to problems" (p. 444). At a basic level, stories drive what we do and what our organizations become. Stories framing the importance of equality of access and success in higher education can support change efforts at the institutional, state, and federal levels. In a democratic society, the education of all SES students is crucial. Narratives that frame the benefits of equity will help create a public higher education system that concerns itself with the well-being of our entire society rather than the wealthy elite.

Conclusion

Stories become part of the cultural fiber influencing individual beliefs and behaviors. Therefore, when left unexamined, stories can further entrench higher education cultures that exclude low SES students. To interrupt the cycle of higher education inequity, new stories should be introduced. The stories that frame higher education as a public good are the stories that warrant celebration and retelling.

At the classroom and campus levels, we see the transformative nature of higher education. These are the stories the public deserves to hear. The public should hear stories about how their investment in public higher education helps low-income students gain exposure to ideas and learning experiences the students thought were out of reach, that their investment makes a difference. We need to tell the stories of financially struggling students who make knowledge discoveries, enrich campus conversations, and propose revolutionizing research. These financially struggling students ultimately improve our communities, our nation, and our world; but in order to do that, the students need support.

As a society we miss out on the talents of low-income students when we do not invest in them. The student that eventually cures cancer or addresses climate change could be low income. However, we miss this realization when our higher education narratives conflate wealth and ability.

Our stories need to describe a public higher education system that is part of a social compact defining us as a nation. The public ought to hear stories of a higher education system that expends resources equitably and values the socio-economic diversity of its students. We should tell the stories of institutions that hold as true north their public mission. Institutions that turn away from the escalating race for elitist rankings change the status quo and their stories merit our telling. Through the telling of these better stories, the public gains reason to trust the value of investing in higher education.

References

Alon, S. (2009). The evolution of class inequality in higher education: Competition, exclusion, and adaptation. *American Sociological Review*, 74, 731–755.

Anderson, N., & Douglas-Gabriel, D. (2016, January 30). Nation's prominent public universities are shifting to out-of-state students. *Washington Post*. Retrieved from www.washingtonpost.com/local/education/nations-prominent-public-universities-are-shifting-to-out-of-state-students/2016/01/30/07575790-beaf-11e5-bcda-62a36b394160_story.html.

Ashburn, E. (2010, December 9). Why do students drop out? Because they must work at jobs too. *Chronicle of Higher Education*. Retrieved from http://chronicle.com/article/Why-Do-Students-Drop-Out-/49417/.

Auvinen, T., Aaltio, I., & Blomqvist, K. (2013). Constructing leadership by storytelling: The meaning of trust and narratives. *Leadership & Organization Development Journal*, 34(6), 496–514.

Boal, K., & Schultz, P. (2007). Storytelling, time, and evolution: The role of strategic leadership in complex adaptive systems. *Leadership Quarterly, 18*, 411–428.

Bowen, W., Chingos, M., & McPherson, M. (2009). *Crossing the finish line: Completing college at America's public universities*. Princeton, NJ: Princeton University Press.

Brubacher, J., & Rudy, W. (2008). *Higher education in transition: A history of American colleges and universities* (4th ed.). New Brunswick, NJ: Harper & Row Publishers, Inc.

Burd, S. (2015). *The out-of-state student arms race: How public universities use merit aid to recruit nonresident students*. New America Education Policy. Retrieved from https://static.newamerica.org/attachments/3120-out-of-state-student-arms-race/OutOfStateArmsRace-Final.b93c2211cdfb4c3da169d668fbb67cc1.pdf.

Collison, C., & Mackenzie, A. (1999). The power of story in organisations. *Journal of Workplace Learning, 11*(1), 38–40.

Cook, B. (2012). *The American college president study: Key findings and takeaways*. Washington, DC: American Council on Education. Retrieved from www.acenet.edu/the-presidency/columns-and-features/Pages/The-American-College-President-Study.aspx.

Denning, S. (2006). Effective storytelling: Strategic business narrative techniques. *Strategy & Leadership, 34*(1), 42–48.

Dewey, J. (1916). *Democracy and education*. Rochester, NY: Starry Night Publishing.

Ford, J., Ford, L., & McNamara, R. (2001). Resistance and the background conversations of change. *Journal of Organizational Change, 15*(2), 105–121.

Gallup-Lumina Foundation. (2016). *Americans value postsecondary education: The 2015 Gallup-Lumina Foundation study of the American public's opinion on higher education*. Retrieved from www.gallup.com/services/190583/americans-value-postsecondary-education-report.aspx?g_source=position1&g_medium=related&g_campaign=tiles.

Gianneschi, M., & Pingel, S. (2014). A hidden cause of rising tuition: Tuition discounting in public colleges and universities. *Progress of Education Reform, 15*(4). Retrieved from http://eric.ed.gov/?id=ED560989.

Heller, D. (1997). Student price response in higher education: An update to Leslie and Brinkman. *Journal of Higher Education, 68*(6), 624–659.

Jaquette, O., Curs, B., & Posselt, J. (2015). Tuition rich, mission poor: Nonresident enrollment growth and the socioeconomic and racial composition of public research universities. *Journal of Higher Education, 87*(5), 635–673. Retrieved from www.researchgate.net/publication/267392513_Tuition_rich_mission_poor_Nonresident_enrollment_growth_and_the_socioeconomic_and_racial_composition_of_public_research_universities.

Jones, J. (2016). *Americans still say postsecondary education very important*. Princeton, NJ: Gallup-Lumina Foundation Poll. Retrieved from www.gallup.com/poll/190580/americans-say-postsecondary-education-important.aspx?g_source=Education&g_medium=newsfeed&g_campaign=tiles.

Jones, M. (2014). Cultural characters and climate change: How heroes shape our perception of climate science. *Social Science Quarterly, 95*(1), 1–39.

Jones, M., & McBeth, M. (2010). A narrative policy framework: Clear enough to be wrong? *Policy Studies Journal, 38*(2), 329–353.

Jones, M., Shanahan, E., & McBeth, M. (Eds). (2014). *The science of stories: Applications of the narrative policy framework in public policy analysis*. New York, NY: Palgrave Macmillan.

Karabel, J. (2005). *The chosen: The hidden history of admission and exclusion at Harvard, Yale, and Princeton*. Boston, MA: Houghton Mifflin.

Karen, D. (1990). Toward a political-organizational model of gatekeeping: The case of elite colleges. *Sociology of Education, 63*(4), 227–240.

Labaree, D. (2016). An affair to remember: America's brief fling with the university as a public good. *Journal of Philosophy of Education, 50*(1), 20–36.

Lambert, M. (2015). Privatization and the public good. *Change: Magazine of Higher Learning, 47*(3), 6–13.

McAuliffe Straus, R. (2004). Restructuring Los Angeles magnet schools: Representations in newspapers. *Peabody Journal of Education, 79*(2), 98–121.

McClenney, K., Marti, C. N., & Adkins, C. (2012) *Student Engagement and Student Outcomes: Key Findings from "CCSSE" Validation Research.* Retrieved from http://files.eric.ed.gov/fulltext/ED529076.pdf.

McKenna, L. (2015, October 15). The allure of the out-of-state student. *Atlantic.* Retrieved from www.theatlantic.com/education/archive/2015/10/the-allure-of-the-out-of-state-student/410656/.

McMahon, W. (2009). *Higher learning, greater good: The private and social benefits of higher education.* Baltimore, MD; Johns Hopkins University Press.

Murphy, R. (1988). *Social closure: The theory of monopolization and exclusion.* New York, NY: Oxford University Press.

National Conference on State Legislatures. (2015, July 31). *Performance-based funding for higher education.* Washington, DC; National Conference on State Legislatures. Retrieved from www.ncsl.org/research/education/performance-funding.aspx.

NCES [National Center for Education Statistics]. (2013). *Educational attainment.* US Department of Education, National Center for Education Statistics (2013). The Condition of Education 2013 (NCES 2013–037). Retrieved from http://nces.ed.gov/fastfacts/display.asp?id=27.

Nussbaum, M. (2010). *Not for profit: Why democracy needs the humanities.* Princeton, NJ: Princeton University Press.

Obergefell et al. v. Hodges, Director, Ohio Department of Health, et al. (2015). United States Supreme Court: No. 14-556.

Oc, B., Bashshur, M. R., & Moore, C. (2015). Speaking truth to power: The effect of candid feedback on how individuals with power allocate resources. *Journal of Applied Psychology, 100*(2), 450–463.

Prueter, B. (2014). *State disinvestment in higher education has led to explosion of student-loan debt.* Washington, DC: Postsecondary National Policy Institute. Retrieved from www.newamerica.org/postsecondary-national-policy-institute/state-disinvestment-in-higher-education-has-led-to-an-explosion-of-student-loan-debt/.

Radwin, D., Wine, J., Siegel, P., & Bryan, M. (2013). *2011–12 National Postsecondary Student Aid Study (NPSAS:12): Student Financial Aid Estimates for 2011–12* (NCES 2013-165). Institute of Education Sciences, US Department of Education. Washington, DC: National Center for Education Statistics. Retrieved from http://nces.ed.gov/pubsearch.

Ramsey, K., & Peale, C. (2010, March 29). First generation students stay the course. *USA Today.* Retrieved from http://usatoday30.usatoday.com/news/education/2010-03-30-FirstGenDorm30_ST_N.htm.

Roe, E. (1994). *Narrative policy analysis: Theory and practice.* Durham, NC: Duke University Press.

Schedlitzki, D., Jarvis, C., & MacInnes, J. (2015). Leadership development: A place for storytelling and Greek mythology? *Management Learning, 46*(4), 412–426.

Schneider, A., & Ingram, H. (1993). Social construction of target populations: Implications for politics and policy. *American Political Science Review, 87*(2), 334–347.

Schneider, A., Ingram, H., & deLeon, P. (2014). Democratic policy design: Social construction of target populations. In P. A. Sabatier & C. M. Weible (Eds), *Theories of the policy process* (3rd ed., pp. 105–149). Boulder, CO: Westview Press.

Selingo, J. (2015, July 30). Do college rankings mean anything? That depends on your perception of No. 1. *Washington Post*. Retrieved from www.washingtonpost.com/news/grade-point/wp/2015/07/30/do-college-rankings-mean-anything-that-depends-on-your-perception-of-no-1/.

Seo, M., Kang, H., Lee, Y., & Chae, S. (2015). Narrative therapy with an emotional approach for people with depression: Improved symptom and cognitive-emotional outcomes. *Journal of Psychiatric and Mental Health Nursing, 22*, 379–389.

Shanahan, E., Jones, M., McBeth, M., & Lane, R. (2013). An angel on the wind: How heroic policy narratives shape policy realities. *Policy Studies Journal, 41*(3), 453–483.

Stebelton, M., & Soria, K. (2012). Breaking down barriers: Academic obstacles of first-generation students at research universities. *Learning Assistance Review, 17*(2), 7–19.

Swartz, D. (2008). Social closure in American elite higher education. *Theory & Society, 37*, 409–419.

Wang, M. (2013). Public universities ramp up aid for the wealthy, leaving the poor behind. *Pro Publica*.

White, M., & Epston, D. (1990). *Narrative means to therapeutic ends*. New York, NY: Norton & Company.

Wines, W., & Hamilton III, J. (2008). On changing organizational cultures by injecting new ideologies: The power of stories. *Journal of Business Ethics, 89*, 433–447.

7
GAINING THE PUBLIC TRUST

Public trust matters to higher education. In this chapter, we argue that the ability to win and maintain public trust is related to higher education's ability to serve diverse SES students. Public trust can influence both the financial support higher education receives, and the quality of relationships between higher education and its stakeholders.

At the outset, we acknowledge that the notion of public opinion is something that scholars can debate (O'Connor, 2004). There are questions about whether a stable, measurable unit of public opinion is identifiable. Arguments can be made both for and against the value of public opinion polling. And perhaps most vexing for our argument that increasing public trust is important is the limited evidence that policy makers are responding to public opinion (O'Connor, 2004). Instead, policy makers are viewed as getting publicity for opinions that suit their agendas.

This suggests a chicken-or-egg dilemma. Which comes first? Does public opinion drive policy makers, or do policy makers drive public opinion? There are no definitive findings of causality in this dilemma. However, while strong public opinion may not guarantee a policy maker will take action, it is unlikely that a policy maker will lobby for increased higher education funding without the confidence that the public feels strongly supportive of that cause. O'Connor (2004) writes

> in order to determine when public opinion should be followed and when it should be led, policy makers nevertheless need to read polls. In doing so, their policies may begin to reflect the majority preference, thus producing a "recoil effect" where public opinion actually does seem to impact policy in academic studies.

(pp. 4–5)

Therefore, if public opinion polls consistently show strong support for funding public higher education at levels that can support efforts to educate low-income students, policy makers may be more motivated to prioritize such spending. Therefore, the topic of this chapter is how public trust in higher education can be increased.

Work is needed to create a strong, trusting public opinion of higher education. Public opinion is currently mixed (Greer, 2013). Without improved public opinion, it is unlikely policy makers will prioritize financial support for public higher education. Research suggests policy makers are generally only responsive to public opinion when the public holds clear majority opinions on issues highly important to them (Monroe, 1998). This means that public opinion is helpful to spark policy change when that public opinion is uniform and the issue is deemed highly important. Throughout this book we have supported the idea that higher education is highly important, so now we turn our attention to creating a universal public trust in higher education.

Why Public Trust Matters

Public trust matters because it influences the funding and relationships higher education needs. Those funds and relationships in turn are assets that can be leveraged to improve the higher education outcomes for low SES students. Unfortunately, real and perceived classism in higher education has contributed to public distrust in the institution. Universities are too often cast as ivory towers where educated people look down upon the masses from their gated community. As discussed in Chapter 2, poor and working-class students often get the sense that they don't belong in college due to norms that conflate academic ability with middle/upper-class cultural capital. When poor and working-class students experience this alienation, it stands to reason they sometimes express it to their parents, friends, and neighbors who in turn come to understand the university as a place of exclusion.

The onus is on university insiders to make our public higher education institutions trustworthy, inclusive, and relevant to the communities with which they ought to be interdependent. This goal may require a paradigm change in faculty and staff who are socialized to understand their constituency more narrowly. Yet there are modest ways universities can leverage existing programs to garner more public support in the small picture. For example, we recently learned state universities in Ohio offer senior citizens the opportunity to audit classes. We work in a state institution and study higher education, yet only recently became aware of this practice that would likely generate more goodwill and public support were it more widely known.

People support services they use. When we listen to our local public radio station, for example, we feel inclined to support it both through our tax dollars and private giving. We experience its value and want it to have the resources it needs to continue contributing to our ability to be informed citizens. National Public Radio (NPR) understands this dynamic and invites our participation through donations, volunteering, and opportunities to call into programs. The last thing this organization would want to do is alienate us as part of its listening public. Interestingly, NPR accomplishes this without pandering to us as customers. We may want them to run more segments about dogs, for example, but they are probably not going to do that. Yet they create a spirit of inclusion that generates public support, allowing them to provide a public good without charging listeners.

We may not seek to replicate NPR's funding model in higher education, but its ability to engage the public and earn its support is instructive. Ultimately, when higher education is less reliant on student tuition fees, more socioeconomically diverse students can be served. However, state expenditures on higher education are often considered discretionary spending (Serna & Harris, 2014). When a budget item is considered discretionary, the public's opinion of that funding recipient will factor significantly on the elected officials' allocation decisions. High levels of public trust could therefore help higher education lobby more convincingly for increased financial support.

Researchers have found a relationship between trust and financial support for education. Alm, Buschman, and Sjoquist (2011) explored how citizen trust in local or state government is related to state spending on K-12 education. The researchers discovered that when citizens have greater confidence in state government to make appropriate decisions, the state provides a larger share of state support for K-12 education. Conversely, when the citizens express more confidence in their local government instead of the state government, the state share of spending on K-12 education is lower. While the research findings cannot address causality, the findings do suggest a relationship between trust and state expenditures.

Unfortunately, trends in polls show the public is losing confidence in colleges' ability to control price and cost (Greer, 2013). But poll trends also show that the public's opinion of the importance of a college education is increasing (Greer, 2013). These trends reveal a precarious relationship between the public and higher education. If people believe they cannot create a good life through stable well-paid employment without a college degree but at the same time do not believe colleges are financially responsible, they may resent higher education institutions taking their money. In this scenario, colleges themselves may be viewed as a barrier rather than a path to a high-quality life. The conflict between believing a college degree is imperative for a good life and believing colleges are unjustly overcharging for that degree can seem increasingly like a "take it or leave it" offer in the mind of the public.

In addition to the potential funding benefits, high levels of public trust would also contribute to an improved relationship between higher education and its many stakeholders. Heightened levels of trust could change the way students, parents, lawmakers, alumnus, taxpayers, and other higher education stakeholders perceive and experience higher education.

For example, high levels of public trust could change the perception lawmakers have about the importance of quantifying higher education outcomes exclusively through workforce returns. Rather than narrowly defining the purpose of higher education as a means to high wages, lawmakers might increasingly embrace a definition of purpose to include broad development of student knowledge with ethics, values, and a commitment to civic engagement as integral. In turn, having a broad definition of higher education's purpose could encourage lawmakers to protect the autonomy and diversity of higher education institutions. This example illustrates the potential benefits for higher education when public trust persuades lawmakers to focus on the support of higher education instead of the policing of higher education.

Public trust also matters because higher education is an integral part of US culture. Johnson and DiStasi (2014) write "At the most fundamental level, decisions about higher education affect every one of us" (p. 2). As a nation, we have valued the higher education of our citizens since our founding. Even before we had a system of K-12 education in this country, we had higher education (Brubacher & Rudy, 1997).

Reporting on increased media obsession with higher education, Cottom (2013) theorizes that to Americans, higher education is symbolic. Cottom writes that college

> has represented economic and social mobility, two things that we increasingly feel are slipping away. We can feel the persistent, growing income inequality in our daily lives. Workers lucky enough to be employed are working longer hours and earning fewer real dollars, adjusted for inflation. Education is supposed to fix that kind of inequality.
>
> *(2013, para. 6)*

In our culture, education *is* supposed to fix that kind of inequality. Having a higher education system that offers the hope of improving our lives means a great deal to our collective psyche. As a society, we need and want to have faith in our institutions of higher learning. Increasing public trust then is not simply self-serving for those of us in higher education. When public trust can be earned and maintained, it provides our populace with a reassuring footing.

Current Levels of Public Trust

Currently, public opinion is mixed on higher education. Some indicators suggest that higher education is viewed positively by the public. For example, in a nationally representative sample of US adults, Gallup (2016) found that colleges and universities are perceived to be the strongest brand internationally. The research participants were asked how they believed people in other countries perceived five US institutions: government, military, presidency, business/economy, and colleges and universities. Thirty-five percent of respondents believed that people in other countries have a very positive opinion of US colleges and universities compared to government (2%), military (8%), presidency (9%), and business/economy (9%). So compared to other institutions that create international perceptions, higher education is far and away considered to have the most positive reputation.

On the other hand, there is a concerning lowering of public opinion. Stelljes (2015) writes that "Public opinion of the mission of higher education is increasingly perceived as a market-driven institution existing for the economic benefit of the individual, the upward mobility of a social class and in turn further sedimentation of the class hierarchy" (para. 5). The poll trends previously mentioned in this chapter (Greer, 2013) support this notion.

Public opinion polling that is representative of the general population may not be convincing evidence to all readers. After all, the most recent census data available reveals that among individuals 25 years or older, about 68 percent of people in the US do not have a bachelor's degree (Fiedler, 2015). Those in higher education may have the desire to dismiss general public polls as simply a matter of poll respondents not having informed opinions. However, a new study of alumni opinions suggests low opinions of higher education exist even from those individuals who graduated college.

The Gallup-Purdue Index Report was introduced in 2014. The study was designed to capture the opinions of alumni who received their education at US universities. In the 2015 Gallup-Purdue study, an item was added that asked alumni to rate on a five-point scale whether they agreed their education was worth the cost. Only half of the graduates responded that they strongly agreed (score of 5) that their education was worth the cost and another 27 percent agreed with a score of 4. However, a more concerning analysis of the responses shows that while overall 50 percent of graduates agree their education was worth the cost, among those who graduated between 2006 and 2015 that agreement percentage drops significantly to only 38 percent. Furthermore, among those recent graduates who took out student loans, only 33 percent strongly agree that their education was worth the cost.

Hunsaker and Thomas (2014) took a different research approach to try to understand public confidence in higher education institutions. They researched the predictors of public confidence in higher education institutions. Based on prior research findings, Hunsaker and Thomas hypothesized that race, income, and marital status had a relationship to people's confidence in higher education institutions. However, their findings suggest that race and political ideology are significant in predicting confidence in higher education institutions while income, sex, work status, age, and marital status are not significant in predicting confidence in higher education. Specific to the factor of race, Hunsaker and Thomas found that African Americans are 36 percent more likely than non-African Americans to express confidence in higher education institutions. The researchers also found that individuals with conservative political ideologies are 10 percent less likely to express confidence in higher education than are individuals with liberal ideology. Again, these findings support that public opinion is mixed on higher education.

Mixed public opinion on higher education is particularly relevant to the issue of correcting inequality in higher education for low SES students. Johnson and DiStasi (2014) report that in both forums and public surveys the country is divided about whether our current higher education system really offers an equal chance for everyone. The researchers report that many Americans believe that even low-income students can graduate from college by going part-time and selecting less expensive public higher education options.

The belief that low-income students can graduate from college by going part-time and selecting less expensive public higher education options is germane to the discussion of higher education inequality. Certainly, some low-income students successfully take this route; however, it is a harder route, representing a double standard for what is acceptable hardship. Until the majority of individuals acknowledge the inequity that is beyond the student's control, it will be difficult to encourage policy makers to provide more support for the higher education of low-income students. Therefore, if we want to interrupt the cycle of socioeconomic inequity, rather than having mixed public opinion about higher education, work is required to build a majority opinion that a two-tiered system of higher education is not helpful to our country's future.

What Contributes to Public Opinion

To build high levels of public trust in higher education, we need to consider what contributes to the current mixed opinions. While the next section of this chapter details how to increase public trust, we first discuss the detriments to public trust of higher education.

Screw Ups

When college leaders make bad decisions, the ill-effects reverberate across higher education. Although a negative situation may be isolated to a specific institution, the public's opinion of higher education as a whole is impacted. Generally, the public does not distinguish like those of us who study higher education between public, private, for-profit, not-for-profit, two-year, and four-year institutions. So when a particular leader or college is found guilty of wrong-doing, the reputational damage is felt across the spread of higher education.

For example, when investigations revealed the University of North Carolina was awarding high grades to students for independent studies courses that required no attendance and no work beyond a single paper, the whole of higher education felt the sting of public scorn. Student-athletes in these so called "paper courses" used the high grades they received to remain eligible for National Collegiate Athletic Association competition (New, 2014). Even though the courses required no attendance and only one paper that was basically guaranteed an A or B regardless of quality, investigations revealed that the papers were at least 25 percent plagiarized (New, 2014). Because the sham courses were used to keep athletes eligible to play, the public scrutinized higher education institutions' mission to first and foremost educate students. If course credit is just given away without even attempting to educate the student-athlete, what mission is being served?

Syracuse University has also been involved with academic scandal (James, 2015). NCAA investigations revealed that athletic staff members portrayed themselves as the student-athletes in communications with faculty members and also completed coursework on behalf of the student-athletes (New, 2015). The investigations found that the academic fraud had been occurring for more than five years.

According to reports, the NCAA is currently investigating more than 20 institutions for academic misconduct (New, 2015). So, new academic scandals may continue to emerge as a result of ongoing investigations. In the cases we already know about, the apparent collusion among diverse campus leaders is worthy of public concern. If bad decisions go unchecked across a campus, and similar bad decisions go unchecked across multiple institutions, then why should the public conclude that higher education leaders are capable of avoiding egregious bad decisions and are worthy of public trust?

Financially Alienating the Majority

When the largest portion of society (79 percent) believes college is not affordable to those who need it (Gallup-Lumina Foundation, 2014), there will be little trust in the mission of public higher education. Financially alienating the majority of society does nothing to instill trust in the mission of public higher education.

Stories of student debt are abundant and they influence public trust in higher education. The accounts of graduates buried in student debt are emotional and concerning. Numerous agencies argue that student debt is altering the whole of our nation's economy (Chopra, 2013). Korkki (2014) reports that individuals with student debt are less likely to start businesses, buy homes, and choose low-paying public-interest jobs. All of which are factors in the overall strength of our economy.

Looking at the 10 years of data between 2004 and 2014, the Institute for College Access & Success (2015) found that the average student debt at graduation had increased 56 percent. In 2004, the average student debt was $18,550. But in 2014 it was $28,950, which represents an increase more than double the rate of inflation (25 percent) over the same time frame.

These averages are troubling, but even more relevant to our purpose of discussing higher education for low-income students is data about "excessive debt"

(Kantrowitz, 2015). Kantrowitz (2015) defines that as follows: "A borrower has excessive student loan debt when 10% or more of the borrower's gross income must be devoted to repaying the borrower's student loan debt, assuming a 10-year repayment term" (p. 1). Using this definition, Kantrowitz finds that 39.2 percent of the lowest annual salaried graduates who borrowed money to attend college are saddled with excessive debt. Only 9.7 percent of the highest annual salaried graduates have excessive debt. Rather predictably, Kantrowitz also finds a correlation between higher cumulative undergraduate debt ratios and increased percent in loan default.

The excessive-debt data illustrates the cycle of socioeconomic inequality currently perpetuated by higher education. Low-income students are aware they need a degree to improve their future prospects. Grants do not cover the full cost of college attendance, so low-income students need to take on student debt to get their degree. Because the low-income student cannot count on significant financial family support, the loan amounts may include money to cover living expenses. Then, upon graduation, the low-income student is saddled with so much debt that even a reasonable first career-job is not enough to cover their costs. The low-income students who set out to improve their life may feel they have not really done so when they are excessively obliged to their moneylenders.

Stories of debilitating student debt are certainly damaging to public trust of higher education. Those in public higher education may want to dismiss the excessive debt stories as those belonging to students attending for-profit institutions. However, while scholars of higher education are quick to distinguish the student debt and outcomes of the students who attend for-profit colleges from those who attend public colleges, unless the general public makes those differentiations, public opinion will remain mixed at best.

Critique of the present level of public trust in higher education highlights necessary changes. Unquestionably, it is important to address issues such as bad leadership decisions and the financial alienation of the majority of society before public trust can be expected to increase significantly. However, we also need to work to increase public trust with additional strategies, as discussed in the next section.

How to Increase Public Trust

Leveille (2006) asserts that "Public trust is the single most important asset of higher education in this nation" (p. 13). The challenge in our era is how to increase that public trust to a level which encourages financial support and strong stakeholder relationships. The recommendations that follow can help increase public trust, which can lead to financial and stakeholder support. With that support, public higher education can improve outcomes for low SES students. Then returning full circle, by serving diverse SES students, higher education receives increased public trust.

Be Transparent

Throughout this book we have tried to draw attention to the choices policy makers have. Being transparent with the policy choices higher education leaders have can foster a trusting relationship. When information to make decisions is out in the open, the public can more accurately determine for themselves if leaders are making decisions that are reflective of the public good.

Being transparent about financial assets could help colleges build public trust. When colleges amass enormous endowments and enroll primarily high-income students, public opinion of college missions lowers. For example, Yale University has an endowment of $25.6 billion, making it the second richest college (Lobosco, 2016). Yet only 12 percent of Yale's students are Pell recipients (Woodhouse, 2015). To put the numbers into perspective, consider that a full 36 percent of all undergraduates in the US receive Pell Grants (Woodhouse, 2015). So, if colleges are sitting on large endowments, shouldn't they do more to support students in financial need?

Here is the rub: most people outside the field of higher education may think elite, "private" institutions can do what they want with their money because it is, after all, their private money. What is left hidden to the general public is that the private institutions are receiving more public support through tax benefits than the public state institutions. The notion that these largely endowed colleges are not publicly funded is misleading.

Klor de Alva and Schneider (2015) conducted comparative research into the level of tax exemptions and appropriations per student of high to moderately endowed institutions, public flagships, regional, and community colleges. Their findings reveal that,

> in fact, many of the richest universities in the country—sitting on hundreds of millions, if not billions, of dollars in tax exempt endowments, and garnering tens of millions of dollars of tax deductible gifts every year—receive government subsidies through current tax laws that dwarf anything received by public colleges and universities, institutions that educate the majority of the nation's low- and middle-class students. For example, we estimate that in 2013, Princeton University's tax-exempt status generated more than $100,000 per full-time equivalent student in taxpayer subsidies, compared to around $12,000 per student at Rutgers University (the state flagship), $4,700 per student at the nearby regional Montclair State University, and only $2,400 per student at Essex Community College.
> *(Klor de Alva & Schneider, 2015, p. 1)*

Prioritizing exorbitant public support of elite, private institutions over the public institutions that are far more accessible for the majority of students is a conscious leadership decision. However, the transparency of such leadership decisions is lacking.

Engage the Public

In the fall of 2017, approximately 20.9 million students are expected to attend American colleges and universities (NCES, 2014a). The total population in America is approximately 324 million (US Census Bureau, 2016). That means approximately six percent of the total population are engaged as students in higher education. How well does public higher education currently engage the remaining 94 percent of the population with its mission? Johnson and DiStasi (2014) write "Whether or not people go to college, they share in providing the resources to support it, and they benefit from its impact on our society. That means a debate exclusively among leaders isn't adequate" (p. 2). Increasing engagement of the public in the challenges of providing higher education to diverse SES students will help build public trust.

The example of climate change teaches us many lessons that can be applied to efforts of engaging the public with the mission of public higher education. Climate change has been described as a "wicked problem" (Hulme, 2009, p. 392): a complex issue that has no obvious solution. Research reveals climate change as "an issue characterized by uncertainty, controversy, skepticism, and limited engagement by individuals" (Ballantyne, 2016, p. 330). The issue of providing higher education to low-income students shares those characteristics.

As mentioned earlier in this chapter, there is skepticism that the current higher education system does not provide viable options for low-income students (Johnson & DiStasi, 2014). The separate and unequal options appear to be acceptable to many. There is also controversy over the mission of higher education. Some argue the mission is to provide broad, transferable education to all students, while others argue that the mission is strictly vocational.

There is uncertainty over whether the US will require more college graduates in the future, or if there are already too many graduates for our economic system to accommodate. For example, Carnevale, Smith, and Strohl of the Georgetown University Center on Education and the Workforce (2010) projected that the US will be three million college graduates short of what our nation will require in 2018. However, a more recent report (2015) from the same center reveals that there were 6.4 million fewer jobs created than were previously projected. Three million of the jobs that have not been created would have gone to workers with at least some education or training beyond high school (Carnevale, Jayasundera, & Gulish, 2015).

On the other hand, the Bureau of Labor Statistics (BLS) (2013) reports that only 27 percent of the jobs in the US currently require an associate's degree or higher, yet according to the US Census Bureau (2012) more than 30 percent of the US adults aged 25 or older already have a bachelor's degree. Additionally, reports reveal that 460,000 Americans with an associate's or bachelor's degree are making minimum wage (Pyke, 2014). While the Georgetown scholars (Carnevale, Smith, & Strohl, 2014) adamantly disagree with the BLS projections and the number of college graduates the US economy can accommodate, this issue still represents an uncertainty for the general public. This is similar to the climate change issue where the general public receives conflicting information from separate authorities who drastically disagree on the data and interpretations.

The issue of providing higher education to low SES students is also similar to the issue of climate change in that there is limited engagement by individuals. In an effort to address this limited individual engagement, scholars researching climate change communication are beginning to focus on communicating for engagement and learning (Ballantyne, 2016). Thus the lessons being learned from scholars addressing similar public policy issues can help higher education improve our communicating for engagement and learning efforts.

For example, from the conservation sciences, we can learn an important lesson on emphasis. Researchers have identified that emphasizing the benefits of conservation to people is now more persuasive than emphasizing the preservation of authentic cultural heritage assets (Lithgow, 2015). From this we can learn the importance of framing the benefits of ensuring higher education for low SES students at the individual level rather than framing just society benefits.

Additionally, climate change communication researchers contend that for increased public engagement it is necessary to bridge the gap between the scientific community being interested in the macro-level and individuals being interested in the local, micro-level (Sadler-Smith, 2015). The take away for higher education in this lesson is that providing higher education for low-income students in the areas immediately surrounding institutions may increase public engagement in the cause. Through coordinated social action and local partnerships, we may be able to exceed simple problem awareness and encourage problem solving.

Engaging the public to help solve the problems associated with ensuring low-income students are successful in higher education will increase public trust. Trust can be built when individuals engage with higher education of low-income students in ways that make them feel they have a personal stake in the issue. Higher education of low-income students can continue to be seen as "their" problem (and who really are "they?"), or it can become "our" problem because each and every individual is affected by it. But, engagement with this issue will require higher education scholars to communicate differently. We must be willing to help the public gain knowledge of the issues low-income college students experience and help the public understand the ramifications of policy decisions for low-income students.

Demonstrate Problem Solving

We build public trust when we demonstrate a willingness to address issues that the public cares about or should care about. Because academia is the single greatest concentration of scholarly minds that exists in the world, it is uniquely positioned to solve societal problems. However, we must demonstrate that great minds working together can solve society's challenges. The societal challenge that faces us now is whether we can work collectively to create an equitable system of higher education for all SES students.

Ironically, the system of higher education that currently exists is a demonstration of academia's ability to problem solve. When federal research support was slashed, institutions forged relationships with private corporations and foundations to continue funding their research efforts. When state investment in higher education plummeted, institutions covered their costs through privatizing measures and raising student tuition. When states implemented funding programs based on student completion, institutions raised admissions criteria to enroll the students statistically most likely to graduate (American Association of Community Colleges, 2014). So, higher education has addressed funding problems, but, unfortunately, the solutions have contributed to a system of higher education that does not serve diverse socioeconomic students equitably.

The body of evidence collected since higher education began in the US demonstrates that higher education will continue to solve the support problems it faces. We have no doubt higher education will continue to thrive in this country, but without increased public support it will not be a system of higher education that is widely accessible to the breadth of our diversity.

Remember, the US has been through challenges of inaccessible higher education before. The Higher Education Act (HEA) (1965) was enacted to provide federal support for college students such as tuition grants, guaranteed student loans, and work-study programs. These types of support were extended to make higher education more accessible to diverse students. The HEA has been rewritten eight times since its inception and is currently overdue for reauthorization. The reauthorization of the HEA was set to expire at the end of 2013, but has been extended through 2016. The next version of the HEA is an opportunity to recommit to the public support of higher education for diverse SES students; however, higher education stakeholders must work collectively to reauthorize an HEA that contributes to the public good.

Although the Baby Boomer generation was the first to benefit from the HEA, some now argue that members of that generation are the largest contributors to reductions in public support. For example, Sellingo (2015) argues that the blame for the growing divide in higher education achievement between the wealthy and poor lies with the Baby Boomer generation. He writes

> when that generation went to college in the 1960s and 1970s, many of them paid little in tuition at nearly-free public institutions or received generous federal and state grants that paid for most of their bachelor's degree. But during the past two decades, as members of that same generation came to power—in Washington, in state legislatures, or as college presidents and trustees—they presided over the decay of the basic building blocks of the Higher Education Act as they drastically increased tuition and pulled back on financial aid.
>
> *(Sellingo, 2015, para. 4)*

That the first beneficiaries of high public support for college are now seen as unsupportive of the initiative is a problem that must be solved.

Higher education must demonstrate the ability to problem-solve the waning interest in public support for college. Now, more than half of the voting-age population is over age 45 (Gurwitt, 2012). And while the Baby Boomer generation is certainly not a voting monolith, the decrease in public support for higher education, as compared to other public policy issues, within the age group is something to address. This issue will be particularly important as the legislative work of reauthorizing the HEA occurs because Baby Boomers make up nearly two-thirds of the Congress (Winograd & Hais, 2015). Specifically, the House of Representatives is 63 percent Baby Boomers and the Senate is 62 percent Baby Boomers (Winograd & Hais, 2015).

To increase public trust, higher education needs to demonstrate it can solve multiple societal problems. But one specific area in which to demonstrate problem solving is within higher education itself. When higher education leaders use the resources they do have in equitable ways, they communicate trustworthiness to the public. When a leader is known to distribute resources equitably, then it can be deduced that giving that leader more resources will contribute to greater equity. Conversely, when a leader is known to distribute resources inequitably, then giving that leader more resources can be presumed to contribute to greater inequity. So addressing socioeconomic inequity on each campus is a demonstration of higher education's ability to problem-solve.

Graduate Low-Income Students

Research reveals the largest financial return from college comes from graduating, not simply attending (Bowen, Chingos, & McPherson, 2009). If higher education graduated more low-income students, the benefits to the students and society would build public trust.

Compared to wealthier students, low-income students are less likely to finish college at every level of academic ability (Weissmann, 2015). In fact, low-income students who tested at the highest ability level in Math only had the same chance (41%) of college graduation as a wealthy student with mediocre Math scores (Weissmann, 2015). Low-income students' high academic abilities do not completely mitigate the challenges facing them in college.

Unfortunately, few low-income students are able to overcome poverty to excel academically. Only 9.8 percent of low SES students in high school achieve the highest quartile of Math scores and only 11 percent achieve the highest quartile in reading (NCES, 2014b). When low-income students have overcome the multiple barriers poverty creates to achieve academically, those students should evoke a heightened response from our system of higher education. With the percentages of low-income, high-achieving students at around 10 percent, higher education should commit to ensuring academically prepared low-income students graduate at the highest percentage possible.

When it comes to building public trust by graduating low-income students, colleges face an additional layer of challenge: accurately communicating success. For the first time ever, the US Department of Education released graduation rates for low-income students receiving Pell Grants broken down by college attended. Unfortunately for everyone involved, the numbers are wrong by an average of 10 percentage points and by as much as 59 percentage points (Butrymowicz, 2015).

To determine the graduation rates of Pell Grant recipients, the US Department of Education used data collected from the National Student Loan Database System. As the name implies, the database is intended to track those individuals with student loans. If a Pell recipient has no additional loans, then that individual would not show up in the database. Therefore, using this particular database meant large numbers of Pell Grant students were not counted.

The US Department of Education released their findings as part of the College Scorecard heavily advocated by the Obama administration. However, after the release of the results, numerous researchers began identifying the inaccuracies in the numbers and conclusions. For example, the Education Trust responded with its own report of college-by-college Pell Grant graduation rates (Nichols, 2015). According to the Department of Education data, Boston University graduates 25 percent of its Pell Grant recipients, but according to the Education Trust data, Boston University graduates 84 percent of its Pell Grant recipients (Butrymowicz, 2015).

The public doubt that the College Scorecard promotes on at least this particular data point is harmful to the efforts to gain public support for low-income students in college. Rather than heralding the successes of graduating Pell Grant students, the College Scorecard data became faulty evidence to argue that money spent on educating low-income college students is wasted. Whereas the Education Trust report highlighted successes like University of Michigan-Dearborn, which enrolls 56 percent Pell Grant students and graduates Pell recipients at rates 6 percent higher than non-Pell recipients (Nichols, 2015), the Department of Education's report promotes doubt that Pell Grant support does anything to help students graduate in higher numbers.

Again, for the sake of public trust, those of us in public higher education may like to call out the low performance rates of select for-profit institutions that graduate too few students of any socioeconomic level. However, as was noted earlier in this chapter, the general public does not think about colleges in the same disaggregated way those of us who study higher education do. So we either need to better educate all students about the risks of attending low-performing institutions, or we accept the shared bad reputation when large numbers of college students are left with debt and no degree.

When it comes to graduating low-income students, Stelljes (2015) writes that "Colleges and universities should linger in the hard work of community development, where engagement means, over the long-term graduating students who, by their example, help to fix the system that created our national conundrum" (para. 5). It is important that higher education learns all it can from the experiences of low-income students. Along these lines, the Education Trust (Yeado, Haycock, Johnstone, & Chaplot, 2014) has created a guide for practitioners that encourages 10 analyses to provoke discussion and action on college completion. One of the suggested analysis points is to ask "How many students who need remediation succeed at our institution?" (Yeado, Haycock, Johnstone, & Chaplot, 2014, p. 7). The experiences of low-income students should provide the insights to help improve the graduation rates for diverse SES students.

Communicate Differently

Increasing public trust to levels that influence higher education funding and stakeholder relationships will require improved communication efforts. The foundation of communicating effectively for increased public trust comes from knowing what to communicate, and then how to best communicate it. Thus, the starting point is identifying what messages the various stakeholder groups need.

Let's start by considering what message low-income students need. In an interview conducted by Amy Scott (2015) of Marketplace, which is distributed by American Public Media in association with the University of Southern California, the Dean of Students at Vassar shared the low-income student responses that sparked change on their campus. The dean, Benjamin Lotto, shared with Scott that "what our students were telling us is that they felt that they didn't belong" (para. 6). Lotto continued that "they were great students. They graduated. They did good work. They got good grades, but they weren't happy here. They felt like the school was for someone else" (Scott, 2015, para. 6).

As a result of the low-income student feedback, Vassar introduced a pre-orientation program for low-income, first generation, and veteran students (Scott, 2015). The students arrive on campus almost two weeks prior to the start of classes and learn about all the different support services available on campus. The program also provides opportunity for student bonding. The head of Vassar's residential life division shared with Scott that his message to the students is "this institution is not a gift to you. You are a gift to us" (para. 10). Six years after the pre-orientation program began, low-income students graduate at the same rate as students overall.

Before dismissing the Vassar example as not applicable to public four-year institutions, consider that Vassar's financial aid budget has doubled in the last eight years. Now, 60 percent of students receive financial aid. However, that means 40 percent of students come from families that can afford to pay the full

$63,000 a year tuition (Scott, 2015). The breadth of that financial disparity is even more significant than for most students who attend a public four-year institution.

It is naive to think that disparities in family income do not show themselves in numerous ways while students are in college. Those disparities show themselves in virtually every aspect of life, so it is not realistic to place blame on colleges for those. However, the message to low-income students should be that the differences between the clothes or spring break trips one student can afford over another student is not a barrier to college graduation. College is a time for finding out who you want to be in the future, for some that will involve strictly a financial goal, but for many it involves a life of pursuing individual values and interests.

The message to higher education institutional leaders should be one of priorities. Without higher education leaders making the support of low-income students a priority, the inequitable system is likely to continue. Campus leaders and those that rank colleges must revisit what faculty behaviors are worthy of praise and reward. If faculty are most highly rewarded for publishing research findings, then the people who have the most direct contact with students are dis-incentivized to ensure diverse students have the necessary support.

Low-income students need additional supports to excel. It is not that low-income students are less bright, it is that they often have not benefited from the extensive support systems that wealthier students had. In an op-ed for the *New York Times*, Madden (2014) writes that coming from a working-class family and attending a private east coast liberal arts college, she understands the transition challenges many students face. For example, Madden writes "I couldn't read the *New York Times*—not because the words were too hard, but because I didn't have enough knowledge of the world to follow the articles" (para. 12). Faculty face these variations in student preparedness in their classes, but are dis-incentivized to prioritize finding solutions. Prioritizing student solutions over research and publishing success is often career damaging.

Low-income, minority students are more apt to need remedial education in college (National Conference of State Legislatures, n.d.). Little more than one third of four-year university students that complete a remediation course actually go on to complete the college-level Math or English course (Complete College America, 2012). Several states are now implementing co-requisite rather than pre-requisite models. Co-requisite courses enroll students directly in the full-credit college course but the students receive built-in support services such as tutoring, or required lab attendance. The point is, the low preparation levels of a growing number of incoming students increasingly challenges the faculty, yet the faculty members' careers are negatively affected if they prioritize helping students over publishing research.

As a former corporate consultant, I (Monica) can assure you that incentive structures are infinitely changeable. As a consultant, I worked with numerous corporate leaders who were disappointed by employee behavior but did not recognize that the employees were doing exactly what they were incentivized to do. My cautionary advice to leaders was to ensure rewards were aligned with goals. If higher education leaders are committed to changing the outcomes for low-income students, then the faculty time spent devoted to that initiative should be rewarded on a level with research publications. Higher education leaders, therefore, need to hear that prioritizing the success of diverse SES students means reconsidering the incentives associated with the initiative.

The message policy makers need to hear is that low-income students can be better served when institutions receive the public support to do so. The public institutions that serve the neediest students cannot continue to be undersupported.

There has been significant attention given to the notion of "undermatching" (Bowen, Chingos, & McPherson, 2009; Bastedo & Flaster, 2014). Matching is the idea that students should attend the most selective institution that their test scores and academic preparation qualify them to attend. Undermatching then is the idea that when students' test scores qualify them for highly selective institutions, yet they attend a moderately selective institution, the student has undermatched. The notion of undermatching is used to argue that we need to get more low-income students to enroll in the highly selective schools with high graduation rates (for example, President Obama at the College Opportunity Summit, 2014 [Pluviose, 2014]).

However, researchers have identified several flaws associated with the notion of undermatching. The notion of undermatching is premised on at least three problematic assumptions according to Bastedo and Flaster (2014). First, the proponents of the notion of undermatching assume they have differentiated colleges in ways that matter for student outcomes. For example, in arguing that undermatching damages low-income student outcomes, Bowen, Chingos, and McPherson (2009) used data that classified colleges as either "very selective" or "less than very selective." However, the difference in measurable outcomes for students comes from measuring the extremes of the selectivity spectrum. There are outcome differences between the most highly selective elite four-year institutions and two-year open access institutions. Yet, in the middle of the spectrum the differences are less distinguishable. This means that, except for at the extreme ends of the spectrum, attending an institution a bit more selective than another one will not yield significant outcome differences for low-income students.

The second assumption proponents of the notion of undermatching operate under is the idea that researchers can accurately predict who will be admitted to the various colleges (Bastedo & Flaster, 2014). All the undermatching research has used standardized test scores to determine a student's college match. However, the reality of elite college admissions is that they use holistic admissions criteria beyond the standardized test scores. Holistic criteria often include rating the strength of the incoming student's curriculum, extracurricular activities, and admission essays. The holistic criteria are highly stratified by SES. The problematic assumption that the undermatching proponents are making is that they are able to predict that a particular low-income student will be admitted based solely on the fact that their standardized test score was equal to a wealthier student who was previously admitted.

Finally, and related to the previous assumption, the undermatching proponents assume that using standardized achievement test results to match a student to a college will reduce inequality and improve student outcomes (Bastedo & Flaster, 2014). However, the relationship between wealth and high standardized test scores has already been detailed in this book. Bastedo and Flaster write that "If perfectly matched purely on GPA and SAT scores, students in the highest SES quartile would actually increase their access to the most selective colleges" (p. 97). Chasing the standardized test results as a way of correcting inequality and improving low-income student outcomes thus has little supportive evidence.

Rather than promoting the notion of undermatching, we should instead promote the notion of greater support for low-income students at the institutions they are choosing to attend. It is a rather false choice to say low-income students must either leave home and family distantly behind to attend the most elite institutions, or they have limited chance at college graduation.

Conclusion

Public trust is easier to keep than to regain; however, in common vernacular, "that horse has left the barn." Now, if we are to increase public funding and improve stakeholder relationships, higher education must recommit to building and maintaining public trust. In discussing his book about why higher education still matters with *Inside Higher Ed* reporter Scott Jaschik (2016), Les Back states "What higher education offers students is an opportunity to be more than what they are already and to learn how to think for themselves about the things that matter to them" (para. 17). I would extend that definition as a reminder that what higher education offers the American public is the hope that each of us can be more than what we already are. Higher education offers the promise that as individuals we can learn to think for ourselves about the things that are important to us. These hopes and promises matter to our national psyche, and the whole of our population deserves to feel that those hopes and promises extend to them.

References

Alm, J., Buschman, R., & Sjoquist, D. (2011). Citizen "trust" as an explanation of state education funding to local school districts. *Journal of Federalism, 41*(4), 636–661.

American Association of Community Colleges. (2014, November 18). Is performance funding changing the open-access model? *Community College Daily*. Retrieved from www.ccdaily.com/Pages/Funding/Is-performance-funding-changing-the-open-access-model.aspx.

Ballantyne, A. (2016). Climate change communication: What can we learn from communication theory? *Wiley Interdisciplinary Reviews Climate Change, 7*(3), 329–344.

Bastedo, M., & Flaster, A. (2014). Conceptual and methodological problems in research on college undermatch. *Educational Researcher, 43*(2), 93–99.

Bowen, W., Chingos, M., & McPherson, M. (2009). *Crossing the finish line: Completing college at America's public universities*. Princeton, NJ: Princeton University Press.

Brubacher, J., & Rudy, W. (1997). *Higher education in transition: A history of American colleges and universities* (4th ed.). New Brunswick, NJ: Harper & Row Publishers.

Bureau of Labor and Statistics. (2013, December). *Monthly labor review: Occupational employment projections to 2022*. Retrieved from www.bls.gov/opub/mlr/2013/article/pdf/occupational-employment-projections-to-2022.pdf.

Butrymowicz, S. (2015, October 9). There's finally federal data on low-income college graduation rates–but it's wrong. *Hechinger Report*. Retrieved from http://hechingerreport.org/theres-finally-federal-data-on-low-income-college-graduation-rates-but-its-wrong/.

Carnevale, A., Jayasundera, T., & Gulish, A. (2015). *Six million missing jobs: The lingering pain of the great recession*. Georgetown University Center on Education and the Workforce. Retrieved from https://cew.georgetown.edu/wp-content/uploads/Six-Million-Missing-Jobs.pdf.

Carnevale, A., Smith, N., & Strohl, J. (2010). *Projections of jobs and education requirements through 2018*. Georgetown University Center on Education and the Workforce. Retrieved from https://cew.georgetown.edu/wp-content/uploads/2014/12/HelpWanted.ExecutiveSummary.pdf.

Carnevale, A., Smith, N., & Strohl, J. (2014, February 21). Too many college grads? Or too few? *PBS Newshour*. Retrieved from www.pbs.org/newshour/making-sense/many-college-grads/.

Chopra, R. (2013, May 8). Student debt drains economy. *Politico*. Retrieved from www.politico.com/story/2013/05/excessive-student-loan-debt-drains-economic-engine-091083?o=0.

Complete College America. (2012). *Remediation: Higher education's bridge to nowhere*. Retrieved from www.insidehighered.com/sites/default/server_files/files/CCA%20Remediation%20ES%20FINAL.pdf.

Cottom, T. (2013, December 26). 2013: The year America went back to college: Why was the media so obsessed with higher ed this year? *Slate*. Retrieved from www.slate.com/articles/life/counter_narrative/2013/12/media_coverage_of_higher_ed_in_2013_the_year_america_went_back_to_college.html.

Fiedler, K. (2015). 70% of Americans don't have college degree, Rick Santorum says. *Politifact*. Retrieved from www.politifact.com/truth-o-meter/statements/2015/apr/08/rick-santorum/70-americans-dont-have-college-degree-rick-santoru/.

Gallup. (2016, May 10). Americans see higher education as strongest US brand abroad. Retrieved from www.gallup.com/opinion/gallup/191441/americans-higher-education-strongest-brand-abroad.aspx?g_source=CATEGORY_EDUCATION&g_medium=topic&g_campaign=tiles.

Gallup-Lumina Foundation. (2014). *Postsecondary education aspirations and barriers: The 2014 Gallup-Lumina Foundation study of the American public's opinion on higher education*. Retrieved from www.gallup.com/poll/182462/postsecondary-education-aspirations-barriers.aspx.

Gallup-Purdue. (2015). *Great jobs, great lives. The relationship between student debt, experiences and perceptions of college worth*. Gallup-Purdue Index 2015 Report. Washington, DC: Gallup.

Greer, D. (2013). *Troubled waters: Higher education, public opinion and public trust*. Higher Education Strategic Information and Governance. William J. Hughes Center for Public Policy, Richard Stockton College of New Jersey. Retrieved from https://talon.stockton.edu/eyos/hughescenter/content/docs/HESIG/Working%20Paper%202%20for%20website(2).pdf.

Gurwitt, R. (2012, September). Baby boomers' impact on elections: Governing the states and localities. Retrieved from www.governing.com/generations/government-management/gov-baby-boomer-impact-on-elections.htm.

Hulme, M. (2009). *Why we disagree about climate change: Understanding controversy, inaction and opportunity*. Cambridge, UK: Cambridge University Press.

Hunsaker, B., & Thomas, D. (2014). Predicting public confidence in higher education institutions: An analysis of social factors. *Research in Higher Education Journal, 22*. Retrieved from www.aabri.com/manuscripts/131565.pdf.

Institute for College Access & Success. (2015). *Student debt and the class of 2014: 10th annual report*. Oakland, CA: TICAS. Retrieved from http://ticas.org/sites/default/files/pub_files/classof2014.pdf.

James, E. (2015, March 6). Syracuse did not control athletics; basketball coach failed to monitor. *National Collegiate Athletic Association*. Retrieved from www.ncaa.org/about/resources/media-center/news/syracuse-did-not-control-athletics-basketball-coach-failed-monitor.

Jaschik, S. (2016, June 13). "Academic Diary": Author discusses his new book about why higher education still matters. *Inside Higher Ed*. Retrieved from www.insidehighered.com/news/2016/06/13/author-discusses-his-new-book-about-why-higher-education-matters?utm_source=Inside+Higher+Ed&utm_campaign=34781723b5-DNU20160613&utm_medium=email&utm_term=0_1fcbc04421-34781723b5-198215325.

Johnson, J., & DiStasi, C. (2014). *Divided we fail: Why it's time for a broader, more inclusive conversation on the future of higher education. A final report on the 2013 National Issues Forums*. Prepared for the Kettering Foundation by Public Agenda. Dayton, OH: Kettering Foundation. Retrieved from www.eric.ed.gov/contentdelivery/servlet/ERICServlet?accno=ED560895.

Kahlenberg, R. (2016, June 7). To really integrate schools, focus on wealth, not race. *Washington Post*. Retrieved from www.washingtonpost.com/news/in-theory/wp/2016/06/07/to-really-integrate-schools-focus-on-wealth-not-race/?utm_source=TCF+Email+Updates&utm_campaign=a5336c8dd1-TCF_Best_June_76_7_2016&utm_medium=email&utm_term=0_e5457eab21-a5336c8dd1-92533381.

Kantrowitz, M. (2015). Who graduates with excessive student loan debt? Student aid policy analysis papers. *MK Consulting, Inc*. Retrieved from www.studentaidpolicy.com/excessive-debt/Excessive-Debt-at-Graduation.pdf.

Klor de Alva, J., & Schneider, M. (2015). *Rich schools, poor students: Tapping large university endowments to improve student outcomes*. San Francisco, CA: Nexus Research & Policy Center. Retrieved from http://chronicle.com/items/biz/pdf/Rich%20Schools%20Poor%20Students.pdf.

Korkki, P. (2014, May 24). The ripple effects of rising student debt. *New York Times*. Retrieved from www.nytimes.com/2014/05/25/business/the-ripple-effects-of-rising-student-debt.html?_r=0.

Leveille, D. (2006). *Accountability in higher education: A public agenda for trust and cultural change*. Berkeley, CA: University of California, Center for Studies in Higher Education. Retrieved from www.cshe.berkeley.edu/sites/default/files/shared/publications/docs/Leveille_Accountability.20.06.pdf.

Lithgow, K. (2015). Communicating conservation science. *Studies in Conservation, 60*(2), 57–63. Retrieved from http://dx.doi.org/10.1080/00393630.2015.1117856.

Lobosco, K. (2016, January 27). America's 10 richest colleges. *CNN Money.* Retrieved from http://money.cnn.com/2016/01/27/pf/college/largest-college-endowments/.

Madden, V. (2014, September 21). Why poor students struggle. *New York Times.* Retrieved from http://mobile.nytimes.com/2014/09/22/opinion/why-poor-students-struggle.html.

Monroe, A. (1998). Public opinion and public policy, 1980–1993. *Public Opinion Quarterly, 62*(1), 6–28.

National Conference of State Legislatures. (n.d.). Hot topics in higher education: Reforming remedial education. Retrieved from www.ncsl.org/research/education/improving-college-completion-reforming-remedial.aspx.

NCES [National Center for Education Statistics]. (2014a). Table 105.20: Enrollment in elementary, secondary, and degree-granting postsecondary institutions, by level and control of institution, enrollment level, and attendance status and sex of student: Selected years, fall 1990 through fall 2014. Retrieved from http://nces.ed.gov/programs/digest/d14/tables/dt14_105.20.asp?current=yes.

NCES [National Center for Education Statistics]. (2014b). Table 104.91: Number and percentage distribution of spring 2002 high school sophomores, by highest level of education completed, and socioeconomic status and selected student characteristics while in high school: 2012. Retrieved from http://nces.ed.gov/programs/digest/d14/tables/dt14_104.91.asp.

New, J. (2014, October 23). Two decades of "paper classes." *Inside Higher Ed.* Retrieved from www.insidehighered.com/news/2014/10/23/report-finds-academic-fraud-u-north-carolina-lasted-nearly-20-years.

New, J. (2015, March 9). Academic fraud at Syracuse. *Inside Higher Ed.* Retrieved from www.insidehighered.com/news/2015/03/09/ncaa-suspends-syracuse-u-basketball-coach-vacates-108-wins.

Nichols, A. (2015). The Pell partnership: Ensuring a shared responsibility for low-income student success. *The Education Trust.* Retrieved from https://edtrust.org/wp-content/uploads/2014/09/ThePellPartnership_EdTrust_20152.pdf.

O'Connor, D. (2004). *Public opinion, rational choice and the new institutionalism: Rational choice as a critical theory of the link between public opinion and public policy.* Paper prepared for Workshop No. 6: "Public Opinion, Polling, and Public Policy," Canadian Political Science Association Conference, Winnipeg, June 3–5, 2004. Retrieved from www.cpsa-acsp.ca/papers-2004/OConnor,%20Derry.pdf.

Pluviose, D. (2014, January 16). Obama seeks to end "undermatching." *Diverse Education.* Retrieved from http://diverseeducation.com/article/60196/.

Pyke, A. (2014, March 31). Half a million people with college degrees are working for minimum wage. *Think Progress: Economy.* Retrieved from http://thinkprogress.org/economy/2014/03/31/3420987/college-degree-minimum-wage/.

Sadler-Smith, E. (2015). Communicating climate change risk and enabling pro-environmental behavioral change through human resource development. *Advances in Developing Human Resources, 17*(4), 442–459.

Scott, A. (2015, September 1). Helping low-income college students feel at home. *Marketplace.* Retrieved from www.marketplace.org/2015/09/01/education/helping-low-income-college-students-feel-home.

Sellingo, J. (2015, November 12). Baby boomers and the end of higher education. *Washington Post.* Retrieved from www.washingtonpost.com/news/grade-point/wp/2015/11/12/baby-boomers-and-the-end-of-higher-education/.

Serna, G., & Harris, G. (2014). Higher education expenditures and state balanced budget requirements: Is there a relationship? *Journal of Education Finance, 39*(3), 175–202.

Stelljes, D. (2015, January 10). US colleges and universities earn a poor grade for civic engagement. *Huffington Post*. Retrieved from www.huffingtonpost.com/drew-stelljes/us-civic-engagement_b_6127608.html.

US Census Bureau. (2012, February 23). Bachelor's degree attainment tops 30 percent for the first time. *Census Bureau Reports*. Retrieved from www.census.gov/newsroom/releases/archives/education/cb12-33.html.

US Census Bureau. (2016, June 15). US and world population clock. *Census Bureau Population Clock*. Retrieved from www.census.gov/popclock/.

Weissmann, J. (2015, June 2). Smart poor kids are less likely to graduate from college than middling rich kids. *Slate*. Retrieved from www.slate.com/blogs/moneybox/2015/06/02/college_graduation_rates_for_low_income_students_why_poor_kids_drop_out.html.

Winograd, M., & Hais, M. (2015, January 5). Boomer dominance means more of the same in the 114 Congress. *Brookings Institute*. Retrieved from www.brookings.edu/blogs/fixgov/posts/2015/01/05-congress-generations-gridlock-millennials-winograd-hais.

Woodhouse, K. (2015, May 22). Doing their fair share? The Harvards of the world are awash in public funds for low-income students. Why aren't they doing more to enroll them? *Inside Higher Ed*. Retrieved from www.slate.com/articles/life/inside_higher_ed/2015/05/wealthy_universities_like_harvard_leave_low_income_students_behind_despite.html.

Yeado, J., Haycock, K., Johnstone, R., & Chaplot, P. (2014). Learning from high-performing and fast-gaining institutions. *The Education Trust*. Retrieved from https://edtrust.org/wp-content/uploads/2013/10/PracticeGuide_0.pdf.

8

CHARTING A MORE EQUITABLE COURSE

Any book that recommends systems change runs the risk of overwhelming its readers. Systemic change does not lend itself easily to daily "to do" lists or even annual performance goals. On too many occasions, we've read many books like our own, felt inspired, and returned to doing the same thing we've always done because that's what we knew how to do. Interrupting this particular cycle is key to addressing some of the larger patterns of problematic policies and practices exacerbating class inequality in higher education today.

Fortunately, systems change includes a notion best described as "the butterfly effect." Instead of the top-down, all-encompassing hierarchical approach to management embodied in Taylorism, a systems perspective allows for the possibility of small changes that have big ripple effects. The goal is not the grand vision that comes down from on high, but rather modest changes that can originate organically in any part of the system. The endgame is to leverage those policies, practices, and/or relationships that show promise in addressing inequality and build momentum for them.

A simple example occurred in my (Laura's) own development as a professor. Like most people who join the faculty ranks, I enjoyed school and did not really understand those who didn't. As a result, my basic assumption about students who did not participate in class and/or turn in quality writing was that they were not trying. I'm not naïve enough to believe this is never the case, but years of researching class inequality in the K-12 education system has given me a deeper and more complex understanding of the issue.

First, I'm just old enough to have dodged the standardized testing movement, so my teachers were not limited by the pressure to teach to a test. As a result, school was interesting enough most of the time, which allowed me to establish a positive attitude toward learning. Also, my parents were financially able to send me to a Catholic school when the public schools in my neighborhood declined. The reasonably sized classes, caring teachers, and rigorous enough curriculum helped me build a good intellectual foundation for college and graduate school.

When college professors challenged me to think critically or support a claim, I knew what they meant because I benefited from a good K-12 education. I finally understand this is not true for many of my students. So I've changed the way I relate to students. I haven't lowered my expectations; in fact, I'm even more committed to high expectations because I believe underperformance generally comes from unequal access to resources, not genetic difference. But I am willing to take class time to teach critical thinking and writing, right down to what is a sentence and what is a sentence fragment. Instead of blaming students for the result of a system they did not create, I try to serve as a corrective to it.

This example demonstrates the power of leveraging small change in one's sphere of influence. In this chapter, we will highlight approaches and practices that show promise in interrupting the cycle of class inequality in higher education. We propose 10 interventions higher education leaders could reasonably work toward within the next academic year to interrupt the cycle of inequality on their own campus.

Ten Ideas for Interrupting the Cycle of Class Inequality in the Next Academic Year

Offer Financial Support

As simple as it sounds, low-income students need financial support. The long-term solution to class inequality surely includes greater public financing of higher education, an argument we've made frequently throughout this work. Many of the structural answers lie outside of higher education; for example, an increase in the minimum wage and single-payer healthcare would most certainly help many low-income students. We must fight the long war for these systemic changes but, in the meantime, there is lower hanging fruit to be picked.

The City University of New York's Accelerated Study in Associate Programs (ASAP) program provides a powerful example of how financial support coupled with strong advising can help. The ASAP program offers students a tuition waiver, free transportation, and free use of textbooks in addition to enhanced advising services. Students who participated in the ASAP program were more likely to enroll in classes the next semester, earned more credits per semester, and graduated at a higher rate than students who did not participate in the program (MDRC, 2014).

The advising component of the ASAP program doubtlessly played a large role in the initiative's success. Yet many institutions offer what is often referred to as intrusive advising; that is, pro-active advising where an advisor will check in on an individual student's progress throughout the semester. TRIO, Upward Bound, and institution-specific programs provide valuable support for low-income students transitioning to college. The mentoring offered through these initiatives has a record of demonstrated success in boosting low-income students' enrollment, grades, credit hour accrual, and persistence in higher education (Perna, 2015).

While we agree quality advising and transition support are important, focusing exclusively on these interventions can support the misconception that the onus should be on the students rather than the systems that contribute to their need for services in the first place. Hence the added financial element offered in the ASAP program goes a step further in addressing both the person and system, an ethos we believe warrants expansion in today's climate of growing inequality in higher education.

Other forms of financial support some universities now offer include food banks, rent subsidies, and emergency grants to their low-income students (Carlson, 2016). The creation of these initiatives requires breaking out of the often class-based assumptions we have about college students' lives. It is still unimaginable to many people that college students would experience food insecurity or homelessness because they assume a certain level of privilege in the university population. That assumption comes from a long history of higher education as a wealthy, then middle-class and wealthy enterprise. Until we acknowledge that the world has changed and most people now need access to higher education, we will continue to do a disservice to low-income students by not anticipating their needs as part of our academic communities.

Even when higher education leaders acknowledge low-income students, they are sometimes reticent to offer direct financial support. There is a tendency to offer the poor advice and services rather than economic resources. We believe there is strong evidence to suggest this proclivity is based on the "culture of poverty," a term coined by anthropologists, Lewis and LaFarge (1965). Former Assistant Labor Secretary Daniel Patrick Moynihan popularized the term in a report describing poor families as "caught in an inescapable tangle of pathology of unmarried mothers and welfare dependency" (Cohen, 2010, para. 2).

The idea is that people are poor because they lack the values that would lead to a middle-class existence. In other words, the road to poverty is paved with sexual irresponsibility and laziness, not gross wage disparities and unequally funded school systems. It is not difficult to see how a person's understanding of how poverty works might influence their comfort level with cash assistance to low-income students. If people take the culture of poverty position, they are likely to believe economic help will be wasted.

University communities tend to be polite places, so people do not usually express the culture of poverty position; they may not even consciously hold it. Yet the dominant discourse of poor people's moral inferiority pervades our national discourse, making it difficult to provide the financial support that would give economically disenfranchised people a real chance.

In Chapter 4 we discussed Doucleff's (2015) research showing that money helps lift people out of poverty, remarking that this should not be a shocking finding. When people take the culture of poverty position, however, this kind of intervention becomes somehow surprising. It's as if poor people are existentially different from those of us in the middle class.

What helped me when I was a student was money. Money came in a variety of forms. I worked for some of it. Some of it came from scholarships. My dad also gave me some of it. My point is that while I needed some financial advice as a young person transitioning to adulthood, mostly what I needed was money. This is no less true of poor people, yet the culture of poverty idea inhibits us from providing actual financial help due to our prejudice that it will be squandered.

Consider Class in Student Affairs Programs

While direct financial assistance is often what low-income students really need, many organizations do better with programs and services. Universities are no exception, so making those programs and services more useful to low-income students should be an important goal for higher education. The co-curriculum has the potential to be relevant to low-income students' success in college. Without intentional inclusion of low-income students when designing the co-curriculum, however, programs and services for students can reinforce class divisions.

For example, higher education environments place high value on the co-curriculum, encouraging students to participate in enrichment activities designed to foster valuable leadership skills. Low-income students access the co-curriculum at lower rates due to their need to make money while going to school. So while they pay for climbing walls, sports, and other student activities, poor and working-class students often face barriers to taking advantage of these things.

We do not advocate erasing the co-curriculum, but we do argue for a more critical examination of all aspects of student life with greater attention to the needs of poor and working-class students. From professors putting textbooks on reserve at the library to some student affairs money diverted to services like childcare, there are modest changes higher education leaders could make to quit centering the middle/upper-class student experience. While higher education has its roots as an enterprise mainly for the elite, society has been encouraging greater participation by low-income students for quite some time. Therefore, we owe it to these students to acknowledge their existence in the planning, budget, and personnel allocations that take place on university campuses.

Jacob Okumu, Coordinator for Student Outreach and Developmental Services at Ohio University, created a program that could be considered a model for those aiming to create co-curricular experiences sensitive to students' SES. When Okumu began his position working with students on academic probation, the foster students in the group shared their struggle of having nowhere to stay over breaks. He dealt with this specific problem by letting the students stay in his home, but explained that the issue prompted him to think about how to address the challenge more creatively:

> This is a group that has been told what to do and where to go for their whole lives. I did not want to patronize them by just handling things. I wanted them to know within themselves that they had gifts to contribute.
>
> *(personal communication, May 31, 2016)*

This goal of empowerment gave Okumu the idea to create a service learning trip with the needs of foster students in mind. He chose Jamaica as a destination due to its low-cost flight options and family connections, which provided students with the opportunity to engage in authentic cultural experiences. As a result, student participants were able to both study abroad and have somewhere to stay over the break.

Many universities provide enriching cultural opportunities and help students with practical matters like housing and food. As more low-income students access higher education, perhaps the next frontier in student affairs is addressing these educational and practical concerns more seamlessly. This seamlessness also has the potential to reduce stigma by positioning low-income students not as clients needing a service but as students making a contribution through service learning. Okumu's words reflect a respect for the students with whom he works, emphasizing both what they need as well as what they offer. This ethos democratizes the relationship, as we all have both needs and contributions as part of the communities we inhabit.

Okumu serves as a "one stop shop" for his students, helping them navigate the maze of financial, emotional, and academic challenges students face in college. These challenges can be formidable for all students, but it is even more important for those students aging out of the foster care system to have an actual human being to whom they can turn rather than being sent to various offices and websites. As student affairs leaders plan for the future, they should consider hiring individuals who understand low-income students and thoughtfully design co-curricular experiences that are truly inclusive.

Make Class Visible

The first two recommendations are rooted in the reality of class's relative invisibility on college campuses. Addressing class inequality in all its various forms necessitates an expanded notion of diversity in higher education. Class and race have been pitted against each other in ways that are both artificial and unhelpful to low-income students and students of color, a theme we explore more fully in the next section. Therefore, we argue for greater visibility of class issues in higher education not at the expense of other forms of diversity, but in true intersection with them.

Social class admittedly presents challenges as a discussion topic on campus. Unlike other demographic categories, it does not lend itself to celebration the way cultural or gender identifications do. Poor and working-class labels carry stigma, leaving students, faculty, and administrators with limited language for discussing the very real ways class manifests on campus. It seems more polite not to acknowledge class differences, especially since class advancement is ostensibly a big reason people go to college in the first place.

The problem, of course, is that silence does not eliminate the class-based challenges many poor and working-class students face in higher education. Without language and opportunity to give voice to their experiences, students from low SES backgrounds often internalize challenges as individual failures rather than structural inequalities. For example, low-income students report high levels of what some scholars call imposter phenomenon, that is, constant worrying about being discovered as not smart or capable despite evidence of one's actual abilities.

Because of the stigma and corresponding imposter phenomenon many low-income students experience, some do not want to be identified as low income, which complicates the visibility issue. For example, Hurst (2007) found some students had complicated relationships with their low-income families and communities and did not claim an identification with them. Others, particularly the low-income students of color in the study, felt their only chance for success required some degree of assimilation into the largely white, middle/upper-class culture of college life (p. 98).

Yet some low-income students in Hurst's (2007) and many other subsequent studies (Soria, 2013) expressed a strong desire for a greater visibility of class consciousness on campus. The diversity within the findings on low-income students' needs for visibility signals the importance of thoughtfulness and nuance in considering how to attend to this population.

Another reason class warrants greater visibility in higher education is the importance of acknowledging the strong tradition of working-class intellectuals. Too often, higher education is positioned as somehow antithetical to working-class communities. We argue throughout this chapter that this misconception is at the root of many challenges faced by low-income students on college campuses.

Yet working-class intellectuals have a long history of championing the idea of education as emancipatory. In *Against Schooling: Toward an Education that Matters*, Stanley Arnowitz (2008) describes how his disenchantment with conventional schooling led him to participate in the founding of the first alternative school in 1965: "The first [alternative school] was a non-degree granting institution that was started by a group of radicals who believed that traditional schools had mostly ruined the passion for learning among young people who deserved another shot at a critical education" (pp. 5–6).

This idea of a critical education has been a central part of liberation movements led by people of color, women, LGBT, immigrant, disabled, and other marginalized groups. Students and faculty continue to advocate for inclusive curricula relevant to a truly diverse academic community. Teaching all students about the contributions of working-class intellectuals is an important function of higher education institutions' educational mission. A crucial part of increasing visibility around class must include a counter-narrative to the notion of higher education as a place created by and for only the wealthy.

Highlight Working-class Faculty and Staff

One way around the complexities of the visibility issue is for faculty and graduate students to take the lead in beginning the conversation around socioeconomic class in higher education. Faculty and graduate students who come from low-income families are uniquely positioned to serve as powerful role models for low-income students on campus. Less vulnerable to imposter phenomenon, faculty and graduate students who grew up in low-income communities can offer empowering interactions to students seeking to have their experiences validated and understood. In her scholarship on working-class students, Hurst (2008) offered an example of how this interaction can happen:

> After the interviews were done I spent a lot of time with several of the students encouraging them to think about graduate school, or explaining what a Ph.D. is and what the process is for getting one . . . I tried to be as honest as possible with students about the costs of education as I've experienced them, but encouraging them all the same, because too often working-class students think they are not smart enough and I wanted to disabuse them of that notion.
>
> (p. 342)

Hurst's identity as a working-class academic allowed her to see the issues that might be impacting her student participants and inspired her to take action. While one does not have to identify as working class to advocate for low-income students, Hurst's story illustrates the importance of having people on campus who understand these students' experiences and are willing to serve as potential role models. The literature is consistent on this point; students need to see themselves represented in leadership roles on campus both to feel a sense of belonging as students and to imagine a path to those kinds of positions as graduates (Young, Rudman, Buettner, & McLean, 2013).

We offer two related caveats here. First, working-class faculty and graduate students experience stigma and imposter phenomenon as well, so their needs must also be part of a greater campus effort to improve the environment for all members of the community. Second, we do not intend to position working-class faculty and graduate students as somehow responsible for the concerns of low-income undergraduate students.

Too often, the dominant group expects marginalized populations to address the concerns of students who share their demographics. For example, the one female engineering professor is tacitly or even explicitly expected to mentor the women students or the one Black professor is called on to explain the concerns raised by Black students in a program. We do not advocate for this practice; in fact, it is one of the cycles we believe needs to be interrupted in order to produce more equitable and hospitable campus climates.

Attending to the needs of low-income students is the responsibility of all faculty and graduate students. At the same time, we acknowledge the particularly powerful role working-class faculty and graduate students can potentially play in this process. Working-class faculty and graduate students' visibility is important, too, for middle- and high-income students who may be underexposed to the possibility of working-class academics. To serve these important roles, working-class faculty and graduate students need institutional support and a culture that pro-actively respects their experience.

How might this look? First, we offer an example of how this does not look. I (Laura) was at a university committee meeting a few years ago when the local schools closed for a snow day. My colleagues spent the first 15 minutes of the meeting speculating as to how the ignorant parents in our university's rural community were going to be able to help their kids do the homework assignments the school sent home. I'm a progressive person who studies inequality and I still didn't know what to say. I'm embarrassed to admit my own inadequate response to the situation, but I share the story because I suspect many readers have been in similar circumstances.

What my colleagues and I needed was an orientation like the one Berea College offers its new faculty and staff. Located in a largely low-income community in rural Kentucky, Berea frequently hires faculty who are unfamiliar with the region and likely to hold stereotypes about its people. The school addresses this reality pro-actively, providing a five-day tour of Appalachia that educates participants about the cultural backgrounds of the vast majority of Berea students. Faculty and staff who take the tour overwhelmingly describe it as highly useful in helping them work effectively with their students. As a result of the tour specifically and a positive institutional culture generally, Berea was ranked the top liberal arts college in the nation for advancing upward mobility (Slavin, 2013).

Address Microaggressions

The experience we described in the previous section can be understood as a microaggression. Harvard psychiatry and education professor Chester Pierce first coined the term in 1969, using it to describe Blacks' experience of subtle, but constant putdowns. His later work expanded the concept to include other marginalized groups, defining microaggressions in the following manner:

> These are subtle, innocuous, preconscious, or unconscious degradations, and putdowns, often kinetic but capable of being verbal and/or kinetic. In and of itself a microaggression may seem harmless, but the cumulative burden of a lifetime of microaggressions can theoretically contribute to diminished morality, augmented morbidity, and flattened confidence.
>
> *(Pierce, 1995, p. 281)*

Low-income students often experience microaggressions in higher education environments where there is silence about the systemic challenges they endure (Stephens, Brannon, Markus, & Nelson, 2015). Poor and working-class students do earn lower grades, experience lower retention rates, report more mental health issues, and express less of a sense of belonging on campus than their higher income counterparts (Soria & Stebleton, 2013). In the absence of robust discourse on college campuses about the structural reasons these differences might exist, it's easy for students and faculty alike to assume they represent personal failing.

Feeling a sense of belonging is critical to students' ability to learn and thrive on campus; the literature is consistent on this point (Strayhorn, 2012). Microaggressions take a toll on low-income students' ability to believe they belong both on a particular campus and in higher education more generally. Sarcedo, Matias, Montoya, and Nishi's (2015) research provides a particularly poignant example that illustrates this point. After being ridiculed for not knowing what the GRE is, a participant describes how she internalized the mocking students' laughter:

> Dot finally said matter-of-factly with clear annoyance in her voice, "I take it you're not going to grad school. The GRE is like the SAT for grad school." She raised a smug, professionally waxed eyebrow as if to question if I even knew what grad school was. Her thin-lipped smile contorted into a grimace as I said, "I'm considering graduate school." Dot audibly gasped. Her shock at my graduate education aspirations made me question my goals. Was graduate school a viable option for me? As Dot shifted uncomfortably in her chair, I felt as if I didn't belong in that conversation, in that classroom, or at that university.
>
> *(Sarcedo, Matias, Montoya, & Nishi, 2015, p. 9)*

Comments like my colleagues' and this student's abound in the qualitative research on poor and working-class students' experiences in college. Perhaps more insidiously, low-income students are often assumed not to even be a part of campus communities, as participants in Smith, Mao, and Deshpande's (2016) research reported. Invisibility added to stereotype creates a perfect storm for denigrating a group whose experience of higher education is already tenuous at best.

Low-income students' erasure from higher education compounds the microaggression issue, empowering people to make insensitive comments due to the group's presumptive outsider status. Of course, the bigger goal is not simply to drive the comments underground, but to address the root cause of the prejudice itself. Achieving this aim requires a bigger effort that goes beyond individuals to the broader campus community.

Educate Campus Communities about Class-based Stereotypes

Class has been discussed as the last frontier in diversity, meaning people can get away with mocking the economically disenfranchised in ways that would be confronted if the comments were about race, gender, or sexual orientation. Williamson's (2016) argument about the rural poor illustrates this point:

> The truth about these dysfunctional, downscale communities is that they deserve to die. Economically, they are negative assets. Morally, they are indefensible. Forget all your cheap theatrical Bruce Springsteen crap. Forget your sanctimony about struggling Rust Belt factory towns and your conspiracy theories about the wily Orientals stealing our jobs. Forget your goddamned gypsum, and, if he has a problem with that, forget Ed Burke, too. The white American underclass is in thrall to a vicious, selfish culture whose main products are misery and used heroin needles.
>
> (para. 30)

We do not take the "class as the last frontier" position because we believe it sanitizes the struggles other marginalized groups continue to face. We do argue that the oppressive attitudes about class are distinct and therefore must be addressed specifically, as is the case with racism, sexism, and other forms of discrimination.

Most books like ours often recommend something along the lines of educating campus communities, but what does this really mean? In our view, integration is the most essential element of effective education. The literature is consistent on the reality that exposure and integration mitigate ignorant prejudices and inculcate empathy. Though admittedly imperfect, college campuses provide one of the few spaces left in our society where people might interact across all kinds of demographic differences. In a nation characterized by increasing segregation in both neighborhoods and K-12 schools, higher education can offer an important corrective.

Integration is particularly important for middle and upper-class students. In the absence of exposure to low-income students, their worldviews are likely to be limited to those produced by the segregated schools and communities from which they came. When there is a knowledge vacuum, prejudices tend to fill it, especially in a culture where the poor are routinely cast as lazy and irresponsible. Given the powerful positions middle- and upper-class students are tracked toward, educating them about structural inequality and sensitizing them to the struggles of others are important roles for universities.

Thomas and Azmitia's (2014) findings illustrate this experience of middle- and upper-class students gaining perspective about class in light of low-income students' experiences of college. One of their upper-class research participants shared the following story contrasting a friend's experience with her own:

> Going with her to the doctor, and hearing that the insurance won't cover it, and that it's going to cost all that money . . . that was a wake-up call for me. I know that if I was in that situation, my parents have secure jobs, and both my parents have health insurance and I have an orthodontist. And that I could afford that money even if it was a ridiculous amount. And so it was a wake-up call for me, seeing her and wanting to help, but not knowing how. And I'm reflecting on my own background and how privileged I am, in a lot of ways.
>
> *(Thomas & Azmitia, 2014, p. 202)*

This student's "wake-up call" represents a powerful contrast to Williamson's (2016) perspective. Universities exist to produce educated citizens who contribute to the public good. Addressing poverty is most certainly required as part of bettering society. Yet even if students embrace that idea theoretically, they are unlikely to succeed if they feel contempt for the very people their work aims to serve. Higher education leaders need to create the conditions under which more students experience wake-up calls.

Integrating class more thoughtfully into the curriculum, including class in diversity programs, and confronting prejudices are the common and important recommendations made whenever there are calls for campus education. We agree with these ideas while arguing integration as the most essential component of any educational initiative. Students and faculty will use the right words and attend required seminars for the most part. But if these programs are not augmented with actual interaction, they are likely to remain theoretical.

Take an Assets-based Approach

Another upper-class student in Thomas and Azmitia's (2014) study reported feeling lazy in contrast to his low-income student roommate, empathizing with his need to work so many hours while in school. Interestingly, the upper-class student also speculated, "I think he's gaining a lot of skills that I am not. He's gaining a lot of independence . . . from the situation he's in, and I see that and I'm realizing that I'm going to have to build that for myself" (p. 203). The upper-class student's insight is a significant one that speaks to another important aspect of educating campus communities: shifting from a deficit to an asset frame.

Lack of education about low-income students sometimes produces the microaggressions and stigma discussed in the previous sections. Other times, the result manifests more in the forms of charity and pity. Viewing low-income students as deficits to be corrected can contribute to their marginalization. When a student repeatedly receives the message that there is something wrong with the family and community from which they come, it is difficult for that student to feel that sense of belonging so vital to their ability to learn and thrive on a campus.

College campuses are generally understood as spaces that reflect middle- and upper-class values. For example, Stephens, Fryberg, Markus, Johnson, and Covarrubias (2012) identified independence as a middle-class value that campus cultures both overtly and subtly reinforce. Students receive many messages about charting their own course, discovering their passions, and doing what interests them. Academic advisors, career counselors, and faculty communicate the importance of independent thinking in ways that do not appear to be ideological or class-based. Yet the reality is that interdependence is often a cultural value in working-class communities, so constant messaging about independence can alienate low-income students.

Interdependence is an asset from which middle- and upper-class members of campus communities might learn. Instead of encouraging working-class students to conform to middle- and upper-class cultural norms, university leaders could more intentionally incorporate this value into their approach to education. For example, middle- and upper-class students abuse alcohol and drugs at higher rates than their low-income counterparts (Patrick, Wightman, Schoeni, & Schulenberg, 2012). Part of this issue likely stems from the privilege they receive; Mohamed and Fritsvold (2010) define wealthy college drug dealers as "non-targets" due to the relative ease with which they are able to operate due to their status.

Part of the disparity, however, might come from working-class cultural values around interdependence. As Luthar, Barkin, and Crossman (2013) found, some upper-class students demonstrate a sense of fragility related to the constant pressure to succeed and acquire. If these students were encouraged to focus more on interpersonal connection, perhaps they would benefit from the ways in which interdependence gets us out of ourselves.

We neither intend to romanticize working-class students, nor denigrate upper-class students. Our point is that applying a deficit lens to one group and a rose colored lens to another creates blind spots when it comes to truly serving all students. Another example of this issue can be examined in the context of respect for authority. While middle- and upper-class cultures tend to encourage students to question authority, working-class communities emphasize respect for authority (Lareau, 2011). This point is often made in the context of low-income students' perceived underperformance in college classrooms where faculty often place a premium on critical thinking and questioning ideas.

Low-income students may in fact need to adjust to this change when transitioning to college. Yet the point ought to be made that middle- and upper-class students might need to learn to balance their comfort challenging authority with a respect for the rules that foster health and safety on campuses. Given universities' current formidable challenges regarding student behavior and mental health, the importance of leveraging the assets all students bring to campus seems even more relevant.

Finding ways to communicate respect for the assets low-income students bring to campus communities is perhaps the next frontier in meeting the needs of students from all socioeconomic class backgrounds. A real barrier to this process is the largely unspoken, but tacit understanding of college as a place where people attempt to change class position. We believe economic opportunity is a legitimate goal of academic endeavors, but further marginalization of working-class communities can be an unintended consequence when moving up the financial ladder becomes the only goal of higher education.

Conflating education and wealth creates a vicious cycle wherein working-class families sometimes send mixed messages about college, encouraging it as a necessity while worrying it will alienate young people from their communities. These concerns are not unwarranted. If campus communities treat working-class cultural values as deficits, they send a negative message about the worlds from which low-income students come.

Attend to Diversity within the Low-income Student Population

An idea related to the notion of appreciating assets is respecting the diversity within a population. While it's important to be aware of the broad issues relevant to any disenfranchised group, there is always the risk of overgeneralizing that knowledge. We therefore advocate an understanding and appreciation of the diversity that exists within the low-income student population.

Our reasoning for addressing low-income students generally in this chapter is due to our goal of not further conflating this population with first-generation students and/or students of color, which frequently occurs in the literature. We acknowledge the need to illuminate the diversity within the low-income student population, though, because treating it as a monolith limits our ability to understand the nuance of each student's experience. While an exhaustive examination of every possible identity a low-income student might inhabit is beyond the scope of this book, we highlight a few of the less visible identities that warrant further consideration.

Rurality and urbanity are under-examined aspects of diversity within the low-income student population. Impoverished rural and urban communities face similar issues, especially in terms of the tensions talented young people express between "getting out" and "giving back" with regard to their communities. For example, Carr and Kefalas (2009) discuss the negative consequences of the rural brain drain; that is, talented young people feeling they have to leave their communities to achieve economic viability. The tension between feeling both rooted in home and pulled toward expanded opportunities is a considerable challenge for those in isolated rural communities. Students receive contradictory messages about expectations and report a great deal of pressure about fulfilling both family and career roles.

Researchers studying predominately first-generation, urban, low-income students of color uncovered a similar ambivalence, which they described as family achievement guilt (Covarrubias & Fryberg, 2015). Students described feeling happy and proud to be in college, yet also worried they were abdicating responsibilities by being away from home. First generation Latino/a students reported the highest levels of family achievement guilt, describing feelings of remorse that they lived on what felt like luxurious campuses while relatives continued to suffer (p. 422).

A related aspect of both diversity among low-income students and the issue of deficit versus asset lenses is the issue of dialect. Dialect is referenced infrequently in the literature, yet is highly relevant in college classrooms where people speak and interpret the quality of speech as part of the daily business of campus life. In their research on this topic, Dunstan and Jaeger (2015) found stigmatized rural accents negatively impacted class participation, comfort in courses, and perceptions of their intelligence for both African American and White speakers.

While the dialect research is relevant to low-income students due to their overrepresentation in rural environments, students with stigmatized accents experienced negative impacts regardless of their SES. This example highlights the need to understand marginalization in the context of intersectionality, a theme we present in the next section.

Approach Class Intersectionally

Many books and articles about socioeconomic class begin with a comparison to race and gender. The general idea is that race and gender have been visible and addressed on college campuses while class remains an issue. We find this characterization unfortunate and worthy of mention because we believe pitting race, gender, and class against each other in some sort of oppression hierarchy hurts these causes.

The hierarchy oppression hinders progress on social justice issues because one group is used as an excuse not to level the playing field for another. The conflicts between race and class-based affirmative action illustrate this point. Politicians have used affirmative action based on class as a tactic for appealing to those who oppose race-based affirmative action. Supporting class-based affirmative action provides political cover as politicians can claim both concern for economically disenfranchised people while appeasing those who fail to acknowledge the racist legacy affirmative action attempts to ameliorate.

Those who work primarily on class issues must acknowledge that racism still exists and work to end it. As we write, the news media is exploding with stories about police killings of unarmed African Americans. Undocumented youth are being deported in record numbers. Recently, a man pulled a hijab off a woman on a Southwest Airlines flight and informed her she was in America. Racism continues to be a real problem on college campuses and in society at large. It manifests similarly to other forms of oppression in some cases, but has its own distinct qualities in others. Sometimes racism and classism intersect; other times they do not. Both issues are problems whether they manifest on their own or in conjunction with another form of oppression.

In his essay "Righting historical injustice in higher education," McPherson (2015) critiques higher education leaders for their selective memory when it comes to discussing their institutions' histories. He argues institutions seek publicity for their achievements while not owning up to their mistakes, particularly where racial injustice is concerned. He highlighted higher education institutions' legacy in failing to take more proactive measures to ensure students of color's access to college. He writes specifically of the GI Bill, which disproportionally benefited whites, thus reinforcing the already sharp racial inequality in access to postsecondary education.

We agree with McPherson's (2015) analysis; initiatives to address class inequality must not exclude people of color and/or other marginalized groups. This is simply a matter of credibility. How can we advocate justice for one group while ignoring the suffering of another? Equally important is the reality that economic marginalization intersects with race, gender, and other identities that can be either privileged or oppressed. Consider the current increased awareness about LGBT college students whose parents cut them off financially out of anger upon learning the news of their identity. A student in this situation may hail from a wealthy background, but receive less economic support than a working-class student whose parents are willing to help them out.

As discussed previously in this chapter, there is a great deal of diversity within the low-income student population. Hence, addressing the needs of this group thoughtfully and in a way that honors that diversity requires a nuanced approach. Crenshaw's (1991) pioneering work on intersectionality provides a useful framework for examining the complexity of the intra-group differences discussed in the previous section.

Museus and Griffin (2011) uses Crenshaw's (1991) and Shields' (2008) works to provide a concise definition of intersectionality as "the process through which multiple social identities converge and ultimately shape individual and group experiences" (p. 7). Museus and Griffin (2011) offer an example of how an intersectional lens might inform higher education leaders' understanding of marginalized students' experiences. They posit a professor who is concerned about the large percentage of Asian American students dropping out of his classes. In this scenario, the faculty member contacts the institutional research office and learns that Asian Americans have the highest GPAs and graduation rates.

Without an intersectional lens, the professor may assume his class is an outlier and cease the investigation. As the authors explain, an intersectional perspective might lead a faculty member in this case to dig deeper. For example, what if the students in his class were first-generation, low-income refugee students whose small numbers on campus were lost in data that lumped them together with large numbers of affluent third-generation Asian American students?

Intersectionality presents some practical challenges in organizing data, writing about specific issues, and designing programs to address the needs of a particular group of students. An intersectional perspective, however, allows us to ask the questions that move us to a more expansive approach in addressing inequality in all its forms. Further, intersectionality allows us to dig more deeply into the complex web of privilege and marginalization the vast majority of us experience. I may experience marginalization as a woman or lesbian, but I also experience privilege as a white, middle-class person. An intersectional lens acknowledges our disenfranchised identities while holding us accountable for using our privileged ones to advocate on behalf of others. If higher education institutions are serious about their mission to create informed citizens, this is an essential part of students' education.

Re-imagine Citizenship

We admit this intervention might require more than an academic year to implement, but we believe it is an important aim for which to strive. In a *Harper's Magazine* piece titled, "Save our public universities," renowned author Marilynne Robinson (2016) wrote:

> There has been a fundamental shift in American consciousness. The Citizen has become the Taxpayer. In consequence of this shift, public assets have become public burdens. These personae, Citizen and Taxpayer, are both creations of political rhetoric. While the Citizen can entertain aspirations for the society as a whole and take pride in its achievements, the Taxpayer, as presently imagined, simply does not want to pay taxes.
>
> *(p. 31)*

Despite decades of corporatization and privatization, most public universities still espouse a commitment to educating students for democratic citizenship. One problem in operationalizing this vision has always been the lack of clarity about what democratic citizenship really means. We've always interpreted the democratic citizenship part of university mission statements in the context of voting. That is, we hope that four years of college gives students the critical thinking skills they need to exercise their vote responsibly and not simply choose a candidate based on height, for example. (Voters choosing candidates based on height is a real example; see Armstrong & Graefe, 2011.)

Robinson (2016) offers a deeper and more complex definition of democratic citizenship beyond the taxpayer and voter roles. Her vision of citizenship starts from a positive position about what we can accomplish as a collective society.

We believe one of these goals must be the reduction of homophily and greater integration of citizens of all backgrounds, especially different socioeconomic classes. As long as the current condition of class segregation remains the status quo, attitudes like those reflected in Kevin Williamson's *National Review* piece will continue to impede higher education leaders' ability to interrupt the cycle of class inequality.

While college campuses do not provide idyllic enclaves of integration, they do have the potential to disrupt the highly segregated worlds that shaped most young adults. Separated by schools, neighborhoods, and activities divided by class, many adolescents come to college having interacted almost exclusively with people in their own family's income bracket. Higher education leaders could use their democratic citizenship mandate to capitalize on the opportunity they have to foster greater integration between students of all backgrounds, including and especially different socioeconomic classes. We do not simply mean it's nice for students to be exposed to people who are different from them; what we advocate is a pro-active role for public universities in shaping students' understanding of integration as essential for citizenship in a democracy.

This fundamental shift in our understanding of citizenship is necessary for any meaningful change to structural inequality. If we continue to allow citizenship to be reduced to the avoidance of paying taxes, we lose what's left of higher education's position as a place that prepares people to contribute to a public good.

Conclusion

I (Laura) began my last book by quoting a retired University of Akron professor commenting on the institution's commitment to providing quality education to a largely working-class population of students. She spoke in the past tense. Now she sends me articles about the University of Akron's president outsourcing academic advising, cutting ill-advised business deals, and purchasing the now famous $556 olive jar for his university-provided home. Under enormous pressure from the university community, President Scarborough did recently step down, but will continue to receive 65 percent of his $450,000 salary in his new role as tenured faculty in the College of Business (Farkas, 2016).

On the surface, it appears we conclude this book on a negative note. Indeed, we feel anger and frustration toward those who would enrich themselves on the backs of students working multiple jobs to pay their lavish salaries. Yet we argue we conclude this book on an essentially hopeful note. Dedicated faculty at the University of Akron stood up to this president, exposing his incompetent and unprincipled leadership. Similarly, brave student journalists at St. Mary's College exposed their president's position on treating students as bunnies who should be drowned. People at these institutions leveraged their respective power as tenured faculty and student-customers to demand positive change. While critiques of both tenure and the student-customer ethos abound, the faculty and students and the University of Akron and St. Mary's College used these tools to improve their communities. We laud them for standing up to those who use their power to perpetuate inequality.

The presidents of the University of Akron and St. Mary's College exemplify what ails higher education. Presidents who return their bonuses and care about the common good like University of Cincinnati President Ono deserve greater attention as examples toward which we should strive. Beyond the president level, there are countless students, faculty, and staff working to uphold higher education's promise as a place where people can thrive regardless of class. Our world faces monumental challenges; our hope for addressing them lies in our ability to access all peoples' talent, not just the elite's.

In all their imperfections, public universities still hold the greatest promise for interrupting the cycle of inequality. We do not believe it's a coincidence that one of the very few US presidents who held the role of teacher is the one who launched the War on Poverty. While four other presidents did teach at some point in their lives, Johnson taught primarily poor children whose conditions drove him to use his power for positive change. President Lyndon Johnson gave the War on Poverty speech on our campus, Ohio University, in 1964. In his speech, President Johnson linked education and opportunity, concluding "Our fight against poverty will be an investment in the most valuable of our resources—the skills and strength of our people" (Johnson, 1964, para. 7).

Over 25 years later, Johnson's words resonate. When we look at our young students, we feel hope in their capacity to address the world's formidable challenges. Our young people will only realize their potential if we invest in them. If we invest only in some of them, we constrict our own ability to create a better future. There are no expendable people in an interconnected world; we will live with the consequences of wealth for the few or investment in us all.

References

Armstrong, J., & Graefe, A. (2011). Predicting elections from biographical information about candidates: A test of the index method. *Journal of Business Research, 64*(7), 699–706.

Arnowitz, S. (2008). *Against schooling: Toward an education that matters.* Boulder, CO: Paradigm.

Carlson, S. (2016, March 6). On the path to graduation, life intervenes. *Chronicle of Higher Education.* Retrieved from www.chronicle.com.

Carr, P. J., & Kefalas, M. J. (2009). *Hollowing out the middle: The rural brain drain and what it means for America.* Boston, MA: Beacon Press.

Cohen, P. (2010, October 17). "Culture of poverty" makes a comeback. *New York Times.* Retrieved from www.nytimes.com/2010/10/18/us/18poverty.html?_r=0.

Covarrubias, R., & Fryberg, S. (2015). Movin' on up (to college): First-generation college students' experiences with family achievement guilt. *Cultural Diversity and Ethnic Minority Psychology, 21*(3), 420.

Crenshaw, K. (1991). Mapping the margins: Intersectionality, identity politics, and violence against women of color. *Stanford Law Review, 43*(6), 1241–1299.

Doucleff, M. (2015, May 15). What it takes to lift families out of poverty. National Public Radio. Retrieved from www.npr.org/templates/story/story.php?storyId=406757551.

Dunstan, S., & Jaeger, A. (2015). Dialect and influences on the academic experiences of college students. *Journal of Higher Education, 86*(5), 777–803.

Farkas, K. (2016, June 3). Former University of Akron President Scott Scarborough will remain on campus and teach. *cleveland.com*. Retrieved from www.cleveland.com/metro/index.ssf/2016/06/former_university_of_akron_pre_2.html.

Hurst, A. L. (2007). Telling tales of oppression and dysfunction: Narratives of class identity reformation. *Qualitative Sociology Review, 3*(2), 82–104.

Hurst, A. L. (2008). A healing echo: Methodological reflections of a working-class researcher on class. *Qualitative Report, 13*(3), 334–352.

Johnson, L. B. (1964). *Public papers of the presidents of the United States: Lyndon B. Johnson 1965*. Washington, DC: Government Printing Office. Retrieved from www.usccb.org/beliefs-and-teachings/who-we-teach/youth/upload/Lesson-2-War-on-Poverty-Speech.pdf.

Lareau, A. (2011). *Unequal childhoods: Class, race, and family life*. Oakland, CA: University of California Press.

Lewis, O., & LaFarge, O. (1965). *Five families: Mexican case studies in the culture of poverty*. New York, NY: New American Library.

Luthar, S., Barkin, S., & Crossman, E. (2013). "I can, therefore I must": Fragility in the upper-middle classes. *Development and Psychopathology, 25*(4pt2), 1529–1549.

McPherson, L. (2015). Righting historical injustice in higher education. In H. Brighouse & M. McPherson (Eds), *The aims of higher education: Problems of morality and justice* (pp. 113–134). doi:10.7208/chicago/9780226259512.003.0007.

MDRC. (2014, January 8). New study shows CUNY's ASAP program boosts two-year graduation rate of community college students who need remedial education. Retrieved from www.mdrc.org/news/press-release/cuny%E2%80%99s-asap-program-boosts-graduation-rate-students-who-need-remedial-education.

Mohamed, A., & Fritsvold, E. (2010). *Dorm room dealers: Drugs and the privileges of race and class*. Boulder, CO: Lynne Rienner Publishers.

Museus, S., & Griffin, K. (2011). Mapping the margins in higher education: On the promise of intersectionality frameworks in research and discourse. *New Directions for Institutional Research, 2011*(151), 5–13.

Patrick, M., Wightman, P., Schoeni, R., & Schulenberg, J. (2012). Socioeconomic status and substance use among young adults: A comparison across constructs and drugs. *Journal of Studies on Alcohol and Drugs, 73*(5), 772–782.

Perna, L. W. (2015, April 30). Improving college access and completion for low-income and first-generation students: The role of college access and success programs. Testimony provided to the Subcommittee on Higher Education and Workforce Training Committee on Education and the Workforce, United States House of Representatives. Retrieved from http://edworkforce.house.gov/uploadedfiles/testimony_perna.pdf.

Pierce, C. (1995). Stress analogs of racism and sexism: Terrorism, torture, and disaster. *Mental Health, Racism, and Sexism*, 277–293.

Robinson, M. (2016, March). Save our public universities: In defense of America's best idea. *Harper's Magazine*. Retrieved from http://harpers.org/archive/2016/03/save-our-public-universities/.

Sarcedo, G., Matias, C., Montoya, R., & Nishi, N. (2015). Dirty dancing with race and class: Microaggressions toward first-generation and low income college students of color. *Journal of Critical Scholarship on Higher Education and Student Affairs, 2*(1), 1.

Shields, A. (2008). Gender: An intersectionality perspective. *Sex Roles, 59,* 301–311.
Slavin, P. (2013, May 21). In Appalachia, a road trip for faculty makes a difference. *Atlantic.* Retrieved from www.theatlantic.com/national/archive/2013/05/in-appalachia-a-road-trip-for-faculty-makes-a-difference/276092/.
Smith, L., Mao, S., & Deshpande, A. (2016). "Talking across worlds:" Classist microaggressions and higher education. *Journal of Poverty, 20*(2), 122–151.
Soria, K. (2013). Creating a successful transition for working-class first-year students. *Journal of College Orientation and Transition.* Retrieved from https://conservancy.umn.edu/handle/11299/150275.
Soria, K., & Stebleton, M. (2013). Social capital, academic engagement, and sense of belonging among working-class college students. *College Student Affairs Journal, 31*(2), 139.
Stephens, N., Brannon, T., Markus, H., & Nelson, J. (2015). Feeling at home in college: Fortifying school-relevant selves to reduce social class disparities in higher education. *Social Issues and Policy Review, 9*(1), 1–24.
Stephens, N., Fryberg, S., Markus, H., Johnson, C., & Covarrubias, R. (2012). Unseen disadvantage: how American universities' focus on independence undermines the academic performance of first-generation college students. *Journal of Personality and Social Psychology, 102*(6), 1178.
Strayhorn, T. (2012). *College students' sense of belonging: A key to educational success for all students.* New York, NY: Routledge.
Thomas, V., & Azmitia, M. (2014). Does class matter? The centrality and meaning of social class identity in emerging adulthood. *Identity, 14*(3), 195–213.
Williamson, K. (2016, March 28). Chaos in the family, chaos in the state: The White working class's dysfunction. *National Review.* Retrieved from www.nationalreview.com/.
Young, D., Rudman, L., Buettner, H., & McLean, M. (2013). The influence of female role models on women's implicit science cognitions. *Psychology of Women Quarterly, 37*(3), 283–292.

INDEX

academic community 89
access to public universities 10
adaptive leadership 57–8, 71
Alexander, M. 51, 53
allocation 7–10
Alon, S. 113
anti-intellectualism 47–8
Ariely, D. 37
assets-based approach 152–4
Astin, A. 19–20
Astin, H. 19–20, 35

Birnbaum, R. 59
Blumenstyk, G. 55
Bowen, W. 8, 102, 110, 132, 136
Buber, M. 73

Chingos, M. 8, 102, 110, 132, 136
class intersectionality 155–7
class-based stereotypes 151–2
classism 28
college readiness 29–31, 49
commercial research and grants 25–6
competition versus collaboration 81–2
cost crisis 40–1
critical management studies 80
cultural and social capital 31–3
culture wars 42–4

Darwinism versus academic community 87–9
deLeon, P. 7, 99–100

Epston, D. 101
equity, definition of 4
ethic of care 35–7

facilities arms race 58
FAFSA 11–12
Farmer-Hinton, R. 65
feedback 10–12
financial aid contradictions 108–10
financial alienation 126–7
financial support 143–5
free community college policy 5
Fry, R. 41
fundraising 24–5

Gallup-Purdue study 124
Grashow, A. 57–8
Guinier, L. 33–4

Heifetz, R. 57–8
homophily 65–7
human capital versus human development 82–5
Hurst, A. 148

I/Thou 73
incentive structures 135–6
incentives 103–6
Ingram, H. 7, 99–100
iron triangle 18

Johnson, L. 159
Jones, M. 110–11

Kelly, E. 93–4
Kendall, D. 67–8
Kerr, C. 90–1
Kezar, A. 91, 95
Kozol, J. 65

Labaree, D. 104
Lareau, A. 28, 32
Lester, J. 91
Lewis, J. 65
Lindholm, J. 35
Linsky, M. 57–8
low-income student diversity 154–5
lucrative students 26–7

making class visible 146–8
managerialism versus shared governance 85–7
massification 60
McBeth, M. 110–11
McMahon, W. 105–6
McPherson, L. 156
McPherson, M. 8, 102, 110, 132, 136
meritocracy 13, 33
Mettler, S. 69
microaggressions 149–51
Murphy, R. 113

Nader, L. 69–70
narrative policy framework 110–11
narrative therapy 101
narratives: definition of 13; impact on social construction 98–101
National Center for Education Statistics 10, 21, 32, 102, 108, 129, 132
Newfield, C. 43
Noddings, N. 36
Nussbaum, M. 83, 103

organizational narratives 114–15
origins 12–17

Patton, L. 65
Pell Institute 61

Piketty, T. 60
policy, definition of 3
privatization 46
problem solving 130–2
public divestment 23–4
public engagement 129–30
public opinion 120–1, 125
public trust 120–5, 127–37
Putnam, R. 50

rankings 107
Reagan, R. 42–3, 48–9
reinvigorating public support 52–4
rent-seeking 62–4
responsibility centered management 88–9, 91–2
Rivers, I. 65

Schneider, A. 7, 99–100
Senge, P. 58
sense of belonging 28–9
Shanahan, E. 111
social closure 113–14
social construction framework 7
social construction of target populations 99–101
Stitch, A. 67
Stone, D. 4
student affairs programs 145–6

technical leadership 57–64
technology transfer 25
transparency 128
Trostel, P. 44–5
Truman Commission 3, 6

undermatching 136–7

victims and heroes 110
Vollmer, J. 46

Welton, A. 31
White, M. 101
Williams, M. 31
working-class faculty and staff 148–9

Taylor & Francis eBooks

Helping you to choose the right eBooks for your Library

Add Routledge titles to your library's digital collection today. Taylor and Francis ebooks contains over 50,000 titles in the Humanities, Social Sciences, Behavioural Sciences, Built Environment and Law.

Choose from a range of subject packages or create your own!

Benefits for you
- Free MARC records
- COUNTER-compliant usage statistics
- Flexible purchase and pricing options
- All titles DRM-free.

Benefits for your user
- Off-site, anytime access via Athens or referring URL
- Print or copy pages or chapters
- Full content search
- Bookmark, highlight and annotate text
- Access to thousands of pages of quality research at the click of a button.

REQUEST YOUR FREE INSTITUTIONAL TRIAL TODAY

Free Trials Available
We offer free trials to qualifying academic, corporate and government customers.

eCollections – Choose from over 30 subject eCollections, including:

Archaeology	Language Learning
Architecture	Law
Asian Studies	Literature
Business & Management	Media & Communication
Classical Studies	Middle East Studies
Construction	Music
Creative & Media Arts	Philosophy
Criminology & Criminal Justice	Planning
Economics	Politics
Education	Psychology & Mental Health
Energy	Religion
Engineering	Security
English Language & Linguistics	Social Work
Environment & Sustainability	Sociology
Geography	Sport
Health Studies	Theatre & Performance
History	Tourism, Hospitality & Events

For more information, pricing enquiries or to order a free trial, please contact your local sales team:
www.tandfebooks.com/page/sales

Routledge Taylor & Francis Group — The home of Routledge books

www.tandfebooks.com